S0-FBC-229

PINK FLOYD REFLECTIONS AND ECHOES

The Music of Pink Floyd

On record, on stage and on film 1965-2005

Through the eyes of the band and the critics

By Bob Carruthers

With additional material by Nigel Cross and Michael Heatley

ABSTRACT SOUNDS BOOKS LTD

Abstract Sounds Books Ltd
Unit 207, Buspace Studios, Conlan Street, London W10-5AP
www.abstractsoundsbooks.com

© Abstract Sounds Books Ltd 2010

Published by Abstract Sounds Books Ltd
Licensed from Archive Media Publishing Ltd
ISBN: 978-0-9566038-4-5

Photography courtesy of Pictorial Press and Rex Features

Chapter 1
THE PIPER AT THE GATES OF DAWN

The mid sixties marked the beginning of the psychedelic era and the burgeoning London "underground" scene was instantly host to a vast array of bands who were busily evolving a dreamy, tripped out sound to fit the mood of the day. After the drab post war era the world was suddenly in glorious technicolor and life was groovy.

One of the less appealing hallmarks of the sixties psychedelic scene was the willingness of some performers to take themselves far too seriously. The litany of new bands ready to turn on and drop out soon gave the impression that an explosion had taken place in the mythology section of the local library as a host of new bands emerged with unlikely titles like Dantalion's Chariot, Jacob's Ladder, Aphrodite's Child and The Gods. Fortunately amidst the stream of portentously named groups striving earnestly to celebrate the age of Aquarius, there were a few who were happy to give a nod to the idea that the whole scene might just be a little too earnest. A few bands were prepared to recognise that the underground scene might just be a huge passing joke and kept one eye firmly on the exit by incorporating a gently self mocking pun into the name of the group. The Tea Set definitely fitted into this category. In 1965 the band in question featured a five piece line up formed from a group of friends from Cambridge in England augmented by newer acquaintances from architectural college in London. Initially the group played gigs in small clubs, private parties and in the safe confines of their own college.

Venturing out into the wider world with a gig at RAF Northolt it was discovered, perhaps rather surprisingly, there were two groups on the London circuit who had chosen to name themselves The Tea Set. The inevitable double booking caused the newcomers to adopt an on the spot alternative. The name quickly chosen by their lead singer was The Pink Floyd Blues Band. From the early summer of 1965 the name began to appear on posters and fliers. The Pink Floyd Blues Band initially included Bob Klose on guitar and vocals. Bob didn't stick around for too long and neither did the Blues element of the name. By the summer of 1965 the band was slimmed down to a four piece and the name too was reduced to match. For the next couple of years the band would be known as The Pink Floyd. It was not until the early 1970's that the band finally managed to shake off the definite article, but by 1971 they had become universally recognised as simply - Pink Floyd.

The initial members of the four piece known as The Pink Floyd were Roger Waters on bass, Richard Wright on keyboards and Nick Mason on drums. Handling both lead guitar and vocals was Roger Keith Barrett, better known to one and all as Syd.

For Syd's group there were no long years of unrewarding obscurity. This was the line up which in 1966 took the London psychedelic scene by storm. The band had by now dispensed with the Rhythm and Blues standards, which had seen them through the early days, in favour of the unstructured improvisations which were the basis for long extended freak outs which were then highly fashionable. By November 1966 word on the band had begun to creep out beyond the cosy world of the capital. The Herald, a local newspaper published in Kent, was among the first to publish an interview with a member of Pink Floyd. Rick Wright was given the job of handling this particular interview and explaining the effect of the band's music on their rapidly expanding audience. "It does sometimes get to a point where it is a wow. That is when it works, which is not always. Then we really feel the music is coming from us, not the instruments, or rather the instruments become part of us. We look at the lights and the slides behind us, and hope that it all has the same effect on the audience as it does on us. It's completely spontaneous. We just turned up the amplifiers and tried it, thought about it, and it developed from there. But we still have a long way to go before we get exactly what we want. It must develop still further. There is probably more co-ordination between the members of our group than in any pop group. We play far more like a jazz group than anything else. Because we have to be together to produce the right sound, we have come to think, musically, together. Most of our act is spontaneous and unrehearsed. It just comes when we are on stage. As we are a comparatively new group and are projecting a really new sound, most people just stand and listen at first. What we really want is that they should dance to the music and with the music, and so become a part of us. When some people do experience what we want them to, it gets a bit of a jungle, but it is harmless enough because they are wrapped up in the music and themselves. It is a release of emotion, but an inward, not an outward, one, and no one goes into a trance or anything."

As a result of the rapidly spreading word of mouth on the underground scene the band soon came to the attention of the mainstream press including the prestigious Sunday Times. Late in 1966 the paper carried one of the first national features on the band interviewing Andrew King in the process. "As for being psychedelic," manger Andrew King stated, "We don't call ourselves psychedelic. But we don't deny it. We don't confirm it either. People who want to make up slogans can do it." Bass player Roger Waters added, "It's totally anarchistic. But it's cooperative anarchy, if you see what I mean. It's definitely a complete realization of the aims of psychedelia. But if you take LSD, what you experience depends entirely on who you are. Our music may give you the screaming horrors, or throw you into screaming ecstasy. Mostly it's the latter. We find our audiences stop dancing now. We tend to get them standing there, totally grooved with their mouths open."

Improvised music can of course be a very hit and miss affair but the addition of a swirling psychedelic light show added to the overall experience and provided a much needed distraction for the frequent moments when the music missed its target. Crucially the band dedicated a great deal of time and effort to the creation of a truly mind bending light show which marked them out from the crowd and produced an all round experience which complemented and, on occasion, excelled the music. As a result of this powerful and immediate impact Pink Floyd were one of the select group of bands which found a ready audience right from the outset. For the Floyd there was to be no extended period of paying their dues. Almost instantly the band found themselves the darlings of the exploding psychedelic scene in London. The Floyd began 1966 with a number of regular appearances at the fabled Marquee club which did an enormous amount for the new group's credibility. Towards the end of the year the equally famous UFO club opened it's doors and The Pink Floyd rapidly became known as the house band for the club which was at the epicentre of swinging London and widely recognised as the barometer for all that was considered hip and trendy. In September 1969 Rick Wright reviewed the experience of the UFO club for the magazine Top Pops and Music Now. "When we started out, you had to have a hit single or nobody would listen to you. In those days, music was to dance to. Now people go to see a group to listen. But it's a pity people don't dance, in a way. At the moment audiences are involved in their heads and not physically. But it's bound to change again. We noticed this at UFO. When we started there, the whole audience used to dance, and gradually they stopped dancing and started listening. UFO played a very big part in the change, I think. It used to be held in a church hall in Powis Gardens, very much a sort of workshop atmosphere. It was all very experimental, and, at that time, we were working things out with music and lights. I suppose our whole life was centered around UFO then, but it was a complete way of life. It all came out in the open, and that was such a nice feeling. The whole thing was an entity in itself, you know, the Floyd were on stage, but the audience and everything else that was happening was just as important. It was an experiment in those days. Money had nothing to do with it. Now we've had to adopt a more professional attitude. We still experiment a lot, but it isn't the same. People know about us now, and they know what to expect. The audience feeling now is nice, but there's that thing behind us that we had to fight through to get established. Then, we just played basically to dig the music, and the future didn't concern us. We didn't think about it. But now we have the confidence in ourselves to know we'll be going for some time."

On January 14, 1967, much closer in time to the UFO experience, Nick Mason and Roger Waters were interviewed by Melody Maker and covered the early days of the band in an interview which revisited much the same territory as Wright but shed a very different light on events. "We were very disorganized then until our managers materialized and we started looking for a guy to do the lights full-time. The lighting man literally has to be one of the group. When we were in our early stages, we didn't play a lot of our electronic interstellar music, and the slides were still rather amateurish. However, this has developed now and our 'take-off' into the mainly improvised electronic scenes are much longer, and, of course, in my opinion, the slides have developed to something out of all proportion. They're just fantastic. You have to be careful when you start on this psychedelic thing. We don't call ourselves a psychedelic group or say that we play psychedelic pop music. It's just that people associate us with this and we get employed all the time at the various freak-outs and happenings in London. Let's face it, there really isn't a definition for the word 'psychedelic'. It's something that has taken place around us, not within us." Roger Waters then interrupted, "I think the reason is that we've been employed by so many of these freak-out merchants. I sometimes think that it's only because we have lots of equipment and lighting, and it saves the promoters from having to hire lighting for the group. A freak-out, anyway, should be relaxed, informal, and spontaneous. The best freak-out you'll ever get is at a party with about a hundred people. A freak-out shouldn't be savage mobs of geezers throwing bottles."

Of course there was more to Floyd than just the hype and freak outs. The group cared genuinely about its stage show which was then at the forefront of combining light with sound to present a genuine audio-visual experience. The early experiments were conducted with the help of college lecturer and landlord Mike Leonard. By the standards of the day the swirling coloured patterns thrown over the performers and audience were both innovative and truly striking. The ever changing light show was synchronised by hand to the hypnotic pulsing rhythms of the music and the results were by turns genuinely disturbing, inspirational and hypnotic. Leonard's light show was considered sufficiently avant garde to be included in an episode of the BBC's popular science programme *Tomorrow's World* which featured The Pink Floyd who were described in the accompanying voice over as providing the background music for the lights!

These early television broadcasts were of course in black and white so the event lost something in translation. For the drugged up portions of the concert audience the show was indeed mind blowing, but it also worked equally well for straight audience members who were prepared to leave their preconceptions behind and embrace the experimental improvised aspects of the performances which could often build to a quite extraordinary crescendo.

The driving force behind the initial incarnation of the band was, of course, Syd Barrett: writer, guitarist, vocalist and focal point of the whole Floyd experience. It's interesting to note however just how small and London focused the underground scene then was. While The Pink Floyd were busy ascending the heady heights of the swinging London scene future Floyd collaborators such as Ron Geesin, co-writer of *Atom Heart Mother*, remained totally unaware of the rising phenomenon as Ron later recalled. "The Pink Floyd with Syd Barrett was outside my field of vision. As regards his own music I suppose you could say, it's a bit ragged, it's individual, but I can't say that it's great form in the sense of structure in composition. In fact the only time I saw Syd Barrett was when he popped into the Abbey Road session when we were doing *Atom Heart Mother* and he kind of spun round a couple of times in slow motion and then went out again and that was all I ever saw of him."

Geesin may have been unaware of the Floyd but the hip London crowd always on the look out for the next sensation were well aware of the music of this amazing new band with it's powerful live show. By early 1967 Floyd were huge news on the thriving underground scene and attracted the attention of Peter Whitehead, an independent film maker, who was the first to capture the Floyd experience on film. He filmed the band in action performing Interstellar Overdrive at Sound Techniques Studios and cut the film to a montage of performances from The UFO club on January 13th 1968 and the 24 hour Technicolour Dream described as a 24 hour "happening" at the Alexandra Palace in London, which took place on April 29th 1967. Interviewed in *Record Mirror* a few weeks later Roger Waters tried to explain the relevance of Floyd's music to these events "We play what we like and what we play is new. I suppose you could describe us as the house orchestra of this new movement because we're the only people doing what the fans want to hear. We're really part of the whole present pop movement. We're not, repeat not, an anti-group. In fact, we're very much in favour of a lot of things, including freedom and creativity, and doing what you want to do, but, of course, tempered by social conscience. We're not really anarchists. Our aim is not to create hallucinatory effects on our audiences. We want only to entertain. We link sounds together which are not usually linked and link lights which are not usually linked. We are relying a lot on our album to show what we're really trying to say. We try to develop. We don't have much time for people who just copy other artists, or get hold of an American record and just put it down, note by note."

With such a strong visual story it was not long before the TV companies too began to take an interest in the wild and wonderful world of the underground scene. In late January 1967 Granada Television also filmed the band performing Interstellar Overdrive at the UFO club for the documentary strand called *Scene Special*. The episode itself was entitled "It's So Far Out It's Straight Down" which may well have been a not so subtle dig at the quality of the music; but for the Floyd the only way was up. On February 1st 1968 the band turned fully professional.

The newly professional Floyd formally appointed a management company called Blackhill Enterprises to represent them. Managers Peter Jenner and Andrew King had formerly booked gigs for the band and were the driving force behind much of the early Floyd activity which included recording the first ever single *Arnold Layne*. In a reflection of the true spirit of the times Jenner and King later divided the ownership of Blackhill Enterprises equally between themselves and the group. Another early champion of the group was American A&R man called Joe Boyd. Joe was keen to lure Blackhill into a deal with a pre-Doors Elektra records. Elektra was rejected as a label, but Boyd soldiered on offering the fledgling Polydor as an alternative. It was with Polydor in mind that the band recorded its first single *Arnold Layne* which was produced by Joe Boyd at Sound Techniques Studios in February 1967. Long before the days of pop video this catchy slice of psychedelia even had a promotional film to accompany it. Produced and directed by Derek Nice, this naïve little short film is basically shot in the fashionable Beatles style featuring the four Floyd's larking around on a beach with a tailor's mannequin. When the film received its world premiere at the UFO club on March 10th 1967 no one could have realised that this unprepossessing film was the forerunner of some of the most intense audio visual experiences in rock music ever to make it on to celluloid.

Arnold Layne's progress towards Polygram was hijacked by the intervention of London Agent Bryan Morrison who steered the band towards the welcoming arms of EMI Records. With an interesting new single already recorded and ready to go EMI knew they were on to a winner. The band were equally happy to be signed to such a prestigious label which was universally recognised as the home of the Beatles.

A very 'English' song, *Arnold Layne* was inspired by a real-life incident encountered by Roger Waters and Syd Barrett in their home town of Cambridge. Syd and Roger's mothers both took in female student lodgers and their washing lines full of underwear were regularly raided by a local transvestite who struck at night. Syd explained the background to the song to *Melody Maker* in 1967. "Well, I just wrote it. I thought *Arnold Layne* was a nice name, and it fitted very well into the music I had already composed. I was at Cambridge at the time I started to write the song. I pinched the line about 'moonshine washing line' from Rog. our bass guitarist, because he has an enormous washing line in the back garden of his house. Then I thought, 'Arnold must have a hobby,' and it went on from there. *Arnold Layne* just happens to dig dressing up in women's clothing. A lot of people do, so let's face up to reality. About the only other lyric anybody could object to is the bit about 'it takes two to know, takes two to know,' and there's nothing smutty about that. But then, if more people like them dislike us, more people like the underground lot are going to dig us, so we hope they'll cancel each other out."

The B side was *Candy And A Current Bun*, another Barrett composition. This track was originally entitled *Let's Roll Another One* and EMI only consented to its release on the understanding that the title was changed. With the band still in it's early days and still willing to toe the party line the name was duly altered. Despite the unusual subject matter of the A side this first release under the band's new contract with EMI was to prove a surprise hit with the record buying public. The surprise element however was somewhat less intense in the offices of Blackhill Enterprises. It was they who, as Andrew King later revealed, had helped the single along with a little discreet chart rigging which hyped the song to a respectable number 20 position in the singles charts. The decision to hype the single was a wise one given the snobby reaction to the lyrics which resulted in calls from some quarters that the single should be banned. The pirate radio station Radio London did formally ban the single; but it is debatable just how much effect a ban by an organisation which was itself banned had on sales of a single which was rigged to hit the charts in any event!

Roger Waters, Rick Wright and Syd Barrett all gave an extended interview at the time of the single's release. Roger took the lead "Let's face it, the pirate stations play records that are much more 'smutty' than *Arnold Layne* will ever be. In fact, its only Radio London that have banned the record. The BBC and everybody else plays it. I think it's just different politics, not anything against us." Rick Wright added his own perspective, "I think the record was banned not because of the lyrics, because there's nothing there you can really object to, but because they're against us as a group and against what we stand for." Barrett succinctly summed up the whole situation, "It's only a business-like commercial insult anyway. It doesn't affect us personally."

Fortunately *See Emily Play*, the follow up single to *Arnold Layne*, was less controversial and proved to be even more commercially successful. *See Emily Play* reached Number 6 in the charts, and is without doubt one of the finest psychedelic songs produced during the brief sixties flower era. It was written for a special concert the band gave at the Queen Elizabeth Hall in spring 1967 called *Games for May*, an event which is name-checked in the lyrics. Shortly afterwards Record Mirror ran a piece based on an interview with Roger Waters which touched on the event "We play what we like, and what we play is new. I suppose you could describe us as the movement's house orchestra because we were one of the first people to play what they wanted to hear. We're really part of the whole present pop movement, although we just started out playing something we liked. We're not an anti-group. In fact, we're very pro lots of things, including freedom and creativity, and doing what you want to do, but tempered by social conscience. We're not really anarchists. But we're in a very difficult position, because the sort of thing we do comes over best in concert, rather than in clubs or dance halls. We gave a concert a short while ago at the Royal Festival Hall, and although we learnt a lot from it, we also lost a lot of money on it. We had to give up a week's work in order to arrange everything, and so on. *Games for May*, as it was called, was on in the evening, and we went onto the stage in the morning to try and work out our act. Up till then we hadn't thought about what we were going to do. Even then we only got as far as rehearsing the individual numbers and working out the lighting. So when it came to the time of the performance in the evening, we had no idea of what we were going to do."

Games For May turned out to be a major milestone in the development of Pink Floyd which marked the first signs of the care the band put into the sound quality of all of their live shows, but as Nick Mason recalled in an interview given at the time, there seems to have been a great deal less consideration for the music. "We just took a lot of props on stage with us and improvised. Quite a bit of what we did went down quite well, but a lot of it got completely lost. We worked out a fantastic stereophonic sound system whereby the sound travelled round the hall in a sort of circle, giving the audience an eerie effect of being absolutely surrounded by this music. And, of course, we tried to help the effect by the use of our lighting. Unfortunately, it only worked for people sitting in the front of the hall. Another thing we found out from giving that concert was that our ideas were far more advanced than our musical capabilities, at that time, anyway. We made a lot of mistakes at that concert, but it was the first of its kind. And we, personally, learnt a lot from it. But it makes us feel good to know that what we are doing, what we have been doing for the past three years, has now been accepted, and has had a great effect upon the sort of thing other groups are doing now. It wasn't until February of this year that everything started happening for us and made us decide to turn professional, and life has been a bit chaotic for us since then. But it was worth the wait. Three years ago, no one knew what it was all about. But now the audience accepts us. We don't feel that we should try to educate the public. We don't want to push anything onto them. But if they accept what we're offering and they seem to be at the moment, then that's great. And we feel good because our ideas are getting across to a large number of people."

Syd claimed *See Emily Play*, the single which evolved from *Games For May* was inspired by a vision he had after he inexplicably woke up in a wood one morning, but there was a real life muse behind this piece, a 15 year-old girl nicknamed 'Far Out Em': Emily Young was the daughter of Labour politician, Lord Kennet and a student at Holland Park school where she was pals with film director John Huston's daughter Anjelica. One night the pair witnessed an early Floyd gig at the Free School in Notting Hill and, afterwards, went back to band manager Peter Jenner's house, where they apparently shared a joint with Syd. Released on June 16th 1967 the charming psychedelic whimsy of the second single cemented the band's growing reputation as a singles act. It also meant that the band had neatly avoided the trap door marked "one hit wonders". The time had now come to record an album.

Piper At the Gates of Dawn was recorded in the spring and early summer of 1967 and released on August 5th 1967. The album was produced by EMI staff producer Norman Smith. Norman had worked successfully with the band on the *See Emily Play* single and had previously earned his spurs as engineer on the Beatles albums. As a veteran of the *Sergeant Pepper* sessions, Norman was used to experimental attitudes, but even he must have been puzzled by a band that had two distinct musical personalities. On one hand were the whimsical very English compositions which climbed the singles charts with ease, on the other side were the extended freak outs which the band performed on stage.

In the July 1, 1967 edition of *New Musical Express* Roger Waters

Pink FLoyd at the Saville Theatre, October 1967.
(l-r) Nick Mason, Rick Wright, Syd Barrett and Roger Waters

gave an interview in which he again attempted to explain the Pink Floyd phenomenon and it's relationship to improvised music, again the Games For May concert was a point of reference. "We recently played a concert at the Queen Elizabeth Hall, and that's usually where string quartets play. The people who came to see us there were a very mixed lot, some really way-out people with bare feet, and a few old women who always go to the Queen Elizabeth Hall no matter what's on. But mostly they were average men and women between 17 and 25, mixed with a few teeny-boppers. We are simply a pop group. But because we use light and colour in our act, a lot of people seem to imagine that we are trying to put across some message with nasty, evil undertones. It sometimes makes it very difficult for us to establish any association with the audience. Apart from the few at the front, no one can really identify us. We're not rushing into anything. At the moment we want to build slowly and I think we're doing not too badly. The important thing is that we're doing what we want to do. We record the numbers we want, and fortunately they seem to be the ones that people want. No one interferes with us when we're in the studio. They just leave us, more or less, alone to get on with what we want. We listen to Radio London and the other stations, but we don't really concern ourselves with what other groups are doing. We'd like to play the major centres like Manchester, Liverpool, and Glasgow, doing our own two-hour show. You see, contrary to what some people think, it's not just the Southern audiences that we appeal to. In fact, the further North we go, the better the reception. We played in Belfast recently, and the reception there was great. The same thing happened when we played in Abergavenny. We had screamers and everything. It really astonished us."

The "screamers" were presumably drawn to Pink Floyd more by songs like, *Arnold Layne*, *See Emily Play*, *The Scarecrow*, *The Gnome* and *Bike*. These flower power driven songs however were in total contrast to the freaked out experimental sounds created in the live arena by the band. As a result the album also had to make room to feature the extended instrumental piece *Interstellar Overdrive* and the general weirdness of *Pow R Toc H*. The two styles sit together rather uncomfortably and Norman Smith had the difficult task of reconciling these apparently incompatible genres. The only time the two styles seemed to come together in one track was the album's opening track *Astronomy Domine*. This album is so steeped in psychedelia it could only have been made in 1967. The overall effect is one of almost palpable confusion as two completely different, and totally irreconcilable, musical personalities battle for supremacy. Not surprisingly, the results are confusing, and by the standards of what was to come later, deeply disappointing. Nonetheless the album did find a measure of favour with the great British public and climbed to Number Six in the charts, this time without any of Blackhill's 'help' along the way.

The title for the new album was taken from a chapter heading in Kenneth Grahame's wonderful children's book *The Wind In The Willows*, one of Syd Barrett's favourite books. The cover for The *Piper At the Gates of Dawn* was based on a photograph by Vic Singh and in many respects was an archetypal Psychedelic era sleeve. It consists of a multiple lens image of the band calculated to achieve the LSD trip effect favoured on so many sleeves at the time.

The Music

ASTRONOMY DOMINIE *(Barrett)* - The album opens with *Astronomy Domine*, the first of eight Syd Barrett compositions on the album. Syd was not exactly a major science-fiction fan, admitting only to liking classic late 1950s/early 1960s films like *Quatermass* and *Journey Into Space* but little else besides. Nonetheless this is a fine piece of early space rock and boasts some very graphic psychedelic poetry - pure lysergic Technicolor. Manager Peter Jenner has suggested that some of the lyrics were inspired by the pages of *The Observer Book Of Planets* especially lines like the chanted 'Jupiter and Saturn, Oberon, Miranda and Titania". Jenner's is the wild, distorted voice recorded through a megaphone at the beginning of the track.

LUCIFER SAM *(Barrett)* - The second track on the album is the cartoon-like Lucifer Sam. The track was slated as the subject of a possible animated film, but given the circumstances of Syd's imminent breakdown, it was understandable that it never got made. The song is about a Siamese cat and is given a sinister tone by the rocking 'secret agent' riff that sounds like it might have been influenced by the James Barry 007 theme. Lucifer Sam was also allegedly a nickname of Roger Waters. It also includes a reference to a Cambridge girlfriend of Syd's, Jenny Spires, and the albums first references to the I Ching.

MATILDA MOTHER *(Barrett)* - is the third track on the album and the third successive Barett composition. It was originally taken word for word from verse by Hillaire Belloc, the 19th-century, Anglo-French writer whose books *The Bad Child's Book Of Beasts* and *Cautionary Tales For Children* were well regarded by Barrett. Indeed the first set of lyrics were taken from a poem called Jim and then re-written in the studio -

however they still retain the style and spirit of Belloc.

FLAMING *(Barrett)* - boasts more trippy lyrics that suggest the influence of the omnipresent LSD during this period on Syd's lyrics. Again very much in a whimsical, fairy-story vein but full of that child-like Barrett mischief, with the line, 'Yippee you can't see me but I can see you.'

POW R TOC H *(Barrett/Mason/Waters/Wright)* - is a bizarre Instrumental written jointly by all four members - both the band's managers Andrew King and Peter Jenner suggest the title was just word sounds, onomatopoeia. *Pow* was certainly in youth culture common parlance at the time from comic books like Batman. Toc H might have related to the charity of the same name the values of whose mission statement - 'committed to building a fairer society by working with communities to promote friendship and service, confront prejudice and practise reconciliation' - would certainly have had a lot of resonance with members of the late-1960s UK alternative society and the band itself.

TAKE UP THY STETHOSCOPE AND WALK *(Waters)* - *Pow R Toc H* is followed by the first Roger Waters composition to appear on a Pink Floyd album; *Take Up Thy Stethoscope And Walk*. This early Waters effort certainly doesn't suggest any trace of the cynical, world-weary wordsmith of a decade later on LPs like *Wish You Were Here* or *The Wall*. Roger seems quite happy to follow his leader and come up with some rhyming nonsense about a patient telling medics that he is still alive.

INTERSTELLAR OVERDRIVE *(Barrett/Mason/Waters/Wright)*- was the second group composition on the album and was the one number on the LP which captured the way the early Floyd sounded live on stage. It was an epic by the standards of the day running to nine minutes of instrumental experimentation. The Coda is built around a riff supposedly based on the melody of a Burt Bacharach song *My Little Red Book* as interpreted by the US West Coast band Love. According to Peter Jenner, he 'd been trying to hum the tune to Syd who then followed it on his guitar and eventually that infamous cyclical riff emerged. Barrett was very influenced by free music such as the British avant-garde outfit AMM and borrowed elements of his sound from their guitarist Keith Rowe which included the habit of rubbing metal objects up and down his guitar neck to produce truly cosmic sounds on the guitar.

THE GNOME *(Barrett)* - Is another Barrett composition and hardly qualifies as Shakespeare, but it is a funny innocent ditty that fitted in perfectly with the whole Syd aesthetic, and became part of the blueprint for the flower-power era. 'I want to tell you a story about a little man if I can, a gnome named Grimble Gromble'. JRR Tolkien whose books

became de rigueur reading for this era springs to mind as one possible influence. It was no surprise that other bands who came within the Blackhill orbit such as Tyrannosaurus Rex would soon be writing and recording songs along these lines. Syd was understandably a huge influence on their leader, Marc Bolan.

CHAPTER 24 *(Barrett)* - is the next track on the album and returns to lyrics which are inspired from I Ching, the Chinese Book of Changes, a 5000 year-old Taoist oracle. The book became very popular with late-1960s youth and Chapter 24 is Fu, Return or Turning Point. One translation of the book by Richard Wilhelm published in 1951 seems to have been the one Barrett consulted - the guitarist lifting lines like 'all movements are accomplished in six stages and the seventh brings return ' verbatim. He was probably turned on to the book by the bohemian mother of Cambridge friend Seamus O 'Connell.

THE SCARECROW *(Barrett)* - The ancient mysteries of the I Ching are left behind for *The Scarecrow*. The song is basically what it says on the tin - a wistful, melancholic ode to a scarecrow. A perfect evocation of the golden age of 1960s innocence and the fabled Summer of Love. The dreamy vision of the title is enhanced by the clip-cloppety percussion and Rick Wright's wispy keyboard fills. The short film which the band shot for Pathe newsreel featuring *The Scarecrow (Barrett)* - is the quintessential psychedelic romp and it's entirely typical of the values of the day. The film made by Pathe for cinema audiences has all the hallmarks of the sixties attitudes to music film making . The master plan for this film seems to have simply consisted of taking the band into the country and asking them to lark about for the camera. The results are predictably uninspiring... as is the music. Songs like *The Scarecrow* were in total contrast to the freaked out experimental sound of the band on stage which was based around a stage show of hypnotic intensity developing the canvas of *Interstellar Overdrive* and the weirdness of instrumentals such as *Pow R Toc H*.

BIKE *(Barrett)* -A magical blend of frivolity and melody closes the album on something of a high. Perhaps the most disconcerting and unexpected element here is the massed ranks of quacking toy ducks which close the song - this was one of Barrett's last recorded performances with the Floyd, but sound effects remained a major component of the music of the band for years to come.

Astronomy Domine has proved to be the most enduring composition on the album and was actually revived by Pink Floyd for the very last shows in 1994, but crucially the album was well received by the critics who included Richard Middleton writing in *Pop Music and the Blues*, "An important characteristic of psychedelic pop is the use of electronic effects and electronically-created noise. One of the best examples of this is the work of the Pink Floyd, a British group well known for their multi-media shows and the vast amount of electronic equipment which they use. The Pink Floyd have developed an improvisational, 'free-form' style, in which traditional pop techniques are mixed with a multitude of electronic effects. It is significant that they share Jimi Hendrix's interest in space and astronomy, many of their songs carrying his obsession much further, both in explicitness and musical implications. So it is not surprising that in their music pop reaches possibly its most 'inhuman' form, man all but disappearing in the vastness of the cosmos. They are not always quite so extreme as this. *Pow R Toc H* alternates sections of chaotic noise with sections of expressive blues piano. Man is set in a non-human context but still exists - though chaos wins in the end. *Take Up They Stethoscope and Walk* seems to be a medical allegory, in which humanity is 'operated on' by horrific electronics and brain-battering noise, beat and ostinato. But here, at the end of the piece, vocal music appears and the patient asserts 'I'm alive'. And *Astronomy Domine*, as the title implies, goes so far as to explore man's control of his environment, his superiority to the cosmos."

It is obvious from the weightiness of the reviews that the critics were beginning to take Floyd seriously and the band continued to take their obligations to their music and their audience just as seriously, as Roger Waters and Rick Wright confirmed in yet another interview with *Melody Maker* late in 1967. "We're being frustrated at the moment by the fact that, to stay alive, we have to play at lots and lots of places and venues that are not really suitable. This can't last, obviously, and we're hoping to create our own venues. We all like our music. That's the only driving force behind us. All the trappings of becoming vaguely successful, like being able to buy bigger amplifiers, none of that stuff is really important. We've got a name of sorts now among the public so everybody comes to have a look at us and we get full houses. But the atmosphere in these places is very stale. There is no feeling of occasion. There is no nastiness about it, but we don't get re-booked on the club or ballroom circuit. What I'm trying to say is that the sort of thing we are trying to do doesn't fit into the sort of environment we are playing in. The supporting bands play *Midnight Hour*, and the records are all soul, then we come on. I've got nothing against the people who come and I'm not putting down our audiences. But they have to compare everybody. So-and-so's group is better than everybody else. It's like marking exercise books. Dave Dee, Dozy, Beaky, Mick and Tich get a gold star in the margin, or 'Tich - very good. On the club scene we rate about two out of ten and 'Must try harder.' We've had problems with our equipment and we can't get the PA to work because we play extremely loud. It's a pity because Syd writes great lyrics and nobody ever hears them. Maybe it's our fault because we are trying too hard. After all, the human voice can't compete with Fender Telecasters and double drum kits. We're a very young group, not in age, but in experience. We're trying to solve problems that haven't existed before. Perhaps we should stop trying to do our singles on stage. Even the Beatles, when they worked live, sounded like their records. But the sort of records we make today are impossible to reproduce on stage, so there is no point in trying. We still do *Arnold Layne*, and struggle through *Emily* occasionally. We don't think it's dishonest because we can't play live what we play on records. It's a perfectly okay scene. Can you imagine somebody trying to play *A Day in the Life?* Yet that's one of the greatest tracks ever made. A lot of stuff on our LP is completely impossible to do live. We've got the recording side together, and not the playing side. So what we've got to do now is get together a stage act that has nothing to do with our records, things like *Interstellar Overdrive*, which is beautiful, and instrumentals that are much easier to play. When the music clicks, even if it's only with ten or twelve people, it's such a gas. We're trying to play music of which it can be said that it has freedom of feeling. That sounds very corny, but it is very free. We can't go on doing clubs and ballrooms. We want a brand new environment, and we've hit on the idea of using a big top. We'll have a huge tent and go around like a travelling circus. We'll have a huge screen. 120-feet wide and 40-feet high inside, and project films and slides. We'll play the big cities or anywhere and become an occasion, just like a circus. It'll be a beautiful scene. It could even be the salvation of the circus! The thing is, I don't think we can go on doing what we are doing now. If we do, we'll all be on the dole."

The difficulties of attempting to put their music across to a hostile audience are there for all to see in the surviving footage of the BBC2 show *Look Of The Week* . On the 14th of May a couple of months before the new album's release a short extract of *Pow R Toc H* and all of *Astronomy Domine* were performed by the band for this BBC2 review of the arts scene. At the conclusion of the live performance of the track the band were joined in the studio for a discussion of Floyd's music by a decidedly frosty Professor Hans Keller who looked on with obvious disdain and was blunt in his criticism of the band's music which he found repetitive and overloud.

Despite the disparagements of the establishment and often bemused dance hall crowds, *Piper At the Gates of Dawn* continued to sell in respectable numbers and the band were also keen to capitalise on a growing following in America; but it was here that disaster struck. In November 1967 Pink Floyd had just released their third single *Apples And Oranges* and it was during North American television appearances to publicise the single on *The Pat Boon Show* and *Dick Clark's American Bandstand* that Syd Barret first began to exhibit the signs of the total mental collapse which would soon engulf him. In the aftermath of a distinctly poor performance Boon's easy going questions elicited only a blank stare and total silence from Syd. Even the most casual observer can clearly see how bad Syd's performance is in these two much bootlegged television clips in which a clearly embarrassed Rick Wright desperately tries to cover for the guitarist.

Not only was Syd performing badly both on stage and in the television studio the material he wrote had also taken a massive dip in quality. *Apples And Oranges* as a composition was well below par. Roger Waters blamed poor production by producer Norman Smith for the failure of this single, although it's difficult to see what could have been done to make it succeed. Barrett though was very pleased with the new release, talking about the new single the singer enthused "It's unlike anything we've ever done before. It's a new sound. Got a lot of guitar in it. It's a happy song, and it's got a touch of Christmas. It's about a girl who I saw just walking around town, in Richmond. The apples and oranges bit is the refrain in the middle." On the subject of the band's live performances Barrett indicated that the band were considering a major change of direction, "We are going to play a lot more songs now. Our organist, Rick, is writing a lot of things, and I am still writing."

Rick Wright was indeed writing at this time but the results were just as uninspiring as Syd's later offerings. *Paintbox* was the B side of *Apples And Oranges* and represents Rick Wright's song writing debut on vinyl. Wright was a less able wordsmith than Barrett, with whom he was closest, both socially and musically in the early Floyd. This is a pleasant enough tune best described as an early commentary on the music business, which would later resurface with far greater bite on the *Wish You Were Here* album.

As Syd had promised there were more songs in the pipeline but sadly events would not justify Syd's optimism. The next projected single *Vegetable Man* was considered too poor even to release, and the accompanying promotional film didn't see the light of day for another thirty years when it surfaced briefly in a BBC documentary with some rather telling commentary by Peter Jennings who described how the piece had been literally thrown together on the spot as a description of Syd himself. Only six months on from recording cheerfully wistful songs like *The Scarecrow* and *Bike,* Barrett's vision had turned extremely bleak as was suggested by the disturbing title of Syd's new offering *Scream Thy Last Scream Woman With A Casket* which only he could have considered a possible single. By late 1967 Syd was continuing to fall apart and his last significant contribution to Pink Floyd was *Jug Band Blues*, but there was very little in this slight composition to suggest that Pink Floyd might be about to arrest the creative decline which was now gripping the band. Syd gave one of his last interviews as a member of Pink Floyd to *Melody Maker* on December 9, 1967. Also present were Roger Waters and managers Andrew King and Peter Jenner. The four had just finished watching the promotional film of Jug Band Blues (See DVD1) which had been shot in order to air in yet another magazine programme. When he spoke to *Melody Maker* Barrett first addressed the thorny issue of the failure of *Apples And Oranges* to dent the charts, "I Couldn't care less really. All we can do is make records which we like. If the kids don't then they won't buy it. All middle men are bad." Manager Peter Jenner was quick to interrupt and qualify Syd's words. "The group has been through a very confusing stage over the past few months and I think this has been reflected in their work. You can't take four people of this mental level, they used to be architects, an artist, and even an educational cyberneticist, give them big success and not expect them to get confused. But they are coming through a sort of deconfusing period now. They are not just a record group. They really pull people in to see them and their album has been terrifically received in this country and America. I think they've got a lot of tremendous things ahead of them. They are really only just starting."

Jenner was clearly papering over the cracks. Although the band's management clearly still had faith in Syd and his ability to pull through, the feeling inside the band was very different. With Syd deteriorating fast and looking increasingly like he was about to take the fledgling band's career with him, the remaining Floyds knew that something clearly had to be done. However there proved to be no need for drastic action, within a few short weeks events took their sad course and Syd Barrett was no longer a member of the band.

Chapter 2
A SAUCERFUL OF SECRETS

With Syd now reaching crisis point Pink Floyd needed a back up singer and guitarist in order to keep functioning during live performances. Finding the additional singer and guitarist was relatively easy. David Gilmour had been a pal of Syd's from their teens in Cambridge. The two were firm friends and had actually gone busking round Europe together. Gilmour had learned his craft in local Cambridge band Jokers Wild who had actually performed alongside The Pink Floyd and a fledgling folk singer called Paul Simon at a birthday party in Cambridge during 1966; not a bad line up by any standards.

Early in 1968 Gilmour was duly drafted in as a fifth member to provide on stage cover and support for the increasingly unstable front man, initially at least there was a genuine intention that the two friends would work side by side in the band. The new look Pink Floyd first performed together as a five piece at the University Of Aston on the 12th of January 1968, but after just five gigs as a five piece it was resolved that Syd was to be allowed to simply drift out of the picture. Syd performed his final gig with The Pink Floyd on Hastings Pier on the 20th of January 1968. En-route to pick up Syd for the sixth gig as a five piece at Southampton University, on the 26th January 1968, a spur of the moment decision was taken not to bother stopping for the increasingly difficult guitarist. It was clearly convenient that Gilmour was already in place as guitarist and singer which made the obvious decision all the easier.

Filling the gap left by Barrett the writer proved to be a bigger challenge which would need much more time to fully conquer. Initial thoughts were that Barrett would take on a role in which he would become, in Gilmour's words, "a kind of Brian Wilson figure" contributing material for the studio which the others would perform live on stage. Sadly the rapid decline in Syd's mental condition ruled out even this possibility. The other members of Pink Floyd have all at various times described the bizarre experience of trying to learn a song called *Have You Got It Yet?* with Syd changing the chords each consecutive time he

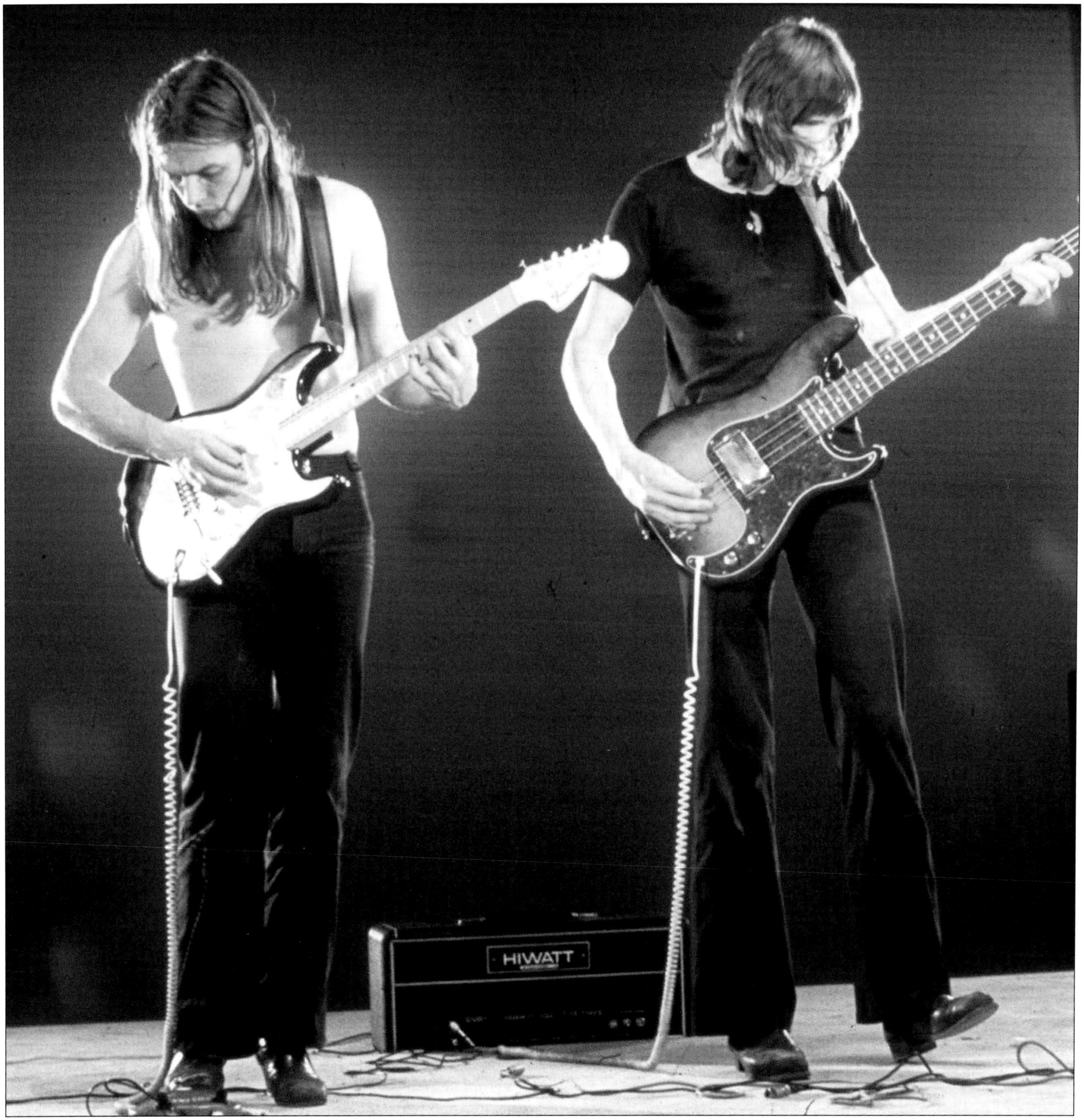

Rex Features

played the song as he unveiled the new piece to his increasingly concerned colleagues.

On taking over his friend's place in the band David Gilmour was faced with the awkward task of performing a set comprising mainly Syd's material. This was embarrassing enough in the live setting where Syd would occasionally turn up in the crowd seemingly just to stare blankly at his friend, an experience which Gilmour understandably recalled with unease in a much later *Melody Maker* interview with Chris Welch. "It took a long time for me to feel part of the band after Syd left. It was such a strange band, and very difficult for me to know what we were doing. People were very down on us after Syd left. Everyone thought Syd was all the group had, and dismissed us. They were hard times. Even our management, Blackhill, believed in Syd more than the band. It really didn't start coming back until *Saucerful of Secrets* and the first Hyde Park free concert. The big kick was to play for our audiences at Middle Earth. I remember one terrible night when Syd came and stood in front of the stage. He stared at me all night long. Horrible!"

Almost as bad as being confronted by Syd was the unavoidable need for Gilmour to actually mime to Barrett's material. On February 19th 1968 RTBF the Belgian television channel were due to film a number of Floyd tracks which had originally been performed by Barrett. The rather painful footage which came out of the session features the new Gilmour line up miming to the backing track of *Astronomy Domine, Apples and Oranges, The Scarecrow, Paintbox* and *See Emily Play*. With the exception of *Corporal Clegg* all of the material had actually been recorded with Syd still in the band. It's small wonder that Gilmour seems to be somewhat detached from the proceedings. The whole feel is tentative, the performance is unconvincing and Gilmour still felt uncomfortable over 30 years later when he was interviewed for the BBC. With his usual flair for understatement, Gilmour described the whole period as "difficult and very odd". At the time of the RTBF recordings the band hid their embarrassment over Syd's absence from *See Emily Play* by using their instruments as cricket bats in a game played with an invisible ball. Quite what a Belgian TV audience would have made of it all was anyone's guess.

The Gilmour version of Floyd were clearly far more comfortable handling the Barrett material in live performance. *Flaming* was one Barrett composition which was occasionally performed by the new line up during 1968. It was performed for two French television specials in September and October 1968.

In the surviving footage from ORTF 2 for the music programmes *Samedi et Compagnie* and *Tous En Forme* the group certainly looks more convincing and a good deal more comfortable performing Syd's material in the live situation. Also perfomed in 1968 for the RTBF cameras was a tentative stab at a new composition, *Corporal Clegg*. Viewing the promotional film again from a distance of almost forty years it's astonishing to see just how far Pink Floyd would ultimately travel; not just in the quality of the material but also in the quality of presentation. There is an uncertain atmosphere to the music and the performance, this is clearly a group who do not yet have the confidence to command their environment. It's amazing the difference a few months can make and Floyd were in much better form when the cameras of German broadcaster ARD caught up with the new line up in Rome where they performed a quite breathtaking rendition of Interstellar Overdrive This land mark performance finally stamped the credentials of the new line up on the older material.

Another piece which was performed regularly for the cameras around this time was *Let There Be More Light*. At this point in their career the group were definitely casting around for material and had to cover the huge gap left by Syd. The quality of the compositions is understandably patchy and it's interesting to note how few even made it into the stage set. At the time, the band had a great deal of misplaced faith in this undistinguished track. It has to be said that *Let There Be More Light* is an example of the mediocre standard of a number of the compositions which emerged early in 1968. The numerous films of live performances from the French archives all serve to illustrate why the track which disappeared from the set in 1969 was never revived.

Despite its many limitations, on the whole *A Saucerful Of Secrets,* the first album recorded by the post-Barrett Floyd, actually represented a step forward in most respects. The album did not sell as well as its predecessor but still reached a healthy number nine in the album charts. This slight dip in sales is possibly because the pop sensibilities of *Piper At the Gates of Dawn* were increasingly buried under layers of avant-garde experimentation as Floyd began to grasp their way towards the sound which would make them world-beaters. Highlights of the album include *Set The Controls For The Heart Of The Sun* and the Heavenly Voices section of the title track. Simple straight formal numbers such as *Jug Band Blues* and *Corporal Clegg* now seem slightly out of place as the main emphasis is clearly on the instrumental heavyweights.

For this album released on July 1st 1968, Norman Smith was moved upstairs to become Executive Producer as the band increasingly sought to control their own destiny in the studio. The results are definitely patchy but there are enough pointers as to where Floyd would go in future to make it worth checking out. New boy Gilmour would later explain how he remembered Waters and Mason drawing the album's title track as an architectural diagram, in dynamic rather than musical forms, with peaks and troughs!

Most of the recording had taken place before the arrival of Gilmour and there is now some debate as to who played what on the album. The uncertainties over the album were not helped by the changing roles behind the scenes. Blackhill chose to abandon Floyd in favour of managing Barrett and in April 1967 the Bryan Morrison Agency took over the management of the band. Besides *Jug Band Blues* Barret himself later recalled that he had played only on *Remember A Day*. Gilmour's role in the group was still very tenuous and he is credited only with writing quarter of the track, *A Saucerful Of Secrets*. It's safe to assume that his is the guitar on the rest of the material although Gilmour himself stated that for the first few months he was so "paranoid" over his status that he limited himself to merely playing rhythm.

The Music

LET THERE BE MORE LIGHT *(Waters)* - opens the album, an hypnotic, slow opening piece with a quirky time signature which signals a return to the cosmic space-rock direction Pink Floyd would now make their own. Roger Waters was always very cynical about the sci-fi tag which the transitional line-up were given. Perhaps this is why later material moved to deal almost exclusively with down-to-earth inner space themes of personality disorder.

REMEMBER A DAY *(Wright)* - Is a light weight throw away Rick Wright song about childhood. Like much of his early material this track wraps up incidents in his life in snapshot form. Childhood and the growing-up process was to become a much-used theme by the band.

SET THE CONTROLS FOR THE HEART OF THE SUN *(Waters)* - was an altogether stronger effort, a number which would become a favourite in Floyd live sets in the late 1960s and early 1970s. This Roger Waters song was characterised by the slow build to the psychedelic crescendo that had first appeared on *Interstellar Overdrive* and was destined to become something of a Floyd hallmark. The song took its name from a line in a William S Burroughs novel and the whispered verses came from a book of Chinese poetry. Burroughs' cut-up techniques had been a big influence on the now departed Barrett. A particularly fine example of the piece in a live setting appeared in the BBC2 documentary *All You Need Is Love* .

CORPORAL CLEGG *(Waters)* - The track which follows is in marked contrast to the spacey atmosphere we have just explored. This is a wacky Roger Waters number full of sarcastic humour. Waters' father had been killed during World War II at Anzio and this event would influence Roger's later writing as he became more obsessed with the obscenity of systemised violence and the pointlessness of war in later material which, ultimately emerges in all it's fully formed bitterness as 'The Final Cut '.

A SAUCERFUL OF SECRETS – *(Waters/Wright/Mason/Gilmour)* A distinct shift in style once more with *A Saucerful Of Secrets*. Originally entitled *The Massed Gadgets Of Hercules*, this was a sequence of pieces that had various sources. It contains no lyrics. The opening *Something Else* had already been used by the band at the Games For May concert, as part of the opener *Tape Dawn* - heavily treated cymbals that produced a series of tones. The next section, *Syncopated Pandemonium*, features a loop of Mason's drumming on top of which Gilmour adds guitar sounds. The maelstrom of the third part, *Storm Signal*, is pure white noise and electronics before the soothing *Celestial Voices*, with its fugue-like organ and heavenly vocal harmonies. The piece suggests four stages of human development - birth, adulthood, death and re-birth.

SEE SAW *(Wright)* After the challenging dynamics of Saucerful comes one of the albums less auspicious tracks written by Rick Wright. Its working title says it all: 'The Most Boring Song I 've Ever Heard Bar Two!' as its author Rick Wright would later say of all his early Floyd contributions: "They're sort of an embarrassment. I don't think I 've listened to them ever since we recorded them. It was a learning process. I learned that I'm not a lyric writer, for example. But you have to try it before you find out."

JUGBAND BLUES *(Barrett)* Was the final track on the album. Sadly it was also Syd Barrett's last recorded contribution to the band he 'd started. This forlorn piece has been accurately described by former manager Peter Jenner as "possibly the ultimate self-diagnosis on a state of schizophrenia." Syd was in bad shape but this is a sad and at the same time scathing portrait of his relationship with the Floyd in the winter of 1967. It directly addresses the drying-up of his song writing, the demands he felt his band mates, managers and record label were placing on him, and an appearance on *Top Of The Pops!* The inclusion of the Salvation Army brass section which Barrett dragged into the studio and invited to perform without scores adds to the sense of anarchy. A total rejection of commercialism and conformity.

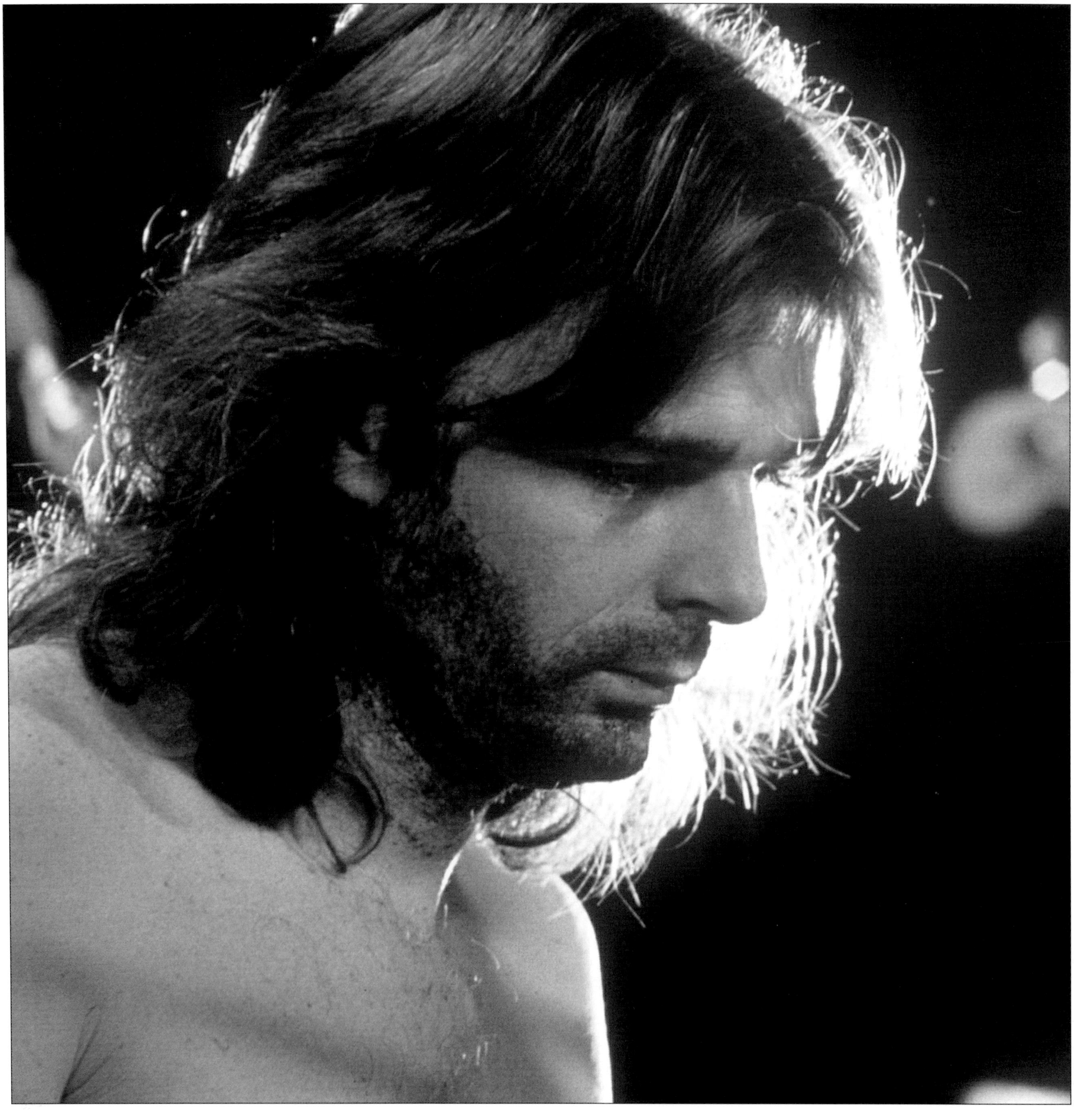
Rex Features

Despite all of the problems, on the whole, press reaction to *A Saucerful Of Secrets* was favourable. One of the journalists who reviewed the album was underground stalwart and Pink Floyd aficionado Miles, his review was published in the "head" magazine *International Times* on 8 August 1968. "The Floyd have developed a distinctive sound for themselves, the result of experiments with new 'electronic ' techniques in live performance. However, the result of most of these experiments was presented particularly well on their first album; there is little new here. The electronic collage on *Jugband Blues,* though it uses stereo well, has been done much better by The United States of America. The unimaginative use of a strings arrangement spoils *See Saw*. The use of electronic effects on *A Saucerful of Secrets* is poorly handled and does not add up to music. It is too long, too boring and totally uninventive, particularly when compared to a similar electronic composition such as *Metamorphosis* by Vladimir Ussachevsky, which was done in 1957, eleven years ago. The introduction of drums doesn't help either and just reminds me of the twelve and a half minute unfinished backing track *The Return of the Son of Monster Magnet* which somehow got onto side four of The Mothers of Invention's *Freak Out* album, much to Zappa's horror and which was left off the British version. In the same way as bad sitar playing is initially attractive, electronic music turns people on at first – then as one hears more, the listener demands that something be made and done with these 'new' sounds, something more than 'psychedelic mood music'. *Let There Be More Light* presents the Floyd at their best as does most of side one. They are really good at this and outshine all the pale imitations of their style. With their *Saucers* track, experiments have a historical place and should be preserved, but only the results should be on record, at least until they bring out one a month and are much cheaper. A record well worth buying!"

In addition to the album the new look Floyd made a couple of attempts to re-ignite their career as a singles chart act. The first stab at making a return to the charts was *It Would Be So Nice - (Wright)* released in April 1968. Looking back this is a big embarrassment… this unremarkable Richard Wright composition starts out promisingly but it's novelty style chorus did nothing to change the fortunes of the band in the singles charts and the group soon disowned the single. On May 18, 1968 *Melody Maker* published an interview with Nick Mason and Roger Waters which explored the difficult relationship between Pink Floyd and the singles charts. Mason was first to explain "It is possible on an LP to do exactly what we want to do. The last single *Apples and Oranges*, we had to hustle a bit. It was commercial, but we could only do it in two sessions. We prefer to take a longer time. Singles are a funny scene. Some people are prepared to be persuaded into anything. I suppose it depends on if you want to be a mammoth star or not." Roger Waters expanded on the difficulty of producing a hit single in the context of the Floyd's album output "Live bookings seem to depend on whether or not you have a record in the Top Ten. I don't like *It Would Be So Nice*. I don't like the song or the way it's sung. Singles releases have something to do with our scene, but they are not overwhelmingly essential. On LPs, we can produce our best at any given time." Mason added, "a whole scene has gone. Light shows have gone well out of fashion, but if people still like them, there must be something in it."

Point Me At The Sky released in December 1968 met with an equal lack of success, small wonder really, as neither the songs chosen for single release are really up to scratch as potential chart contenders. The promotional film for *Point Me At The Sky* kept up the Floyd tradition of half hearted film making. Grabbing a plane and shooting off some film may have been considered acceptable in 1968 but there was no great forethought or any sense of real film making craft on display, the results are uninspired photo-journalism. The days of the applied use of the language of film in Pink Floyd's promotional films and stage shows still lay far in the future.

Interestingly the B sides of both of the later singles proved better than the A sides. *It Would Be So Nice* was backed by the evocative *Julia Dream*. Originally called *Doreen's Dream*, this Roger Waters song mined the same kind of flower-power sound that, a year before, had been fresh and innovative, but which now was beginning to sound stale and clichéd. It was however the first Pink Floyd arrangement to be properly recorded with Dave Gilmour on guitar.

The lack lustre *Point Me At The Sky* was backed by *Careful With That Axe* which was to become a stage favourite for the next four years. Here was a track that showed the way forward and which, in various forms, was to become a staple of their live show for years to come. Ultimately the piece would develop into a perfect example of the Floyd's sound scapes, all textures and moods with Gilmour's whispered 'words' and that bloodcurdling scream. *Eugene* was also known as *Murderistic Woman* and *Keep Smiling People*.

Interviewed by Record Mirror on September 21, 1968 Roger Waters and David Gilmour seemed happy over the progress of the band without the need to chase success in the singles charts as Waters said. "We're not making our fortunes, but we're doing all right. We can survive by playing the kind of music, and recording the kind of LPs, that we like. And there are enough customers to make it worthwhile." Gilmour continued the up beat thread, "We're beginning to find that we're booked on concerts, particularly on the continent, where we get top billing over famous groups that we looked up to as the big stars when we were starting. It's not easy to adjust to this. We keep thinking there must be some embarrassing mistake."

Chapter 3
MORE

If it was an uphill struggle to re-establish the group's credibility in the aftermath of Syd's departure, one possible option to solving their short term economic problems and also establish some much needed credibility in the process was to produce film scores. The band had always embraced film as a medium of expression and during the Barrett era the group had contributed music to films such as The Committee and Tonight Let's All Make Love In London. Certainly the sounds they were now making lent themselves effortlessly to the moving image. At a time when most groups did not dream of using film as a promotional tool The Pink Floyd had also had the foresight to understand the need for promotional films hence the Derek Nice directed Arnold Layne.

In the main interview at the time Rick Wright expanded at length on the subject. "We're going more and more into films, doing film music. We've always wanted to get into that, and now it's beginning to happen for us. We did the music for More, and that's doing well abroad. It's supposed to be the most popular film in Paris at the moment. In the beginning, it was important for us to play to earn money, gigging all over the country. But now we're trying to work things out film-wise. It's a good way of working because it leaves us a lot more time than if we had to travel all over the country every night, and we can go into other things. It'll leave us more time for recording and writing. We want to release a lot more albums than we have done in the past. We'd like to do more concerts rather than straight club venues. Eventually, we'd like to make our own films. Doing the music for films is a very challenging thing. It means that we have to express facts ands scenes in music. And, as I say, financially it pays off, and so it leaves us more time on our own to develop our own individual ideas. Gigs take up so much time, and they're very hard work. I'm not saying that gigs aren't satisfying. We 'd never give up playing clubs. There's a good feeling when you 're playing to an audience in a small environment."

The much needed work on the film score for More (See DVD1) had materialised when Barbet Schroeder, who'd worked with French New Wave director Jean Luc Goddard, asked the band to score his debut feature, More. The film was already completed and edited and just needed music. For the reasons set out by Mr Wright the band readily agreed. Money aside, the band accepted the commission because they reckoned the film also projected the right message about drugs and the band were never particularly drug-orientated, especially after Barrett's departure. The film follows the fortunes of a beautiful junkie princess played by Mimsey Farmer who draws German drifter Klaus Grunberg into her sunny world of Mediterranean beach parties, retired Nazis and heroin pushers. The music is far better than the film, which is pretty lame.

Fortunately the band's fortunes did not rest too much on the success or otherwise of the film. Although Floyd wrote the new material ostensibly for the movie, the resulting material from the soundtrack was also worked into the live act. Many of these became integrated pieces in the highly ambitious live show that the band continued to develop during 1969. The live show was entitled The Man and The Journey (The Massed Gadgets of Auximenes... More Furious Madness from Pink Floyd) and had by now expanded into a lengthy suite which also borrowed from earlier numbers such as Pow R Toc H and most importantly A Saucerful Of Secrets.

The beautiful instrumental Quicksilver, for example, which was written for the acid trip part of More, was now fitted into the first half of this live show as Sleeping, while Up The Khyber was used as the part of the live suite that chronicled the act of copulation. Cymbaline (the first expression of Roger Waters' disillusionment with the music biz) became Nightmare. Green Is The Colour was incorporated as the opening of The Journey, though its second verse refers directly to heavy drug use by Estelle, the heroine in the film.

Unusually for a film soundtrack there were a large number of songs in addition to the expected mood pieces. As well as being incorporated into the Auximines suite both Green Is The Colour and Cymbaline became staples of the live set over 1970 and 1971 and both were performed for the cameras of KQED in 1970.

Recorded over a very short period of time in early 1969, the album exhibits all of the disadvantages that would suggest, nonetheless *More* did yield a few stand out tracks in the form of *Cirrus Minor, Cymbaline* and *The Nile Song* all of which were excellent examples of the increasing confidence in writing and recording within the band. On the whole it is unfair to judge the soundtrack albums by the same standards as the studio albums. It was never intended for albums like *More* to be representative of the band's regular output. The short time scales over which the album was recorded really shows in compositions like the lacklustre *More Blues* which was certainly not destined to become a Floyd classic.

The Music

CIRRUS MINOR *(Waters)* - The album opens with *Cirrus Minor* a woozy acoustic gentle mannered piece which uses recorded birdsong. This is one of the earliest examples of the musique concrête motif that would crop up regularly in Pink Floyd music over the next twenty years.

THE NILE SONG *(Waters)* - Next up is *The Nile Song*, a very untypical composition with Gilmour's heavy metal guitar and aggressive vocal pre-dating the vocal styles of grunge and garage and nu-metal which would not arrive on the scene until 20 years later. In the film this piece appears as a background piece in heavily compressed form which suggests that it is being played back on a record player during the party. There is no connection with the Nile in the film.

CRYING SONG *(Waters)* - After the fury of the Nile Song we come to a complete contrast. *Crying Song* is a return to the gentle dreamy territory driven by the keyboard from Rick Wright and heralds a soft acoustic number, which deliberately follows an unexpected melodic and acoustic line, but not terribly successfully.

UP THE KHYBER *(Wright/Mason)* - Another unsuccessful number was *Up The Khyber*. Nick Mason's distinctly un-jazzy drums and stabbed jazz chords from Rick Wright combine to little effect before the organ attempts to engage our flagging interest with equally limited success.

GREEN IS THE COLOUR *(Waters)* - is a folk tinged acoustic number which buries Gilmour's tentative vocal in the middle of a muddy cluttered mix. The amateurish tin whistle fails to convince and neither does Rick Wright's piano solo.

CYMBELINE (Waters) - Fortunately the next track, *Cymbaline* arrives just in time to lift the quality of the album. A fine example of the quieter more reflective side of Pink Floyd with a memorable and uplifting chorus, *Cymbaline* is justifiably regarded as one of the four standout tracks on the album. With more time, care and attention this track could really have been developed into something special.

THE PARTY SEQUENCE *(Waters/Wright/Mason/Gilmour)* - is a very short percussion interlude which heralds the grandly entitled *Main Theme*. Disconcerting cymbals and organ set the mood for the arrival of the mysterious main theme featuring a typically Floydian rhythm track and a melody line which pre-dates Jean Michele Jarre but which contains much that would later characterise his work. A real gem and sadly overlooked.

IBIZA BAR *(Waters/Wright/Mason/Gilmour)* - is a short variation on the theme first heard in the *Nile Song* and treads very similar ground. The production here is muddy and feels especially hurried.

MORE BLUES *(Waters/Wright/Mason/Gilmour)* - On *More Blues* trademark guitar from Gilmour introduces a slow blues which threatens, but never quite develops into a full fledged blues work out. The blues soon disappear into a layer of weird sonic effects, avant-garde gongs and discordant keyboards, which are the main feature of the piece.

SPANISH PIECE *(Gilmour)* - Next up is *Spanish Piece* which features interesting Spanish guitar flourishes from Gilmour underneath a layer of spoken words.

DRAMATIC THEME *(Waters/Mason/Wright/Gilmour)* - The album concludes with *Dramatic Theme*. An unsettling Waters bass line introduces a more recognisable Floyd back in firm melodic/instrumental territory before the track peters out like so many that have gone before. An undistinguished end to an undistinguished album.

The *More* album was not terribly well received by the critics, reserved is probably the best word to describe the overall reaction. This review in the *The Record Song Book* published on 1 August 1969 is untypical in its enthusiasm for the album. "Pink Floyd were commissioned to compose the musical score for the film *More*, shown at the Cannes Film Festival recently. The film was directed by Barbet Schroeder and stars Mimsi Farmer and Klaus Grunberg. All thirteen titles on the original soundtrack recording were composed and played by the group. The music is sometimes purely instrumental, sometimes both instrumental and vocal, always extremely interesting and arresting. Quite weird in parts too. Try the *Main Theme* on side two, for an example. But it's not all like this. There's a super little Spanish bit that sounds almost traditional and there are other equally contrasting tracks. They did a great job."

Chapter 4
UMMAGUMMA

Ummagumma (pronounced Ooma-gooma) is a difficult album to rationalise. It's a strange hybrid double album which features an album's worth of live recording and a whole studio album for which each of the four members contributed unique individual pieces.

The opportunity to write and produce each of the four pieces was in theory divided among the four contributors (although it is interesting to note that even in 1969 Roger contributed two pieces compared to the others who got one each!). On February 15, 1969 while the album was still at the recording stage Nick Mason met with *Disc and Music Echo* for a progress report, at this stage it's interesting to note that there was still some uncertainty as to whether the album would be a double or a single. The idea of using live recordings does not seem to have presented itself at this stage. "It's our usual annual album, but it is quite an elaborate affair. What we've agreed to do is take a quarter of the album each, on which we can all do the things we really want to do. It's hard to say what's going to come out of it at the moment, because everyone's being incredibly secretive about their bit till they've got it all together. I've done my quarter twice over. The difficulty is, doing something so totally egocentric as this, you keep wanting to go back and do something completely different. There's still hope we could do our quarters on one album, and on the other have one side of straight songs and one side of a major work involving all of us."

In the studio at least the band were definitely struggling for ideas. Roger Water's *Several Species Of Small Furry Animals Gathered Together In A Cave and Grooving With A Pict* was a great title for a musical joke, but it was a joke which unfortunately lacked any kind of a punch line. The overall weakness of the studio album is amply demonstrated by the fact that *Grantchester Meadows* is arguably the best of the studio tracks. The piece is gentle and pleasant, but it lacks a stand out melody or the innovative instrumental flourish which would mark out the later Floyd from the rest of the world. With this track we are reaching the end of the pastoral era of Pink Floyd which flowered briefly with tracks like The Scarecrow and ends with the gentle wistful melodies of If and Fat Old

Sun on *Atom Heart Mother*. Although the song marks the end of an era in that particular sense, the prominent use of sound effects again looks forward to the future of Pink Floyd.

Those who viewed the band as serious space-rock explorers believed the title was inspired by Frank Herbert's hugely popular sci-fi epic *Dune*, but the real story couldn't have been more down to earth - it was simply local Cambridge slang for sex.

Retrospectively the album has been described as a "disaster" by Roger Waters; and who are we to argue? The prospects of a possible debacle were always there from the moment it was decided to allocate half a side of one disc to each member. The rather indulgent studio experiments of the studio album definitely sit uncomfortably against the excellent live recordings on the first disc. Overall the experiment strays too far towards free form instrumental exploration without enough of the melodic counterpoint which was to make the next album so successful.

By April 1969 when Beat Instrumental came calling Nick Mason was still full of enthusiasm for the Ummagumma album which the band had begun hard on the heels of the *More* sessions.

"We've just completed the music for a film, which we did in a week, really hard at it, but we are working on an album which will be split into four quarters, each one of us doing what he wants on his piece. Mine, naturally, will be purely percussion and very much stereo orientated, using a wide range of instruments. If you can hit it, I might use it. I have tried to hang it together, it has movements and so forth, a construction. Few drum solos move me on record and I'm not as good as many other drummers, so it would be pointless for me to hammer away as fast as I can for ten minutes. There is a problem here, though. *Saucerful* was more than just the sum of the four of us. It was us and what we make together, which is more. We would like the new album to be a double one, with half of it live or semi-live, us as a group. This would then show both what we can do together, and what each of us can do individually." Individually there was not a great deal to show and the only piece which still survives on film from the time is a short snippet of promotional film featuring Rick Wright's *Sysyphus* .

In November of 1969 *Disc and Music Echo* interviewed David Gilmour on the progress of the band to date. It's interesting to read between the lines of the piece which dealt with the creation of new Pink Floyd pieces in the aftermath of the Ummagumma debacle. The reader gets the clear impression that Pink Floyd had still not found a strong musical direction in the studio and were to an extent drifting along hoping to find the muse from somewhere. "I don't know how it's going to go. It's tended to get a little less spacey lately. It's just a matter of doing new things, new pieces of music, and seeing what happens. You can have an idea, then, when the whole group gets together, it will change completely. How a song is originally, and how it eventually turns out, may be two different things. The group has changed a lot since the early days, and come a long way. The worst period was after the two hit singles. We went right down then because people expected us to do them and we wouldn't. Now we are as busy as we want to be. We do two or three gigs a week and that keeps us going. But I never seem to have any cash. It's such an expensive business. We are also a bit slow, especially on recording. It takes us months to get out an LP. We get in the studio for a couple of days, then someone like the Beatles wants to record and we get shoved out. So a couple of weeks later we go back and we've forgotten the mood. It takes a lot of time getting back into the thing. What we really need is a block session to get something done in one go. We have great fun in the studio mucking about. But I don't think I could go on recording without doing appearances. It's great to do a live gig, but we can do so much more recording. I don't see why we should limit ourselves on record to what we do on stage. There are a lot of things we haven't really touched on yet, television, for instance, which is good publicity. We have been approached about doing programs, but nothing's ever come of it. I thought we had some nice ideas for a TV show, they'd probably still be OK. But TV generally is so boring. I suppose everybody's ego would be satisfied by a lot of fame, but it seems that if you have a record in the charts, you are rejected by the so-called underground movement. Hit parades do spell death for our sort of group. But if we did a single, I'd be quite happy if it got into the charts."

The Music

ASTRONOMY DOMINE *(Barrett)* - The live album opens strongly with *Astronomy Domine* which was one of Barrett's strongest compositions. At the time Waters and Gilmour had just produced the final sessions for Syd's first solo album and it was fitting that Syd's song was still a staple in the Pink Floyd set at this time and played perfectly into the preconceived audience expectations of a band which played 'music of the spheres'!

CAREFUL WITH THAT AXE, EUGENE
(Waters/Wright/Mason/Gilmour) - was the second track on the live album. On

stage the band had transformed this rather unpromising material which had first appeared a year previously. No longer a humble half forgotten B-side, *Careful With That Axe* had become a central part of the live show and the Floyd really began to develop the piece to it's limits. An extended studio cut was later used to stunning effect to enhance the climactic scenes of Antonioni's Zabriskie Point in which a building exploded over and over again to it's unearthly strains. *Careful With That Axe* was something of a workhouse for Floyd at this time. The same number, re-titled *Beset By Creatures Of The Deep*, had also been incorporated into concerts as part of *The Man and The Journey* opus.

SET THE CONTROLS FOR THE HEART OF THE SUN (Waters) - is the next track on the live album. Roger Waters did little to help the band shake off the space rock tag when he described the number as being "about an unknown person who, while piloting a flying saucer, is overcome by suicidal tendencies!" *Set the Controls* was a stage favourite and was frequently performed for cameras in television studios around Europe. Notable appearances include the BBC Omnibus programme *All My Lovin'* and *Samedi et Compagnie* for ORTF1. In the USA the band performed the track for the PBS station, KQED. There were also numerous radio broadcasts but without doubt the best surviving example is the performance in the magnificent ruins of Pompeii where the piece provides an unexpected highlight of the film. *A Saucerful Of Secrets* demonstrated that the band had developed this ever evolving musical soundscape over the intervening year and it was now a live piece de resistance. The reviewer at *Rolling Stone* commented on the great distance the band had covered with the track since the studio recording. He noted that the group, and particularly Wright, had achieved a complexity and a depth, building nuances into the main line of the music, far beyond the studio version.

SYSYPHUS PARTS 1-4 (Wright) - opens the studio album and represents a significant departure for keyboardist Rick Wright. After the rather uninspired flower-power numbers he had composed for previous records, this serious slice of prog-rock was more indicative of where the band would go in future. Sysyphus was the hero of Greek mythology whose penance was to roll a rock to the top of a mountain, every time he reached the summit, the gods would cast the stone back down and Sysyphus would have to repeat the task. Here Wright is in positively avant-garde mode, a bizarre piece that owes more to composer John Cage than to rock music, employing a range of instruments and effects from guitar and percussion to piano and, significantly towards the the end of the piece a plaintive solo mellotron.

GRANTCHESTER MEADOWS (Waters) - As previously noted *Grantchester Meadows* is the highlight of the studio side of the album - Waters' paean to the eponymous beauty spot south of Cambridge and a meditation on summer and the immensity of nature. The track features a number of sound effects perfectly integrated into the structure of the song - the twittering of a skylark, the honk and splash of a swan landing on the River Cam. The final sequence with the bumblebee being swatted with a newspaper in full stereo by Roger became a great favourite among stoned listeners everywhere.

SEVERAL SPECIES OF SMALL FURRY ANIMALS GATHERED TOGETHER IN A CAVE AND GROOVING WITH A PICT (Waters) - Next comes Roger Water's humorous sound collage which suggests Pinky & Perky on acid. Various voices are sped up and slowed down in a series of tape loops (an art form US composer Terry Riley was pioneering at the time), many listeners assumed this track was completed with the assistance of Ron Geesin. Ron certainly was doing similar performance art at the time but he later confirmed he had no direct input into this piece, though he did point out with reference to the ranting Scotsman that both he and Roger had Scottish mothers! Nick Mason, writing almost 35 years later finally put the record straight when he acknowledged the Geesin influence.

THE NARROW WAY PARTS 1-3 (Gilmour) This was David Gilmour's first ever solo composition. It was also used as an instrumental passage in the live concept the band had been touring throughout the first part of 1969, *The Man and The Journey*. Unfortunately when he rang up Waters and asked for lyrics, the bassist just said 'no' and the resultant recording suffers from Gilmour's lack of confidence in his lyrics, especially in the buried vocal.

THE GRAND VIZIER'S GARDEN PARTY; ENTRANCE/ ENTERTAINMENT/ EXIT (Mason) - The album ends on a rather puzzling and pretty flat note. Despite the portentous titles this piece is little more than an extended nine-minute drum solo by Mason with electronically treated percussion. Anyone who had suffered the album this far in the expectation of some programme music was likely to be severely disappointed but by this stage most listeners had long since given up the ghost.

In January 1970 following the release of the album, *Beat Instrumental* interviewed Rick Wright and sought his thoughts on the album "The four pieces on the LP are very different, though there are pieces in all of them which link together. There wasn't actually any attempt to connect them all. We didn't write together, we just went into the studios on our own to record and then we got together to listen to them. We all

Rex Features

played alone on our pieces, in fact. Again, we couldn't all agree on this. I thought it was a very valid experiment and it helped me. The result is that I want to carry on and do it again, on a solo album. But I think that maybe Roger feels that if we'd all worked together, it would have been better. That's something you just don't know, whether it would or not. I think it was a good idea. The live part of the album we had to record twice. The first time, at Mother's in Birmingham, we felt we'd played really well but the equipment didn't work so we couldn't use nearly all of that one. The second time, at Manchester College of Commerce, was a really bad gig, but as the recording equipment was working well, we had to use it. Parts of *Saucer* on *Ummagumma* came from the Birmingham gig, which we put together with the Manchester stuff. But the stuff on the album isn't half as good as we can play."

Chapter 5
ATOM HEART MOTHER

The experimentation of Ummagumma was soon recognised as a failure and the album was quickly disowned by the band. Ultimately the orphan bore fruit with Atom Heart Mother. This was the album which gave the band its first UK number one. The title track was a bold, innovative piece with a very stylish arrangement for choir and orchestral elements by Ron Geesin. Sadly the group have come to dislike the piece intensely, and it is without doubt a work of it's time, but it still has the power to enchant the listener with its unexpected twists and turns.

Side Two of the original vinyl disc is a simpler down to earth affair with the pastoral delights of *If* and *Fat Old Sun* providing an elegant contrast to the pointless studio noodlings of *Alan's Psychedelic Breakfast*, a track which again underlined the fact that musique concrête needs more than just an intriguing title to make it interesting. Mercifully, this was the band's last foray into sound collage for the sake of it.

Side one was co-written by Ron Geesin who had become friends with first Nick Mason then Roger Waters. Ron's friendship with Roger was cemented by, of all things, a mutual love of golf, probably the most un-rock 'n' roll of all pastimes. In addition to the golf there was also a mutual background in architecture, another unusual interest for an aspiring musician. Geesin felt that there was some merit in that particular choice. "I can sympathise with the view that the architectural background of Roger and Nick shaped the way they created their music. I myself was also put into an architect's office because my father didn't know what to do with me before I left Glasgow, so I've had experience of architecture also, but at a much lower level. I've always thought architecturally, I've always thought in shape and shape and form is the basis of art. Look at Bach, one of the great sound architects."

By the time the band came to record Ummagumma a tiny piece of the Geesin influence had already rubbed off on Roger Waters as Nick Mason writing in his book *Inside Out* recalled some thirty years later, "Ron had been working on his own for quite some time, so his idiosyncratic techniques and modus operandi were entirely his own. He had interested both Roger and me in home production and his influence can clearly be detected in one element of Roger's contribution to *Ummagumma*, namely *Several Species*.

Despite his minor contribution to the final shape of *Ummagumma*, the music of Pink Floyd as a whole left very little impression on Geesin. Ron has always walked a decidedly idiosyncratic path and it was no real surprise that his musical tastes did not run to psychedelia. When he was finally exposed to the work of Pink Floyd the main criticism for the music from the veteran composer appears to have centered around the absence of melody in much of the band's early output. "I don't remember thinking anything much about their music except a drifting of clouds, a pleasant drifting but not something for me to get off on. I always thought it lacked melody, of course the words, in the Floyd's case, were the melody. You could convert those words into melody in the future one could do that as an artistic exercise or project. What happened then in *Atom Heart Mother* was that because they were kind of exhausted, because of commitments and demands by the manager and EMI Records, they needed some other input. So because I was friends with them all, I was asked to be that input.

"As an artist, I kind of caricatured and parodied a lot of what was going on then. So even when I was kicking about, friends, with the individual members of Pink Floyd, I was gently ribbing them, gently taking the piss, but it was all friendly because I think everyone has to be redressed in a way, everyone has to be bought to some kind of level, doesn't matter who they are. We were just friends and I think they appreciate me for my individuality of thinking and indeed doing. That was the main thing. I didn't see much of Dave Gilmour at that time because he was more of a part of the 'rock scene' a straight musician if you like as was Rick Wright really. The other two, Nick Mason and Roger Waters were much more out going, more multi-dimensional I suppose. They were looking at shape and form in a social circumstance and in an audio-visual way, not just an audio way, so maybe I related to them much more."

Despite the commercial success of the Pink Floyd output, by 1970 the band had yet to make a real coherent musical statement. Geesin had certainly got close to the heart of the problem with his observation that Floyd's output lacked melody. There was definitely an emerging Floyd style, but there was, as yet no masterpiece; no show stopper. Pink Floyd had long since given up performing the poppy Barret material and were working on epic tracks such as *Set the Controls* and *Careful With That Axe*. Taken as a whole the material produced a highly satisfying concert experience, but it definitely lacked the twists of melodic genius that would characterise *Meddle* and *Dark Side Of The Moon*. The band was still suffering from the loss of their key creative force and even in 1970 was still finding it's feet as a compositional team. The new Floyd had not yet begun to really fly as a creative writing force. *Ummagumma* was at best a patchy affair, but at least as regards the live album it was clear that there was a cohesive approach to making music on stage which centred on the interplay of dynamics and repetition. There was a specific Floyd sound which took time to develop and had it's own distinct atmosphere, but they certainly weren't tunes you could hum in the bath.

Although Pink Floyd are today remembered for the brilliance of their work in the studio it's important not to overlook the fact that the band was very much a working touring live unit. This is particularly important when one considers how much of Pink Floyd's output was routined on the road. It was in the concert hall where emerging new compositions would be tested and refined over a long series of live dates. During this process familiar tracks would often be given working titles. As we have seen *Careful With That Axe* was one example which was originally known as *Murderistic Woman*. In 1970 the band began trying out an extended piece known as *The Amazing Pudding*. Once *The Amazing Pudding* emerged from the development process it had metamorphosed into *Atom Heart Mother* and had gained additional instrumentation in the form of a ten piece brass section and full choir. The piece was performed live by the four piece band on dozens of occasions. In it's full scale incarnation it was transmitted live on the BBC and on the Europa satellite. As regards live performances the full scale work was toured extensively in Europe and America. It was also performed live at the Bath Festival where the surviving film footage demonstrates just how difficult it was to get the thing right. *Atom Heart Mother* was an incredibly difficult piece and the studio version which finally saw the light of day on the album was simply not designed with the live arena in mind. The surviving examples on film and radio both demonstrate the problems synchronising the band with the orchestral elements. As a result of the awkward opening time signature in the introduction the brass in particular tended to sound ragged and undisciplined.

The process of composition which led to the birth of *Atom Heart Mother* seems to have been rather vague with the result that there was also a certain vagueness in the results.

Writing in his book *Inside Out* Nick Mason described the vague genesis of the piece. Clearly the rather woolly approach to creating the music was unlikely to bear any great fruit given the confused beginnings of the work as recalled by Mason. "*Atom Heart Mother* had been assembled during a number of rehearsals. Once we settled on the nucleus of the piece (a theme supplied I think by David), everyone else had contributed, not only musically, but also in devising the overall dynamics. I can't remember now if we had decided to create a longer piece or whether it just snowballed, but it was a way of operating we were starting to feel comfortable with. After some lengthy sessions in early 1970, we had created a very long, rather majestic, but rather unfocused and still unfinished piece. One way to develop such a piece was to play it live, so we played shortened versions, sometimes dubbed *The Amazing Pudding,* at a number of gigs. Gradually we added, subtracted and multiplied the elements, but still seemed to lack an essential something. I think we had always intended to record the track, but the songwriters must have all felt they had hit a specific block, as in the early summer we decided to hand over the music as it existed to Ron Geesin and asked him if he could add some orchestral colour and choral parts."

The Amazing Pudding was certainly a piece that needed something. There are quite a few surviving recordings of the piece and none really has a great deal to recommend them. In 1970 the band laid down an hour long television special for KQED which began with a complete performance of *The Amazing Pudding.* It is tempting to over do the culinary metaphors, but let's just say it was at best unappetising and leave it there. The diligent searcher will also have come across a DVD version of Floyd performing *Atom Heart Mother* which purports to have been recorded at The Hakon Festival. In reality it is actually the sound from the 1970 Montreux performance cut to pictures of the Japanese performance shot by the promoters. The audio performance is much better than many from the time, but the effect is spoiled by the clandestine long lens shots of the accompanying visuals which clearly do not match the performance on stage.

Nick Mason's hunch that Ron Geesin was right for the project proved to be correct. For his part Geesin also agreed with Nick's general impression that the piece lacked form. Much later Ron Geesin recalled the process of beginning to bring some sense of order to the proceedings. "It was Roger who actually suggested to me that I should help Floyd with their next album. He proposed the idea that I should write the brass and choir pieces. Floyd were off to the States then, and Roger left me with a skeleton tape of rhythm and chords. Nobody had a clear idea of what was wanted, they didn't read music and didn't have to, so it was never an easy musical dialogue. The group was mostly receptive to my ideas. There were murmuring and frowns and puzzlement at times, but rather like the way I had to accept their tape, they had to accept what I did because none of them could write music and I could only write it very slowly. I was only one page ahead in the book really from that point of view."

This last statement by Ron seems a little unfair to Rick who was the band's resident musical theorist, having studied keyboards and trombone before joining the nascent Pink Floyd while a student at architectural college. Bored of life as a trainee architect Rick left and enrolled at music college before finally joining Floyd full time, so the keyboardist at least was well grounded in musical theory. Summer '68 demonstrates Rick's own skills for brass arrangement.

In any event the piece which would ultimately become *Atom Heart Mother* had by now been performed many times on the road. With a structure now beginning to take shape it was time to really get down to work in the recording studio which was once again EMI's Abbey Road now something of a second home for the band. It was to prove eventful to say the least as Nick Mason recorded in *Inside Out..* "Unfortunately, *Atom Heart Mother* is twenty-four minutes long. Roger and I embarked on what can only be described as an Odyssean voyage to record the backing track. In order to keep tracks free for the overdubs we had bass and drums on two tracks, and the whole recording had to be done in one pass. Playing the piece without any instruments meant that getting through it without mistakes demanded the full range of our limited musicianship; matters such as tempo had to be left in abeyance. The delights of quantizing - using computers to digitally adjust tempos without affecting pitch - were still some twenty years in the future. "Once this preliminary process had been completed the band handed the tapes to Ron Geesin and went off to tour America. Working from the tapes supplied, Geesin scratched his head for a while before he finally took the plunge and got down to work. He later recalled the creation of the piece. "The recording process for *Atom Heart Mother* was a collage. They had five or six little sections that they had recorded at EMI Abbey Road, of what I call a backing track. It was quite a thick texture but it was a backing track. They had then stuck these together, as you do with magnetic tape. They'd come up with a tape which was an accompaniment tape lasting 23 minutes and they gave me a rough mix of that tape and we had some discussions about what might go on it. They said they wanted a big sound, they wanted a choir section here and probably some kind of louder, raucous section here, possibly brass, and we had a very short session, and I'm talking a morning and another bit of an afternoon somewhere, where Rick Wright came round to my studio in Ladbroke Grove, London and we looked at the choir section. He suggested maybe some notes, but there was nothing written down for the choir at that time and then Dave came round with a sort of arpeggio, which in Italian, means 'steps'. It wasn't a melody, it was a pattern and he suggested that for what was in fact the opening, the main theme. The rest of it was me. It's a concoction, an assembly. The tapes of the sections were stuck together. Because they were stuck together and they didn't have the energy or time to re-do them, because they were off on tour, I remember those little briefing sessions happened and then they were off to America or some other place, the speeds were all wrong. When you're moving through a piece you know when it should speed up and when it should slow down. In fact the reverse happened with some of the sections. When they stuck the sessions together they didn't actually really work, so my job was to craft something sensible on top of this rather cobbled collage or montage and make it look like it was working. To me that's craft, not art, although we could have a long discussion about the relationship between craft and art. The art bit was getting a couple of melodies that really worked and I believe that the opening theme melody really works and the cello melody really works. They are entirely out of my head, except as I say, Dave doing a little arpeggio piece. So we had the cobbled together tapes, which was the best they could do at the time, given the restraints of time and energy. My job was to make something sensible on the top so as not to appear like it was the same as the joins that they had made. I consider that to be a crafting process, not particularly an art process, but the art is in the making of original melodies and structures."

As we have seen, the album was recorded in a very curious way with Nick and Roger laying down the whole of the twenty odd minutes of backing track in a single take. To obtain a result from this strange way of working certainly requires someone with a particuar approach to music. More than thirty years on, Nick Mason writing in *Inside Out*, remains highly complimentary concerning Geesin and his work "Ron Geesin is a talented musician and arranger, as well as a virtuoso performer on banjo and harmonium, when his style might best be described as ragtime poetry on speed. The good news was that with Ron at the helm, it was unlikely that we'd end up with 'The London Symphonic Philharmonia Plays Pink Floyd'. Ron set to work on our piece, and with little further input from us, he arrived at Abbey Road armed with a sheaf of scores ready to record. He immediately ran up against a major hurdle. The session players balked at being directed by Ron, who they perceived as belonging to the world of rock music. As Ron waved his baton hopefully, they made as much trouble as they could. Ron had not only written some technically demanding parts, but the phrasing he wanted was unusual. The musicians hated this even more. With microphones open they knew every comment would be noted and their discreet laughter, clock-watching, and constant interruptions of 'Please sir, what does this mean?' meant that recording was at a standstill, the chances of Ron being had up on a manslaughter charge increased logarithmically by the second."

Ron himself has never made any secret of the problems encountered during the recording process by a young and fairly inexperienced composer finding himself confronted with the grizzled veterans hardened by years of session work. "I didn't choose whether to use or not use anything. Pink Floyd and EMI Records dictated the limits and how there would have been so many session players etc. The brass players were session players, EMI-type of session players, who were of a high quality but not to my standards of best orchestral players. I had been doing very tiny pieces before in TV commercials and short films, where I used sections of the Philharmonia Orchestra of London. The whole of the trumpet section I used for one. Now I would have booked them in like a shot because they would have known how to interpret the piece just right but the players that were on *Atom Heart Mother* were rather hard. Brass players are known to be rather hard and it's been told already in some books that I had a bit of a go at a horn player because he was mouthing off. He could see that I was nervous because I didn't have much experience of directing professional musicians. I knew a lot about how to make a good form, but not about directing. So he could see this and that suited him to have a bit of a go and I said 'Another word from you mate and I'm over there'. And in the box they're all going 'Christ Almighty - Ron's lost it', so I had to be taken off doing the conducting bit, which, to be honest, I wasn't best suited to because I was green, I was definitely a new boy with all these well-worn session players. So it was a tense moment. So that was why John Aldiss, the choirmaster, was asked to conduct the rest of the whole session and I just sat at the side and said 'You want a bit more punch into that,' or, 'Do this.' I actually pretty well cracked up, due to the strain of working. I'd done a lot of work that year - films, an album, so I was ready for a bit of a rest so he took over. But the main point about him taking over was that he, as a classically trained person, didn't have that punchy drive that a Duke Ellington, standing up in front of the band would have had, and I really needed that kind of direction. If I could have held on for a bit or gone and had a breather for a couple of days, I would have done it and it would have been punchier. The delivery of the brass section was a bit woolly for me but it worked. And it may have been more suitable for the Pink Floyd cloud-drifting aspect. But that's the fact of it."

Overall the recording process was very far from smooth which inevitably affected the results. To Nick Mason it seemed as if it was one problem after another, even the introduction of new technology was to prove a hindrance rather than a help as he later recalled in *Inside Out*. "This was not his only problem. At the time the piece was recorded

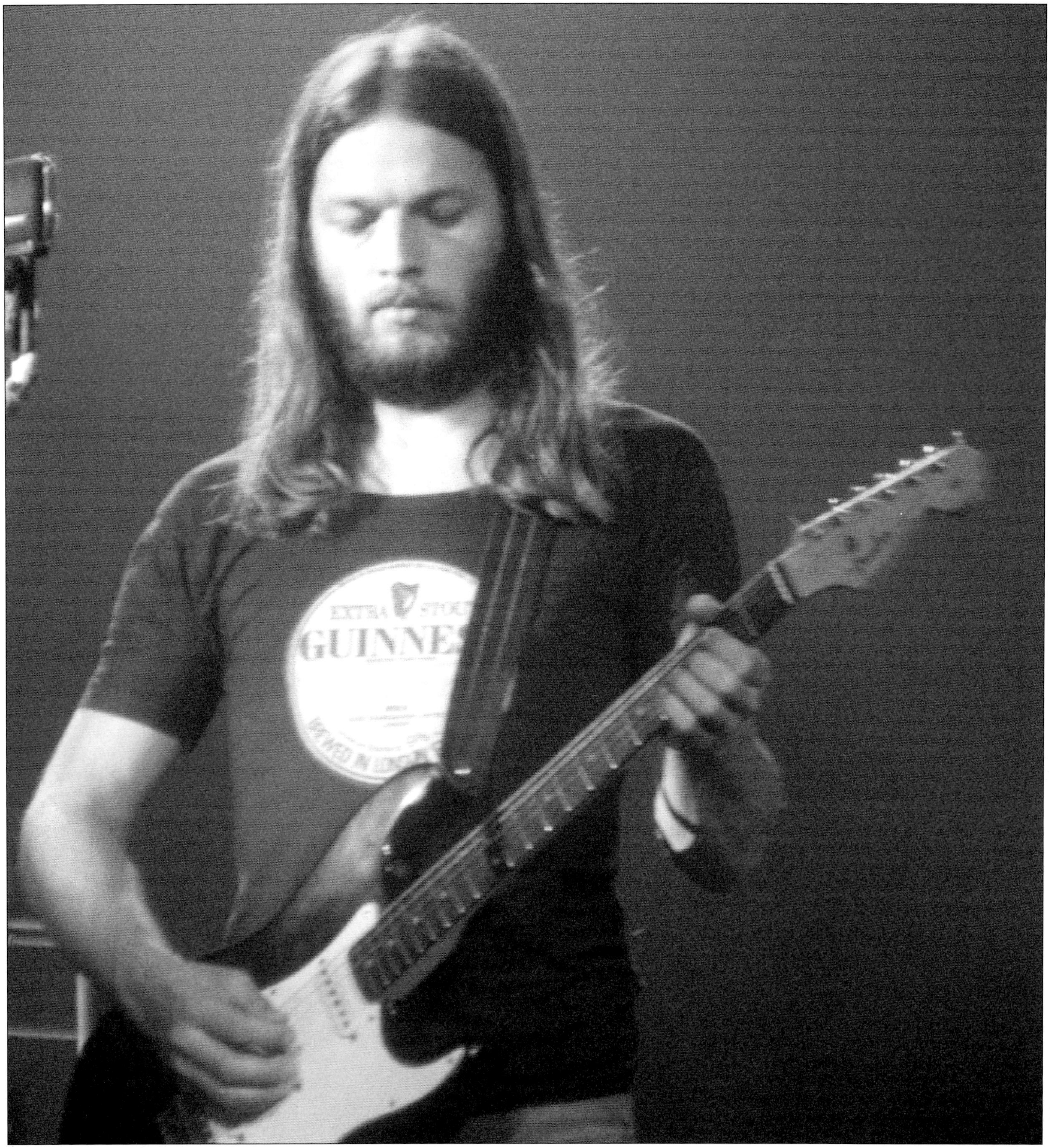

Rex Features

EMI had just taken delivery of the latest in recording technology, the eight-track Studer recorders. These utilised one-inch-wide tape, and with admirable caution EMI issued a directive that no edits were to be done on this, as they were worried about the quality of the splicing." Naturally all of this made things rather difficult for a band for whom cutting and re-cutting tape had become a way of life particularly when it came to the inclusion of the sound effects as Geesin later recalled. "There's the motorbike and the electronic area and a train. They used a lot of sound effects in those days. They weren't pioneers of ambient music or found objects stuck together because some of the American classical electronic music composers had done that before, so the Floyd were borrowing some of those techniques, but they work very well and I've always said that Roger Waters was a grand master at timing. He was not a great bass player, he didn't need to be. His art is in timing and in knowing exactly what is required and when. Although the piece as a whole is still a pleasant curiosity the timing is most definitely out. There's the famous case of the lost beat where I had written a whole section thinking that beat one was on a certain beat, reading from the tape, but when Nick Mason saw that and we got to the session - this was a choir section - he said 'No, beat one's not there, it's one beat back,' so he said 'you'll have to move everything one beat back.' I said no, why not take that as one beat, it's only where the bar lines are written on the score and I didn't have the time to go away and overnight move the bar lines one beat because that's what you'd have to do. The phrasing's all correct for what was I in the backing, which was an off-beat punchy section. It's the funky section. So no-one has ever heard that section as I wrote it and that's something that could be done in the future. Put that section back and in fact, I was talking to the Italians, who have not yet been able to do this piece, about doing it and making the whole thing longer and bigger - in other words more performers. And actually doing that section, doing the backing twice and have the choir section moved on for one beat, for once through, and in the original position for the second time through. I don't know if that would ever happen."

It will come as no surprise to the alert reader to discover that these unpromising factors conspired together to further reduce the chances of achieving an acceptable result. This was confirmed by Nick Mason writing in *Inside Out*. "Sure enough the finished piece lacked the metronomic timekeeping that would have made life easier for everyone. Instead the rhythm track accelerated and then lurched back to the correct tempo in a volatile fashion that Ron now had to take into account. The day was saved by John Aldiss, the choirmaster, whose disciplined classical choir had (it must be noted) a far more positive attitude and plenty of experience of dealing with orchestras. With their unruffled help, the recording was completed. However, there was another problem we were unaware of at the time. We had been forced to supply relatively high levels of backing track to the orchestra of monitor speakers, some of which had been picked up by their microphones. This unerasable spill forever ensured that *Atom Heart Mother* lacked the sonic clarity we have always strived for."

Although he was under considerable pressure, Geesin was aware of the below par aspects of the work and despite all of the trials and tribulations would willingly have put himself through the whole ordeal again. "Because of all these non-perfections, I said to Steve O'Rourke, the manager, after the recording session had finished 'Well that was a good rehearsal, can we do it for real now?' That was never to be. The money had run out, the energy had run out. EMI said we've got to get it out. The speed fluctuations would all have been put right but there was no energy there. Reality prevailed. On the whole it's not a bad little number. It's rather obvious, but it was all that could be done with the material and confinements." Ron Geesin also confirmed the origins of the title which today sounds somewhat grand and portentous but the truth is all rather prosaic. "We were sitting in the control room and John Peel had his newspaper, the *Evening Standard*, and we were sitting round with Nick, Roger and the others. I think they were all there saying, 'We haven't got a title for this,' and I said, 'If you look in there you'll find a title,' and then Roger picked up the paper and said, 'Atomic Heart Mother' and the others said, 'Yeah, that sounds good.'"

The Music

ATOM HEART MOTHER *(Mason/Gilmour/Waters/Wright & Geesin)* — Whatever the band may now think this piece is definitely worth revisiting. Based around a theme which was designed to evoke the atmosphere of a western movie, the piece moves effortlessly through a range of contrasting moods and styles. The playing is superb and the music is by turns both melodic and atonal. The choral section is particularly inspired with the rhythmic qualities of the unformed words harnessed to great effect. The piece is now openly despised by the band and although that may well be justified in the case of *Ummagumma* there are certainly enough plus points in *Atom Heart Mother* to merit a re-evaluation by both it's creators and the listening public.

IF *(Waters)* - Side two of the album was much easier to record and it is an altogether different experience. It opens with If, the first of two tracks by Roger Waters. This is a gentle bucolic sounding piece in the same pastoral vein as *Grantchester Meadows* from *Ummagumma*. Gentle, reflective and unchallenging it provides a total contrast to the breathless hustle and bustle of the first side. If can be described as one of the last echoes of the pastoral Pink Floyd which had blossomed briefly on the *More* soundtrack with gentle tracks like *Cymbeline. Julia Dream* is another good example as is *Grantchester Meadows* from *Ummagumma*. By now the band clearly felt that this gentle bucolic style had run its course and If was destined to be something of a swansong for the acccoustic mellow Floyd sound. Despite the gentle mood of the music the lyrics are much darker, full of self-analytical imagery and self doubt like, "if I was a man I'd talk with you more often" - the first suggestion that Waters would make an art out of his own self-loathing.

SUMMER OF '68 *(Wright)* - is an unusual piece written by Rick Wright which feels like a very British slice of late sixties pop music complete with a rather snappy brass arrangement, often overlooked and never played on stage this is the forgotten moment of the album, but it is a very pleasant track which surprises the listener in its own very English unprepossessing way.

FAT OLD SUN *(Gilmour)* - Next up came *Fat Old Sun*, another understated piece, but one which has nonetheless become something of a favourite among the Floyd fraternity. Clearly the band had exhausted its stocks of creativity at this point and Nick Mason later recalled the difficulty the band had in bringing forth new music at a time when the studio experience seemed to be "endless." It would appear that the threat of being incarcerated in Abbey Road for life, with no chance of parole, was sufficient to galvanise even the most reticent songwriters to perform. *Fat Old Sun* utilised the same chord structure as the main piece but the similarity ends there. This is another piece of what Geesin would term "drifting". The listener is transported effortlessly along on an undemanding journey into the sunset. The quality of the song is enhanced by the effect of Rick Wright's sweet harmony vocal intertwined with Gilmour's equally smooth voice. Gilmour always seems to sound at the very limits of his vocal ability, there is a real fragile quality to the Gilmour vocal and this song is no exception. The only tension which comes from the piece is the listener wondering if Mr Gilmour will be able to hold it all together. A rare live recording of the piece by the BBC surfaced on *Top Gear* .

ALAN'S PSYCHEDELIC BREAKFAST
(Waters/Mason/Gilmour/Wright) - Side two of the album closes with one of the more famous Floyd tracks though one suspects it is as a result of its unusual title as much as for its unusual musical content. The Floyd were often criticised for being po-faced but here was more mischievous humour, based on a thing they sometimes did live where the front rows of the audience would be treated to the sound and smell of bacon and eggs sizzling on a cooker on stage. A mixture of music, sound effects (the dripping tap at the end ran right on to the run-out grooves on original vinyl copies) and mumbled spoken word - at one point a list of favourite breakfast dishes is mumbled in a rather stoned voice by the character of the title, roadie Alan Styles. Roger Waters explained the development of the piece in an interview with *Sounds* from October 1970. "It was the usual thing of an idea coming out of the fact that we'd almost finished an LP but not quite and we needed another so many minutes. We were all frantically trying to write songs, and initially I thought of just doing something on the rhythm of a dripping tap, then it turned into this whole kitchen thing. On the record it's a carefully set up stereo picture of a kitchen with somebody coming in, opening a window, filling a kettle and putting it on the stove. But instead of the gas lighting, there's a chord, so he strikes a match and there's another chord, and so on until it finally goes into a piece of music. The logistics of doing it live are quite difficult - we can't obviously take a set of a kitchen round with us and do it all, but we'll have to have some table arrangement to fry eggs on and boil kettles and everything."

One of the most controversial aspects of the album was the packaging. In stark contrast to the dramatic rollercoaster of the music the cover was filled with a simple unadorned image of a cow in a field. Writing in *Inside Out* Nick Mason recalled the feathers which were being ruffled at EMI Records. "Storm remembers that when he showed the cover to EMI, one of the executives screamed at him, 'Are you mad? Do you want to destroy this record company?'"

With the album at long last in the can and an innovative promotional campaign ready to swing into action it was finally time to allow the British public to form their own judgement. The response was overwhelmingly positive and the album unexpectedly rose to number one in the UK album charts. Ron Geesin had certainly not expected the album to do so well and had not even insisted on a co-writers credit on the sleeve of the album. "Yes, I was definitely surprised by the commercial success. That was a surprise, when I'd slaved away for years at projects and not got much obvious return or reward. We're talking spiritual reward here - not just money, so it was a great surprise and nice. But I'll never understand why they did not put my name on the cover, or at least give me a proper acknowledgement. It's on as a composer credit. To me that also showed the part of the Floyd that not too many people know which is the giant money-making machine. It gradually grew on me that I should have had credit for that because from my career point of view it would have helped a bit and it would probably have stopped me from the rather galling activity of self-publicity. I should just be playing stuff and making my art without having to say 'I did that.'"

Despite the complexity of the piece the band were undaunted by the prospect of taking the piece on the road, but it was still not something to be taken lightly as David Gilmour confirmed in an interview given in 1970 when the band was preparing to take the show over to America. "Something on the scale of *Atom Heart Mother* really takes a lot of getting together. The problem is that we've never done it more than twice with the same people. The choir is usually all right because they're used to working together, but some of the brass people have been really hopeless. We had problems with the sound equipment, getting it miked up and balanced and stuff. The trouble was also not having enough rehearsal time everywhere we did it, because we used a different brass and choir group in Europe than the one we used on the East Coast, and another one on the West Coast. So we used three completely different sets of people performing it. We tried to hire musicians from local symphonies, if possible. Often we couldn't get them all from local symphonies, so we'd just get session musicians. We found our conductor, Peter Phillips, by coming over and looking for someone a couple of months before the tour..."

The results of the live performances were highly variable ranging from mediocre to diabolical. Geesin found the live experience excruciating. "From what little I saw of them, I hated the live performances. The brass and choir were not up to live performing, the conductor did all he could to keep the thing together but it was pretty ragged and I know that I left Hyde Park in tears and I don't know what went on in America. I could stand seeing *Atom Heart Mother* performed again but only properly and that means re-instating the original missing beat in the funky section and enlarge the choir by a factor of ten, from 20 to 200 and probably the brass from 10 to at least double, so there would be two instruments on each."

It was not just *Atom Heart Mother* which presented difficulties in respect of possible live performances. On June 3, 1972 *New Musical Express* published an interview with Rick Wright in which he explored the difficulties presented by other tracks on the album.

"We have had difficulties. For example, *Alan's Psychedelic Breakfast* we tried on our English tour and it didn't work at all, so we had to give it up. None of us liked doing it, anyway, and we didn't like it on the album. It's rather pretentious. It doesn't do anything. Quite honestly, it's a bad number. A similar idea, in that idiom, we did at Roundhouse another time, I thought was much better. Practically on the spot, we decided to improvise a number where we fried eggs on stage and Roger threw potatoes about, and it was spontaneous, and it was really good. *Alan's Breakfast* was a weak number. We don't have that much problem producing things on stage. We work on our four instruments, which is all we have on stage, and adapt accordingly."

Chapter 6
MEDDLE

For all of it's supposed faults Atom Heart Mother had finally produced the breakthrough which had been threatened for so long. The task now was to consolidate their new found position as commercial and artistic heavy weights. As well as their status, the word heavy could equally be applied to Roger Water's state of mind. Long before the angst-ridden albums which would appear later in the decade, as early as October 9, 1971 in a Melody Maker interview, Waters gave a glimpse of the factors which would come to characterise the man as an artist. "I work to keep my mind off a doomy situation. All over the globe, it gets crazier every day. And the craziness seems to be accelerating at a fantastic rate. But it might just be that, as you get older, your perception gets faster, until the whole thing seems unreal."

The next album had to be a major step forward and the band were all too aware of the pressure. They rose to the challenge magnificently and the result was *Meddle* which marked a huge leap forward in compositional terms and also in the contributions and performances from the individual members of the band collectively. Three highly significant factors simultaneously came into play to ensure that *Meddle* would be an outstanding album. It was highly significant that Roger Waters had at last blossomed as a lyricist. As a result the lyrics of *Echoes* are mature, confident and meaningful. The point of transformation in Echoes is particularly well handled with a magnificent economy of language and a strong poetic sense which was to develop strongly from here onwards.

> *"Strangers passing in the street*
> *By chance two separate glances meet*
> *And I am you and what I see is me."*

These three brilliant lines can almost be viewed as the moment when Waters finally emerged as a fully formed lyricist. From this point onwards there would be no stopping the man who would become recognised as one of the greatest wordsmiths in rock. It is also in *Echoes* that we see the first use of the device of repetition in Water's lyrics.

The most effective use of this particular technique would be shortly unveiled in *Eclipse* where it is used to best effect, but we see it first in Echoes where the receptiveness of the lyrics blends wonderfully with the music to create a stunning tour de force. As the great cyclical theme soars upwards it is propelled by the repetitive pattern of the unforgiving lyric

> *"And no-one calls us to move on*
> *And no-one forces down our eyes*
> *And no-one speaks and no-one tries*
> *An no-one flies around the sun."*

Just as Waters was developing his craft so too was David Gilmour who had also had time to mature as an artist. Gilmour now boasted his own distinctive guitar technique and we are first introduced to this new found mastery on *Echoes*. It was certainly not a style of playing based on technical wizardy with lightning fast fretboard runs of Jimmy Page or Ritchie Blackmore, but Floyd were never judged by the number of notes played. Like a master craftsman, Gimour's great skill lay in an amazing ability to select the perfect note at the perfect time, and *Meddle* was the first evidence of his new found confidence on the instrument. As a band Floyd had taken on board the hard earned lessons of *Atom Heart Mother* and they were now a highly experienced studio recording ensemble constantly seeking out new and innovative ways to enhance the sound of their recordings. Nothing was sacrosanct or too unlikely to be worth trying.

Most important of all however, the Floyd collectively had finally flowered as composers of outstanding melodies. To date the Floyd albums had demonstrated a mastery of dynamics but had consistently lacked the sublime melodies which would come to characterise their later work. Much of the *Meddle* album is still very much rooted in the mid-tempo four beats in the bar which Floyd tended to favour, but where earlier albums had relied heavily on repeated patterns with varying loud and soft passages, *Meddle* was constructed around the sublime melodies of *Echoes*, the stand out track of the album. Although both albums differ radically in form, in retrospect *Meddle* owes a great deal of it's success to the band's work with Ron Geesin on *Atom Heart Mother*. It was on the previous album that the Floyd had first discovered how even the most unpromising piece could be transformed when the stylistic hallmarks of the Floyd sound were married to really strong expansive melodies for the first time in their career. The success of the huge main theme of *Atom Heart Mother* and the haunting cello section were reflected in the sales of the album which had pushed a Floyd disc to number one for the first time. These lessons were swiftly learned and adapted for *Echoes* which proved to be the first major composition from the band itself which measured up to every musical standard. With *Meddle*, and Echoes in particular, Pink Floyd demonstrated that the group had learned how to take the innovative sound effects which the band had made their own and weave them together with the music to create a seamless blend which was to become synonymous with Pink Floyd. The results are best seen in *Echoes* which is still a classic slice of Floyd today.

One Of These Days is another masterpiece which succeeds in blending sound effects into the music to create a unified whole. The band were keen to unveil their work as soon as possible and gave strong performances which included the BBC *Top Gear* show . This hard earned skill developed over the previous four albums was to become a hallmark of the Pink Floyd sound of the future. This is the record that finally began to define Pink Floyd's image and sound. As we have seen, *Atom Heart Mother* represents the transition point at which, with Ron Gessin's help, Pink Floyd finally managed to marry strong melody to their dynamic ideas. *Meddle* represents the moment when the Floyd discovered the ability to create melody for themselves. From this point on, the band would never look back. In an article published on December 11, 1971 in *Disc and Music Echo* magazine David Gilmour set out his views on the mood of the music created for *Meddle*. "We're really making emotional music. I wouldn't say it's intellectual. In England it's different. We can do anything we like, really. We've often gone onstage and done material that we've never done before and the audiences are used to us and they love it. But in the States, it's more or less like we have to play our hits. At the concert, the crowd yelled for Pink Floyd to play *Astronomy Domine* and *See Emily Play*, to which Rogers replied, 'You must be joking!'"

The Music

ONE OF THESE DAYS *(Waters/Wright/Mason/Gilmour)* - The album opens with *One Of These Days,* a group collaboration credited jointly to all four members. So named because everything was going wrong in the studio the day they recorded this piece (AIR studios January 1971). *One Of These Days* builds into a furious space rocker with great use of Mason's backwards recorded cymbals. The hugely impressive bass sound is actually achieved by using two bass guitars played through the Binson echo unit. The second of the double tracked basses is actually played by David Gilmour following Roger Waters' lead a bar behind. Nick Mason's is the treated voice saying 'one of these days I'm going to cut you into little pieces.'

A PILLOW OF WINDS *(Waters/Gilmour)* - is next up. It takes the form of a restrained, ethereal, predominantly acoustic ballad written by Waters/Gilmour that makes ample use of a wind machine. This is a classic Floyd lyric, which follows a daily cycle in human life: bedtime, sleep, dreaming and rising to greet another day. The song itself is one of the more disposable moments in the Pink Floyd cannon and does not appear to have been played live on stage.

FEARLESS *(Waters/Gilmour)*- Fearless composed jointly by Roger Waters and David Gilmour is a piece that seems to presage the themes of the next album with references to someone who could well evolve into Syd in lines like 'fearlessly the idiot faced the crowd '. The Floyd play off the song's strong melody line against the recorded sounded of Liverpool FC fans on the Anfield Kop, chanting their anthem *You'll Never Walk Alone*.

SAN TROPEZ *(Waters)* - is a cocktail jazz paean to the French resort beloved of the jet set and Hollywood stars. The Floyd were frequent visitors to the French Riviera and the Med. However many fans regard this as the worst Floyd track of all time.

SEAMUS *(Waters/Wright/Mason/Gilmour)* - A short throwaway acoustic blues written about a dog whose whining and barks are part of the lead vocals throughout. A Floydian joke that seemed funny to the band but ultimately backfired. Seamus was a real-life mutt that belonged to Humble Pie's Steve Marriott - the connection being his band mate Jerry Shirley who played with Dave Gilmour in Jokers Wild and also appeared at Gilmour's invitation on the 'Barrett' album. When Steve was on tour in the summer of 1970 Syd and his girlfriend apparently looked after Seamus at the Pie man's gaff in Essex!

ECHOES *(Waters/Gilmour/Mason/Wright)* - The whole of side two is dedicated to the group composition *Echoes, which* has been described by Roger Waters as 'an epic sound poem'. With this piece the Floyd shifted their direction from outer space to the world above and beneath the ocean waves. The lyrics abound with references to Albatrosses and choral caves, the eerie sound of a repeated submarine ASDIC bleep. With Floyd finally unchaining the keys to the melody cabinet this is a bleakly beautiful and darkly terrifying piece, especially famous for the middle sequence with its myriad of sound effects like crows cawing. The number started out as a single note played on the piano by Wright and then put through a microphone and a Leslie cabinet. Parts of the track were also used as the soundtrack to the Crystal Voyager surfing movie.

Michael Watts was given the job of reviewing the album for the respected British music journal *Melody Maker* which duly published his review in November 1971. Unfortunately Mr Watts found little to cheer about and his piece was entitled "Pink's muddled *Meddle*" which gives something of the flavour of the following critical ire. "One can't help but feel that Pink Floyd are so much sound and fury, signifying nothing. Their achievement has been to create a space rock sound, which revolves around the use of electronic effects combined with the usual musical instrumentation of four-piece rock bands, i. e. drums, guitar, bass and organ. Frequently, they have utilized this concept to good effect, right from the early days of *Interstellar Overdrive* and *Astronomy Domine* to the *Atom Heart Mother* and *Ummagumma* albums, but how much of this, in fact, has been pure effect? Stripped of the sense of etherea, the music hardly stands up as more than competent rhythmic rock, while even the use of electronics and spacey atmospherics is not as adventurous as it may seem at first hearing, especially when considered alongside such as *Zero Times* by *Tonto's Expanding Headband*.

"*Meddle* exhibits all their faults, as well as their most successful points. The first side is taken up with songs, as opposed to long instrumental pieces, and it's in this area that they most expose themselves to criticism. Since Syd Barrett left, there has been no one in the band able to cope with the sort of pithy statement that is necessary to the five-minute pop track, which undoubtedly explains why they have ceased to work to the single format. The vocals verge on the drippy, and the instrumental work-outs, which rely heavily on Dave Gilmour's guitar, are decidedly old hat. Listen to *One of These Days*; it's a throwback to *Telstar* by the Tornados. The second side, *Echoes,* is the one where the concept comes in. It encompasses the whole side, starts off with a passage of Asdic pings and lots of soaring guitar before settling into a genuinely funky organ riff, and then there is introduced some wind effects and the sound of cawing rooks (or it could be cows; that's how it comes across). It follows on with some beautiful cello set against further use of the Asdic, before the whole piece crashes out in a crescendo of volume and rattling cymbals. Far out, you may say. Not really. Although there appears to be some continuity in the work – the Asdic echoes, get it? – my basic impression was of a series of effects without any underlying depth. Interesting, even aesthetic, they may be, but superficial ultimately, like background noise in a Radio Three play. When there is little real musical substance to sustain those effects, how can the result be anything but a soundtrack to a non-existent movie?"

On February 19, 1972 *New Musical Express* published a much more positive interview with Nick Mason in which he explored the relationship between *Atom Heart Mother* and *Meddle*. "Yes, I think there are similarities between *Atom Heart Mother* and *Meddle*. I don't think we could have done *Meddle* without doing *Atom Heart Mother*." Isn't the construction of the two pieces very similar? Mason answered, "You're obviously right about the construction. There are various things that have a Pink Floyd flavour, but are also very dangerous Pink Floyd clichés. One is the possible tendency to get stuck into a sort of slow four tempo. And the other thing is to take a melody line, or the chorus, or something, and flog it to death. Maybe we'll play it once slow and quiet, the next time a bit harder, third time really heavy, which tends to come a little bit into *Meddle* and in *Atom Heart Mother*. But it's slightly more forgivable with the choir and orchestra because it's nice building an orchestra and bringing in extra brass and playing more complex lines. There are various sections on *Atom Heart Mother* that I'm very happy with. I love the choir section, both the singing and the spoken choir section. The constructing of *Echoes* is rather similar in terms of it running through various movements. But the movements are so different that I don't feel that we've had to milk *Atom Heart Mother* to produce *Echoes*. *Echoes* was a specific attempt to sort of do something by a slightly different method. What we did, in fact, was book a studio for January, and throughout January we went in and played. Anytime that anyone had any sort of rough idea of something, we would put it down. At the end of January, we listened back and we'd got 36 different bits and pieces that sometimes cross-related and sometimes didn't. *Echoes* was made up from that."

Chapter 7
POMPEII

Echoes also formed the foundations of the superb film Pink Floyd at Pompeii directed by French director Adrian Maben. The bulk of the film was shot between October 4th and 7th 1971 with some additional filming in Paris between the 13th and 20th of December.

Pink Floyd had always been greatly appreciated in Europe and the Pompeii film is the result of a European co-production. It is still rightly regarded by many as the best evocation of the Floyd in the live environment. Elegantly directed and brilliantly shot, the success of the Pompeii film rests on the fact that in Echoes the Floyd had at last created a musical masterpiece. The flawless performance served up in the empty ruins only served to underline the strength of the material. Another stand out moment in the Floyd film and the *Meddle* album is, of course, *One Of These Days*. Once again the superb quality of the direction and photography combine with a quite remarkable performance to produce a record of the Floyd at their very best. Interestingly for a band which relied so strongly on stage effects this simple unpretentious presentation is remarkably effective.

The public launch of the film was an embarrassing fiasco. After a successful screening at the Edinburgh Film Festival in the summer of 1972, the film was slated for a London premiere at a sold out screening at the Rainbow theatre on November 25th 1972. Unfortunately the whole event had to be cancelled at the last minute for contractual and licensing reasons with 3000 fans being turned away at the door. The film finally enjoyed a general release in 1973 and was well received by audiences composed naturally enough of Pink Floyd fans.

On February 5, 1972 *Disc and Music Echo* ran an interview with Rick Wright in which he explained the reasons for the film. "We did get into a lazy period. There was a point when we sat about not knowing what to do. That was before and during *Atom Heart Mother*. After that, we wondered what to do. Then *Meddle* came, and since then we've been quite excited about what we've been doing. I think our best music comes from that method of working because, in a studio, everyone is throwing in ideas and rejecting ideas. *Saucer* was done in the same way. But there is this schizophrenic half to the group, definitely a sort of macabre relish of titles like that."

Chapter 8
OBSCURED BY CLOUDS
(Music from the film La Vallée)

By the time the Pompeii film had finally been launched the Floyd had completed another foray into film soundtrack music. Their old chum Barbet Schroeder had again come up with a sufficiently lucrative offer to justify the band taking time out to have yet another tilt at the world of film. Time was incredibly tight but the money was attractive and the music for La Valée was accordingly written and recorded in two one week sessions. The first was squeezed in, in February 1972 after a two week UK tour.

The second session was shoe horned in during March 1972 following a short tour of Japan and before the band left for America. Given the haste of the recording sessions the album was never likely to come up to the standards of a regular studio album. However the soundtrack album certainly worked better than the film which was justifiably lambasted by the critics. Sandwiched between two stunning studio albums *Obscured by Clouds* is often overlooked, but nonetheless rewards the listener with it's understated elegance. Musical highlights are the title track, *Mudmen* and *Free Four*.

Barbet Schroeder had asked the Floyd to come back and compose the soundtrack for *La Vallée* (The Valley), a feature about French longhairs communing with nature in New Guinea, while looking for the mythical place of the film's title and seeking the meaning of life. The album was recorded at the Chateau d'Herouville (Elton John's Honky Chateau!). Originally called *La Vallée*, the soundtrack album was re-christened after a dispute with the film's producers. The switch of name was made in order to prevent the film makers from riding on the back of the Floyd angle. Undettered however, the film makers simply re-named the film *La Vallée Obscured By Clouds* and carried on regardless. *Obscured By Clouds* makes for a magnificent title piece, and the psychedelic throbbing pulse from the VCS3 soon became the curtain-raiser at Floyd gigs in 1972.

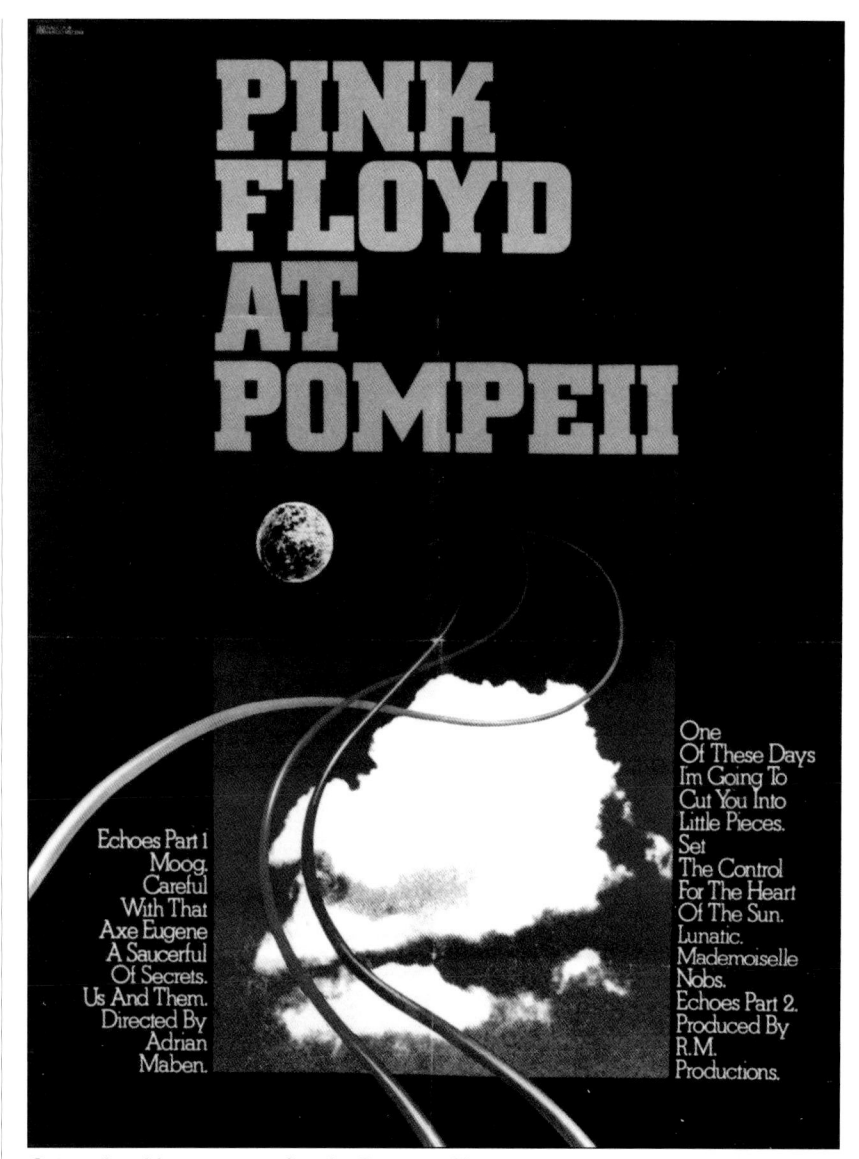

Original publicity poster for the Pompeii film.

Although very much a soundtrack album, the album did have an untypically large proportion of regular songs, Nick Mason would later comment, "I thought it was a sensational LP, actually." There are some fine Floydian moments in between the passages written purely to enhance what was going on up on the big screen. There's Gilmour's ace rocker *Childhood's End*, inspired by Arthur C. Clarke's eponymous novel, but the real gem and another pointer to the band's future was *Free Four*, as in the 'one two three four' count-in to playing a number. This song featured an old man out of his mind on his deathbed, rambling on about the shortness of life - the bleak and cynical tone, belying the almost breezy musical accompaniment.

The Music

Obscured By Clouds features a stunning instrumental introduction with an ominous bass section overlaid with trademark Floyd guitar and some truly inspiring VCS3 synthesiser work.

WHEN YOU'RE IN *(Waters/Mason/Gilmour/Wright)* Next up is *When You're In,* a number written by the entire band. We move up tempo for a riff driven instrumental featuring Gilmour and Wright doubling up on the riff, an unusual moment in the Floyd canon.

BURNING BRIDGES *(Waters/Wright)* A rare Waters/Wright collaboration provides some welcome contrast featuring a soft gentle acoustic interlude with a gentle Gilmour/Wright vocal and some tasteful, mournful guitar.

THE GOLD IT'S IN THE… *(Waters/Gilmour)* is a typical rock song but very untypical of Pink Floyd. We seem to have strayed into Eagles territory with this straight forward mid-tempo slice of American sounding AOR written by Waters and Gilmour.

WOT'S…UH, THE DEAL? *(Waters/Gilmour)* The second consecutive Waters/Gilmour number which features a warm acoustic guitar intro over a softly sung Gilmour/Wright vocal which had by this stage become somewhat over familiar in Floyd recordings. Some nicely understated piano from Rick Wright raises this one out of the ordinary.

MUDMEN *(Wright/Gilmour)* - Features some excellent guitar work which majestically rises above the generally plodding nature of the track.

CHILDHOOD'S END *(Gilmour)* - Composed by David Gilmour, this is another of those tracks which utilises the ominous build up before the song settles into an interesting driving rhythm with shades of Native American drumming, big organ chords and excellent guitar work from Gilmour which looks forward to *Wish You Were Here*.

FREE FOUR *(Waters)* - This is Roger Waters in uncharacteristically good time, feel good mode with a number from the mould of the Beatles or at least what the Beatles might have sounded like with a VCS3. The title is a phonetic pun on the standard drummers count in "one, two, free, four!"

STAY *(Waters/Wright)* – is the second Waters/Wright composition, this is more gentle mellow Floyd in an otherwise unremarkable confection sung by Rick Wright.

ABSOLUTELY CURTAINS *(Waters/Wright/Mason/Gilmour)* - closes the album with a stylish Mellotron and organ intro gives way to a long outro comprised of music from the natives of New Guinea. After *Green Is The Colour* on *More,* this is arguably Floyd's second foray into what would later be termed "world music".

At the time of the album's release, *Sounds*, then the third most popular music magazine in the country, ran an extended interview with a very enthusiastic Nick Mason. "I thought the album was an amazing improvement on the film music, and I thought the film music was really good. But then I thought the same about *More*. It's one of the annoying things, in a way, that the difference between something we've spent a week on and something that takes nine months isn't that great. I mean, the thing that takes nine months isn't thirty six times as good. Obviously, nine months doesn't mean nine months solid recording, but even so. I thought it was particularly good from that point of view. It had a good, together feel. It was a fairly relaxed album, but it was, well, tight. I like that sort of short, scheme thing. It's less disappointing in a way. Whenever we finish an album, I always think it could have been better. But with things like *More* and *Obscured by Clouds*, I tend to think it's really not bad for the time. Perhaps it's just there's more excuses."

Sadly there were no excusue for the accompanying film . It is a truly wretched, appalling effort. So bad in fact that film critic Tim Healey selected *La Vallée (Obscured by Clouds)* as one of The World's Worst Movies, in the book of the same name published in 1986.

"A personal reminiscence: many years ago I went to see a double bill of 'youth' films at a crowded cinema in Islington, North London. The first movie was a Jimmy Cliff's raw reggae triumph *The Harder They Come* (1972) – arguably the most powerful rock film ever made – which kept the audience enthralled throughout. The second movie, which boasted a soundtrack by Pink Floyd, perhaps suffered by comparison with the Jamaican classic. Nevertheless, I still think of it as positively the least powerful rock film ever made: a flaccid farrago of pretentious poop about a bunch of boulevard hippies seeking Shangri-La in the jungles of New Guinea. It was called *La Vallée* (1972); in translation, The Valley or, more preciously, *The Valley (Obscured by Clouds)*.

The film was made by Barbet Schroeder, a director already notorious at the time for an opportunist documentary he made about Idi Amin. The plot introduces beautiful Bulle Ogier as Viviane, wife of a French diplomat, who is on the look-out for exotic native artefacts to stock a chic boutique in Paris. Her particular desire is for some rare bird-of-paradise feathers and, in the company of a young Englishman called Olivier (Michael Gothard) and his wealthy friend Gaetan (Jean-Pierre Kalfon), she embarks on an expedition to the remote interior of New Guinea, heading for an uncharted declivity referred to on the maps as a valley 'obscured by clouds'. During the portentous quest we are treated to much lushly scenic photography by the distinguished

Pink Floyd captured at the time of recording 'Dark Side of the Moon'. At this time the group was still very much a unit in terms of creating the albums together in the studio.

Nestor Almendros, a certain amount of erotic loveplay in the jungle and the druggy experiences among primitive villagers, all backed by what has kindly been referred to elsewhere as the 'appropriately trancelike' droning of the Floyd. Wow, veteran longhairs may find themselves breathing, far out. But what no brief review can possibly communicate is the tedium of the movie's soulful stares and meaningful conversations about life, nature and civilization presented by our band of boulevardiers.

The finale comes somewhat abruptly as, weary and depleted, the adventurers stagger to the misty and barren brow of the hill beyond which lies the valley of the quest. Will they reach it? What will they find there if they do? We are left with many tormenting questions; chief of which is, did the film-makers run out of money? It is all very well to end with an enigma, but after the rich cinematography of the earlier sequences, the finale looks suspiciously as if it may have been filmed on the embankment of some French municipal reservoir.

Back to that Islington cinema: I watched through to the end in the company of two friends, all of us hypnotised by the movie's awfulness. And when the lights came on and we rose to leave, we found ourselves in an almost empty cinema: the packed crowd of the earlier movie had simply melted away."

Chapter 9
DARK SIDE OF THE MOON

The Dark Side of The Moon is universally recognised as a rock masterpiece. The darling of every hi-fi shop on the planet and still harnessed into service to sell a million hi-fi systems every year around the globe. This, the ultimate Floyd album captured just the right blend of lyricism, inspired instrumental passages, innovative use of sound effects and some genuine musical innovation. All of it allied to a uniformly high standard of composition and performance.

Previous outings had all been let down by the presence of weaker almost throw away numbers, but on this album there was no *Seamus* or *San Tropez*, every single track worked like a dream forming a near perfect suite of songs linked by a common theme based around the mental stresses and strains of living in the twentieth century.

With the launch of the new multi-channel SACD version in 2003 this remarkable creation looks set to impose it's grip on the multi-channel world just as it's predecessor did in the stereo age.

The Floyd's magnum opus was developed at the rehearsal studio in Broadhurst Gardens, West Hampstead. The basic idea was to make a record about the different pressures of modern life - it would go on to spend 700 weeks in the charts. It was no great surprise in 2005 when the reformed Pink Floyd began their short set at Live 8 with the sound of the heart beat from *Speak To Me* heralding the arrival of *Breathe*. The opening sequence of the album with it's pulsing heartbeat had been the sound which had introduced millions of new listeners to the genius of Pink Floyd. For a group which hadn't performed together in 20 years, the Live 8 performance was incredibly assured. After the show Floyd swept every single poll as the band of the day. The performance was unexpectedly strong and confident; but the material the band chose to draw on is nothing short of sublime.

The material on the *Dark Side of The Moon* album was universally powerful but it also translated brilliantly into the live arena. On this album the sonic experiments which had gone so disastrously wrong on tracks like *Several Species* came together brilliantly for *On The Run*. David Gilmour was by now emerging as a world class player with his own distinctive style.

Money provided the ideal show case for those remarkable skills when the ungainly 7/8 time signature of the early part of the song gives way to a straight ahead 4/4. This is also the time that Gilmour chooses to unleash some of the finest guitar work of his career. *Dark Side of The Moon* had such strong material and worked so well as a suite of songs that it came as no surprise that the album was revived by Pink Floyd for the band's last tour in 1994 when the album was performed in it's entirety.

Back in 1972 when Nick Mason was interviewed for *Sounds*, Mason seemed to be less than 100% comfortable with the album. "I think the thing that bothers me more than anything is that we seem to get stuck into a slow four tempo for nearly everything we do. Like the speed of *Meddle* is the speed of nearly everything we've done for too long. That has something to do with it, that penchant for slow tempos. But again, I think, in some ways things are becoming more aggressive. There's more aggression in the way we do *Careful With That Axe, Eugene* on stage now than there ever was when we first recorded it. Our original recordings of that were extremely mild, jog along stuff. Even if it doesn't always come off, there's meant to be a lot of very heavy vibes coming off the stage during *Dark Side of The Moon*. We're well into putting on a lot of effect in order to make the whole thing heavy, really, in the true sense of the word. I'm not expressing that very well, but I don't think it's getting any lighter, and I don't think the intention is to make it light, either. It's all a bit abstract, really."

The Music

I SPEAK TO ME *(Mason)* - The overture, a sound collage, saw Waters generously give Mason a song writing credit and later bitterly regretted it. The various spoken pieces about madness come from roadies Pete Watts and Chris Adamson, and from Jerry Driscoll, the doorman at Abbey Road studios where the album was made! Waters had devised a series of cards containing 20 questions which ranged from 'what does the phrase *Dark Side of The Moon* mean?' to 'are you afraid of dying?' Everyone the band could get their hands on in Abbey Road from Paul and Linda McCartney who happened to be making an album there to doorman Jerry Driscoll was asked to respond and then taped. The McCartney answers were discarded as being too measured.

BREATHE *(Waters/Wright/Gilmour)* - Adapted from a piece Waters had written for The Body documentary back in 1970. Roger claimed that the lyrics 'are an exhortation directed mainly at myself, but also at anybody else who cares to listen. It's about trying to be true to one's path.' Gilmour provided the vocals, both lead and harmony, and the guitar - an open-tuned Stratocaster played across his knees.

ON THE RUN *(Waters/Gilmour)* - The number came from Waters and Gilmour experimenting with a VCS 3 synthesiser - creating an eight-note sequence similar to the things Pete Townshend had been doing on *Baba O'Reilly*. The point of the track was to express the stress and pressures of everyday life - and so a whole menagerie of sound effects were added such as airport sounds over the footsteps of a passenger desperately rushing for the plane and a train sound which was actually played by a guitar. It was another roadie, Roger the Hat, who is heard speaking the line, 'live for today, gone tomorrow' - a response to one of Waters' card questions.

TIME *(Waters/Wright/Mason/Gilmour)* - A stunning group composition. Waters would later admit that during the making of the record - he was 29 at the time - he suddenly felt as if he'd grown up, that childhood and adolescence were just training for adult life. Ultimately it's about making the most out of life, not wasting it. Again the song is characterised by a dominating sound effect - clocks ticking - the basic sound created by Waters' Precision bass and Mason's Rototoms. However it was engineer Alan Parsons who added all the real timepieces after Waters told him the song's title. The other dominating characteristic about this number was the backing singing to Gilmour's lead vocal provided by Barry St John, Doris Troy, Liza Strike and Lesley Duncan.

THE GREAT GIG IN THE SKY *(Wright/Torry)* - This stunning composition keeps up the progression of power. For many years this song was credited solely to Rick Wright until an out of court settlement in 2005 finally resolved that the piece should be jointly credited to Clare Torry. Based on a sequence of piano chords written by Wright, this song addresses the omni-present fear of death and mortality in life. Originally intended as an instrumental sequence and featuring some blinding guitar from Gilmour, the vocals were only added literally a couple of weeks before the LP was finished. The improvised vocal was provided by Clare Torry - a young EMI staff songwriter who had only recently begun to do a few sessions as a singer - her gutsy vocals take the song to an orgasmic climax! This number subsequently became notorious as great music to bonk to, while Wright later adapted it for a Neurofen advert.

MONEY *(Waters)* - is a Roger Waters composition in the unusual 7/8 time signature. The track has self-explanatory lyrics about the evils of greed and rock-star wealth - Waters certainly saw some of the songs on this LP as being about the lately departed Barrett. The rhythmically-sequenced loop of the cash-till sound effect gives the song a lot of its bite…and a touch of irony in as much as record store cash registers around the world would soon be ringing up millions of sales to its tune. Also featured is Dick Parry - an old Cambridge mate of Gilmour's - whose sax solos added a new dimension to the Floyd sound.

US AND THEM *(Waters/Wright)* - is a superb piece co-written by Waters and Wright. In time-honoured Floyd fashion this composition was based on another piece that had been lurking around for ages - the song's origins were in a piece rejected by Antonioni for Zabriskie Point called *The Violence Sequence*. Based on a chord sequence by Wright, Waters claimed the song was about, "the political idea of humanism, and whether it could or should have any effect on any of us." The lyrics range from going to war in the first verse, to themes of civil liberties, colour prejudice and civil rights in the second, and the thought of passing a down-and-out on the street and not helping in the third. The voices of sundry roadies and Wings guitarist Henry McCullough and his wife can be heard responding to Roger's flash cards. Dick Parry shines again on sax - Gilmour asked him to get the breathy sound similar to that on *Gandharva* by US electronic duo Beaver & Krause.

ANY COLOUR YOU LIKE *(Wright/Mason/Gilmour)* - written by Wright, Mason and Gilmour, this was an instrumental filler bridging *Us And Them* and *Brain Damage*. Originally called *Scat*, it features the ubiquitous sound of the VCS 3 synthesiser with a long tape echo as well as more conventional instrumentation. The final title came from a favourite catchphrase of roadie, Chris Adamson: "You can have it any colour you like'.

BRAIN DAMAGE *(Waters)* - A Roger Water's song that is perhaps up to this point most strongly identified with Syd Barrett, as Waters later told *Mojo*: "That was my song, I wrote it at home. The grass (as in the lunatic is on the grass) was always the square in between the River Cam and Kings College chapel. I don't know why but when I was young, that was always the piece of grass, more than any other piece of grass that I felt I was constrained to keep off. I don't know why, but the song still makes me think of that piece of grass. The lunatic was Syd, really. He was obviously in my mind. It was very Cambridge-based, that whole song." The final line name checks the title of the album, "I'll see you on the *Dark Side of The Moon*," and the maniacal laughter was by Pete Watts.

ECLIPSE *(Waters)* - *Eclipse* was tacked on to the end of the album in a moment of inspiration by Roger Waters purely because he sensed that the album needed a proper ending. The lyrics suggest that while the human race has the potential to live in harmony with nature and itself, this is depressingly never usually the case. However the song has an uplifting feel - sung by Waters with Gilmour's harmonies and Doris Troy's voice thundering alongside them. It is Jerry Driscoll who adds the cryptic final spoken-word coda about the real nature of the *Dark Side of The Moon*.

On the whole critical reaction was favourable and it was only later that retrospective niggles began to creep into reviews such as this piece by the respected American rock journalist Robert Christgau best known for his pioneering work with *Village Voice* magazine who wote about *Dark Side of The Moon* through post-punk eyes when it was chosen as one of the Rock Albums of the '70s. This controversial review was published in 1981. "With its technological mastery and its conventional wisdom once-removed, this is a kitsch masterpiece – taken too seriously by definition, but not without charm. It may sell on sheer aural sensationalism, but the studio effects do transmute David Gilmour's guitar solos into something more than they were when he played them. Its taped speech fragments may be old hat, but for once they cohere musically. And if its pessimism is received, that doesn't make the ideas untrue – there are even times, especially when Dick Parry's saxophone undercuts the electronic pomp, when this record brings its clichés to life, which is what pop is supposed to do, even the kind with delusions of grandeur."

Mr Christgau was definitely an atypical reviewer. Most were agreed that the cumulative effect of the brilliance of the compositions and the pristine quality of the recording served to position *Dark Side of The Moon* as a landmark in popular music. The problem for Pink Floyd was that at some stage they would have to produce an album to follow their own masterpiece. The standard had been set so high by *Dark Side of The Moon* in every respect. It was clear that the follow up had to be nothing short of a second masterpiece.

During the course of an intrview published on May 19, 1973 in *Melody Maker* David Gilmour declared that he was not unduly concerned by the pressures brought about by the phenomenal sales of The *Dark Side of The Moon*. "No, success doesn't make much difference to us. It doesn't make any difference to our output or general attitudes. There are four attitudes in the band that are quite different. But we all want to push forward and there are all sorts of things we'd like to do. For Roger Waters it is more important to do things that say something. Richard Wright is more into putting out good music. And I'm in the middle with Nick. I want to do it all, but sometimes I think Roger can feel the musical content is less important and can slide around it. Roger and Nick tend to make the tapes of effects like the heartbeat on the LP. At concerts we have quad tapes and four-track tape machines so we can mix the sound and pan it around. The heartbeat alludes to the human condition and sets the mood for the music, which describes the emotions experienced during a lifetime. Amidst the chaos, there is beauty and hope for mankind. The effects are purely to help the listener understand what the whole thing is about. It's amazing, at the final mixing stage we thought it was obvious what the album was about, but still, a lot of people, including the engineers and the roadies, when we asked them, didn't know what the LP was about. They just couldn't say, and I was really surprised. They didn't see it was about the pressures that can drive a young chap mad. I really don't know if our things get through. But you have to carry on hoping. Our music is about neuroses, but that doesn't mean that we are neurotic. We are able to see it, and discuss it. The *Dark Side of The Moon* itself is an allusion to the moon and lunacy. The dark side is generally related to what goes on inside people's heads, the subconscious and the unknown." Despite Gilmour's confidence there was still no sign of a new album. A year later on November 16, 1974, *Melody Maker* published an interview with Rick Wright which was quick to touch on the increasingly large gap between the *Dark Side* and the next album "It'll be a two-year gap between *Dark Side* and the next one, and that's too long in my opinion. We have never been a prolific group in terms of records. We average about one a year over our whole career. It's not a policy to work like that, it's just the way it happens. We have a deal with the record company that makes us do about seven albums in five years, which is one album a year and maybe a couple of film scores. It's very easy to make that deal. *Dark Side of The Moon* has been in the English charts ever since it was released, which is quite amazing. We all felt it would do at least as well as the other albums, but not quite as well as it did. All our albums have done well in this country, but *Dark Side* was number one in the U. S. ad we never dreamed it would do that. It was probably the easiest album to sell in that it was the easiest to listen to, but it's success has obviously put some kind of pressure on us, and that is, what to do next. We have always tried to bring out something different with our next release and it would be very easy now to carry on with the same formula as *Dark Side*, which a lot of people would do. It's changed me in many ways because it's brought in a lot of money and one feels very secure when you can sell an album for two years. But it hasn't changed my attitude to music. Even though it was so successful, it was made in the same way as all our other albums and the only criteria we have about releasing music is whether

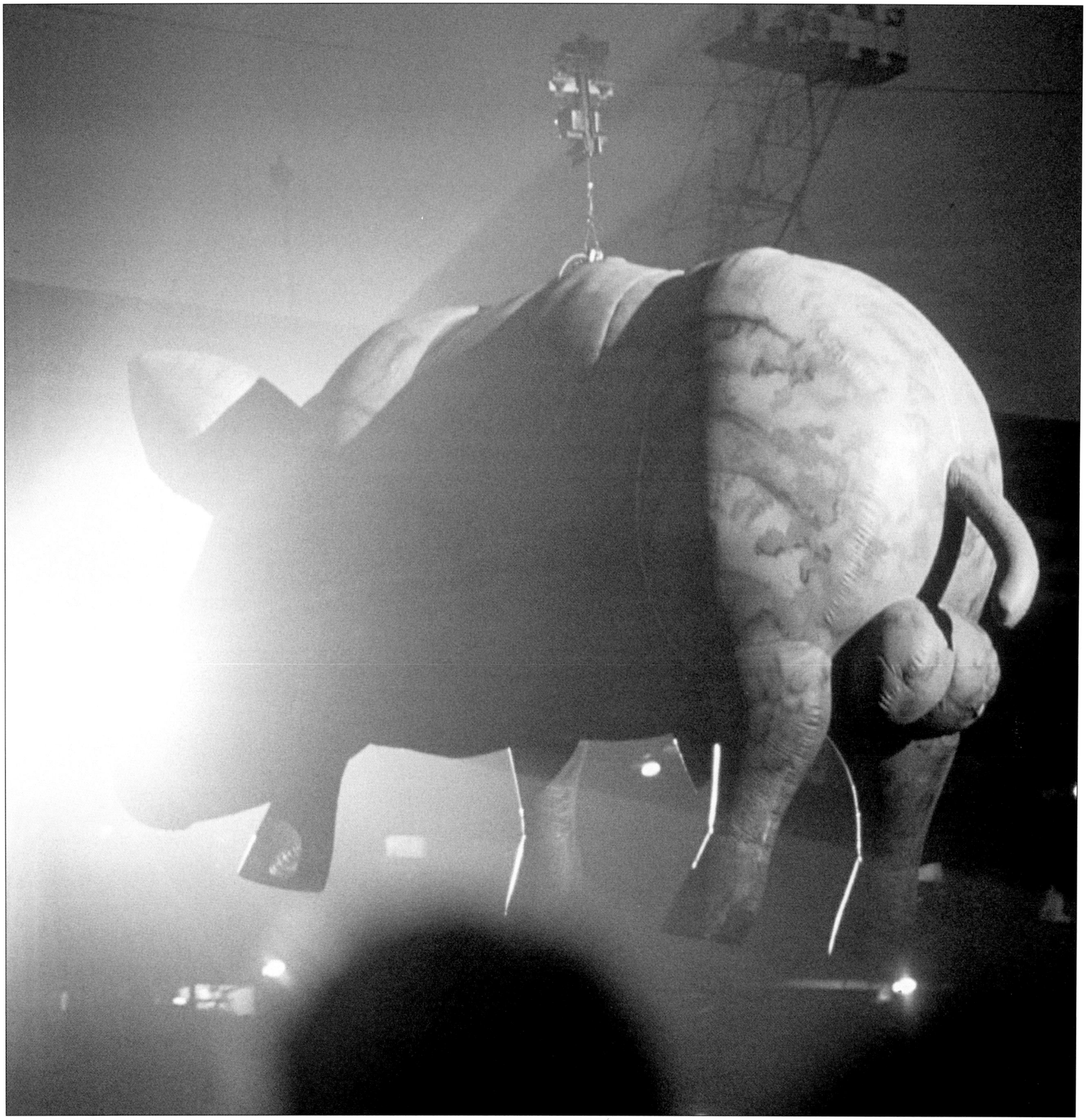

Rex Features

we like it or not. It was not a deliberate attempt to make a commercial album. It just happened that way. Lots of people probably thought we all sat down and discussed it like that, but it wasn't the case at all. We knew it had a lot more melody than previous Floyd albums, and there was a concept that ran all through it. The music was easier to absorb and having girls singing away added a commercial touch that none of our other records had."

Chapter 10
WISH YOU WERE HERE

Fortunately for Pink Floyd time was now on their side. Dark Side had opened the doors to the financial gold mine and there was to be no unseemly scramble to produce a follow up. By 1974 Pink Floyd were undoubtedly masters of the recording studio, but they were first and foremost a live band. Long before it was committed to vinyl, the music of Dark Side of The Moon had been honed and refined on the road.

As the compositions for *Wish You Were Here* began to take shape the band had little hesitation in unveiling a key part their new work in progress in the live arena. The astonishing track which concert audiences first heard in 1974 was then simply entitled *Shine On*. Under its formal title *Shine On You Crazy Diamond* it was to become one of the most celebrated pieces in the Pink Floyd catalogue. The overall theme of *Dark Side of The Moon* dealt with madness as a human condition from the perspective of humanity as a whole. *Shine On You Crazy Diamond* stayed with the same theme but shifted the focus on to the individual …that individual was Syd Barrett.

As we have seen Syd had contributed only a single album to the story. Nontheless Syd was an enormously influential figure who was the inspiration for the early Pink Floyd. The seeds of Syd's problems were possibly there already in the shape of a fragile artistic ego, but it was a condition which cannot have been helped by a massive intake of drugs such as LSD. Despite the fact that he had left the band after a very short tenure, the spectre of Syd and his tragic condition continued to haunt the group. It seemed as if Syd had left an indelible imprint on the heart of the band which could never go away.

The spirit of Syd Barrett was to become a kind of lost soul haunting the collective memory of Pink Floyd. In 1970, David Gilmour made an attempt to exorcise the ghost by trying to help Syd to get back onto the rails and producing music again. Gilmour produced the solo album *Barrett* for Syd but this therapeutic approach to music making was doomed to failure, and Syd drifted off into the background surfacing only very occasionally. By 1975 Syd's physical presence was just a memory but recollections of Syd continued to haunt the consciousness of Pink Floyd. Remembrances of Syd were to surface as the key subject matter on the album which many consider to be the band's greatest work .

The Music

SHINE ON YOU CRAZY DIAMOND *(Waters/Wright/Gilmour)* - was written as a testimony to the young Syd Barrett. Lyrically it is an exploration of the factors which had conspired to crush the delicate flame of Syd's genius. The piece has been misinterpreted as romanticising the Syd Barrett story. The wistful tale of a lost mind sounds attractive in the idealistic sense, but as Dave Gilmour is still at pains to point out, there is clearly nothing attractive or uplifting about mental illness. In creating *Shine On You Crazy Diamond* Pink Floyd set about deflating the myth that there was anything positive in the sad decline of Syd Barrett but ironically the huge success of the piece both creatively and artistically has only served to escalate the process of romanticising the Syd Barrett story. Lyrically the song may have found itself on thorny ground, but musically *Shine On You Crazy Diamond* encounters no such difficulties. *Shine On* is one of the undoubted highlights of Pink Floyd's career.

The piece has been compared to an immense sonic cathedral, and it has certainly stood the test of time. *Shine On* begins with a haunting keyboard introduction which utilises an understated horn motif over an extended electronic drone. This perfectly sets the mood of melancholy reflection which underpins the opening section of the piece.

The keyboard intro is followed by the soaring guitar solo in which every note seems to have been carefully considered weighed and tested by David Gilmour, the master craftsman responsible for the musical fabric of the stunning introduction.

We are then introduced to a short four note figure which seems to capture the essence of the lost life of Syd Barrett. Gilmour's four note theme heralds the introduction of the drums which have been absent for the first four minutes of the piece.

The opening section of the piece is in a sedate 4/4 time but it gains extra interest and colour from the unusual and ever changing pattern of emphasis which is placed on different beats in the bar by the rhythm section of Mason and Waters. There is a subtle change in time signature to 6/4 to herald the introduction of the vocals which enter in an equally restrained manner. The piece now develops a flowing, almost waltz like quality which carries the listener through the first two verses. As the emotion builds, female voices are used to harmonise with the male voices and help to build the ethereal quality of the song. This device had been used extensively on *Dark Side of The Moon* and was to become something of a hallmark on Pink Floyd's later material.

With the piece now well into its stride the guitar eventually gives way to the saxophone. The sax had been used to great effect on *Dark Side of The Moon* where it brought extra colour to the instrumentation on tracks such as *US And Them* and *Money*. Mid way through the saxophone solo the composition changes gear and the tempo lifts for a 12/8 double time section. *Shine On You Crazy Diamond* had originally been conceived as a single piece but the constraints of vinyl meant the piece couldn't fit on a single side and had to spilt into two where it acted as the musical book ends, opening and closing the album. Initially the piece was divided into 16 parts. On subsequent releases the first part of the track was listed on the sleeve as *Shine On You Crazy Diamond (Parts 1-5)* with the remainder of the track named *(Parts 6-9)*. More recent CD pressings have relented and simply credit the tracks as *part one* and *part two*. Live performance of this majestic piece surfaced on *The Delicate Sound Of Thunder* and a brilliant live version was performed against the elements as the introduction to Pink Floyd's one off appearance at Knebworth House in 1990 .

WELCOME TO THE MACHINE *(Waters)* - The subject matter of the album now shifts away from the tragedy of Barrett's sorry tale to deal with the industrial face of the music business which engulfed the young Syd for *Welcome To The Machine*. This is an inspired piece of composition by Roger Waters, the compelling rhythm of *Welcome To The Machine* is driven by sounds of synthesised heavy industrial machines which fuse together and form the rhythmic pulse of the song. The savagery of the lyrics and the relentlessly bleak sound of the heavy machinery combine to create a real sense of menace. When asked in an interview for *Street Life* magazine of Canada what the *Machine Song* was about, Roger Waters had to pause for a while before replying. "Let me think. It begins with a saxophone that fades into the distance and the appearance of a machine. It's really a song from the point of view of our hero, of an individual. And the opening of the door, if you like, symbolically you know. It's a phrase that gets used all the time in English, 'and the doors open to...' The symbol of doors, keys, the symbol of discovery, of advancement, of progress, of agreement. But progress towards what? Towards discovery, or something else? In this song its in the direction of nothing at all, except the aim of becoming part of a dream that's trapped you, and to follow this road first and foremost. And the Machine is self-perpetuating, and so much so because its fuel consists of dreams. The rock machine isn't oiled and doesn't actually run on people's appreciation of the music or on their wish to interest themselves in music and listen to it, in my opinion. At the base of it all, it runs on dreams. It's for that reason people throw themselves into it, not to make music. And that's faulty reasoning. Many people believe in it, but I don 't. That's not why I got into it at all. But I still haven't explained the song of the Machine. It's a question of what causes a feeling of absence. *Wish You Were Here* is a song about the sensations that accompany the state of not being there. To work and to be with people whom you know aren't there anymore. The song of the Machine is about the business situation, which I find myself in, which creates this absence. One's encouraged to be absent because one's not encouraged to pay any attention to reality, everywhere, not only in the rock machine, but in the whole mechanism of society. This mechanism encourages you to reject things. From the moment you 're born, you 're encouraged to reject the realities of the things that surround you and to accept the dreams and the codes of behaviour. Everything is coded. You 're asked to communicate through a series of codes, rather than to communicate directly. And that's called civilization, the crowd noise was put in there because of the complete emptiness inherent in that way of behaving, celebrations, gatherings of people who talk and drink together. To me, that epitomizes the lack of contacts and of real feelings between people. It's very simple, obvious even. He gets up from where he was, ready to confront the festivities, and he's ready because that's what he was trained to do. He's surfacing if you like. The idea's that the Machine is underground. Some underground power and therefore evil, that leads us towards our various bitter destinies. The hero's been exposed to this power. One way or another he's gone into the machinery and he's seen it for what it is. And the Machine had admitted the fact, telling him that he's being watched because he 'knows', and informs him that all his actions are Pavlovian responses, that everything's only conditioned reflexes, and that his responses don't come at his own instigation. In fact, he doesn't exist anymore, except to the extent that he has the feeling deep down inside himself that something just isn't at all right. That's his only reality. So he goes off, leaves the machinery and enters the room. The doors open and he realizes it's true, the people there are all zombies. That's now very serious, you see. As for the album, critics have said it was very cynical."

HAVE A CIGAR *(Waters)* - With the global success of *Dark Side of The Moon* Floyd were now very much an integral part of the music industry, nonetheless the next piece *Have A Cigar* is infused with such a sense of savagery and loathing that there is a real possibility that Waters could arguably be biting the hand that feeds him. On the album, Roy Harper was drafted in to handle the vocals. It's a workaday tale of an insincere record executive and the platitudes he peddles to the artists signed to his label. The song includes the infamous line "by the way which one's Pink?" David Gilmour had initially tried to lay down the vocal but according to Roger Waters, Gilmour's interpretation lacked the neccessary bite. It's actually quite hard to see what was gained from the introduction of Harper. The vocal style is remarkably similar to Gilmour in any event. In his extended interview with *Street Life,* Waters was untroubled with regard to potential criticism. "I don't know. *Have a Cigar* isn't cynicism, it's sarcasm. In fact, it's not even sarcasm, it's realism. I know a guy who works in a clinic for drug addicts, alcoholics, and child molesters. I met him in my local pub and he'd heard the song *Time* where there's the phrase 'hanging on in quiet desperation.' That moved him a lot because it had a bearing on what he himself felt. That made me realize if I were to express my feelings, vague and disturbed as they are, as honestly as I could, then that's the most I can do. At present, I'm not very interested in art, and I only interest myself in music insofar as it helps me express my feelings. I wrote all the words and organized all the ideas for the pieces we've done in the last few years. And it's hard to say what we'll do now. I know that Dave and Rick, for example, don't think that the subject matter or theme of the record and the ideas developed are as important as I think they are. They're more interested in music, as abstract form as much as anything else. There's something unavoidable about each of us working on his own solo project. Three of us, certainly. As for Nicky, I don't know. Personally, I've got enough material to start making a record straight away. I don't know where Dave'll find the necessaries to make a record, but I'm sure he will find them. I think he'll make a fantastic record, but nothing like we've done

ourselves. We'll see."

WISH YOU WERE HERE *(Waters/Gilmour)* - One of the undoubted highlights of the album is *Wish You Were Here*. The song itself feels spontaneous and unplanned. It doesn't seem to fit thematically with the rest of the album and it comes as no surprise to learn that the song was arrived at by a happy accident. This simple easy going track began from Gilmour's country bluegrass motif and was worked up to something truly spectacular. Despite the forcefulness of the anti-war lyrics the song always maintains that warm feeling of impulsive artlessness. It feels unforced and natural and it was. Interviewed on January 24, 1976 by *Street Life Magazine* of Canada Roger Waters was asked to confront the unusual possibility that in *Wish You Were Here* he had actually written a love song. "Yes, that's true it's a love song, and still one on a very general and theoretical level. If I was undergoing psychoanalysis, my analyst would tell you why I don't write love songs. In fact, I've done one or two others, but always in a very impersonal way. If I haven't really spoken about love, perhaps it's because I've never really known what love was. I'm just like someone who's had a constant love relationship since the age of 16 and who then changes all that 15 years later. What can I say about love that'd be meaningful? To write love songs, you have to be sure about your feelings. Maybe I could write about it now, but maybe just for myself, not for Pink Floyd."

SHINE ON YOU CRAZY DIAMOND *(Waters/Wright/Gilmour)* - The album closes with the second half of *Shine on You Crazy Diamond*. This was originally listed as parts 6 to 9 but in more recent years this has simplified and appears on recent CD releases as Part Two.

Often overlooked in favour of the brilliance of the introduction this is a powerful slice of Floyd at their best with some inspired playing by Rick Wright. Events in the studio took a surreal turn when, after an absence of six years, Syd Barrett suddenly re-appeared in the studio. Legend has it this event took place during the creation of the very track written about him. The unsettling effect of Syd's arrival on the remaining band members seems to have translated itself into the music which grows even more bleak and poignant. Despite Roger Water's protestations, the presence of the long lost Syd must surely have had an influence on the recording process even at a subliminal level. The spirit of Syd was suddenly there in person, it was almost as if he heard the call.

In an extended interview with *Street Life* magazine of Canada, Waters dealt with the difficult subject of Syd's relationship to the album. "For my part I've never read an intelligent piece on Syd Barrett in any magazine.

Never. No one knows what they're talking about. Only us, the people who knew him, who still know him a bit, only we know the facts, how he lived, what happened to him, why he was doing certain things. They make me laugh, these journalists with their rubbish. In actual fact, I wrote that song, *Shine On* above all to see the reactions of people who reckon they know and understand Syd Barrett. I wrote and rewrote and rewrote and rewrote that lyric because I wanted it to be as close as possible to what I felt. And even then, it hasn't altogether worked out right for me. But, nonetheless, there's a truthful feeling in that piece. I don't know, that sort of indefinable inevitable melancholy about the disappearance of Syd. Because he's left, withdrawn so far away that, as far as we're concerned, he's no longer there."

Hipgnosis had produced the sleeves for all of Pink Floyd's studio albums since *A Saucerful Of Secrets*. Floyd had recognised the importance of strong imagery and had developed a strong series of iconic record sleeves which was just as well as from the record company point of view the band had a maddening tenancy to leave the Pink Floyd name off the sleeve. This was particularly infuriating for executives who knew they owned one of the biggest brand names on the planet. Storm Thorgeson had been moved by the music and also by the unexpected appearance of Syd. He too had known Syd for many years and felt that the achingly beautiful music was infused with a sense of loss. There was the loss of Syd, but Thorgeson also sensed the loss of togetherness in Pink Floyd. Storm focused on the word "absence" to encapsulate the melancholy mood of the album and set about depicting a sense of absence in his images for the album sleeve. In his *Street Life* interview Roger Waters confirmed Thorgeson's statement that the album is all about absence. "*Shine On* is not really about Syd. He's just a symbol for extremes of absence some people have to indulge in because it's the only way they can cope with modern life and how sad it is; which is to withdraw completely. We didn't start out with the idea of making a record based on the theme of absence. What happened was that we began to put the music for *Shine On You Crazy Diamond* together, and from that we got a very strong feeling of melancholy. That's what happened first. Anyway, when I wrote the words, I don't know why, but I began to write about Syd's demise. And then a few other sections got written. I wrote one of them, 'Raving and Drooling', and another with David called 'You Gotta Be Crazy'. Then we began to record *Shine On*. The first six weeks in the studio were extremely difficult. I felt that, at times, the group was only there physically. Our bodies were there, but our minds and feelings somewhere else. And we were only there because this music allows us to live and live well, or because it was a habit, to be in Pink Floyd and to operate under that banner."

The packaging for the initial launch of the album was an elaborate affair. The album was released in enigmatic black plastic wrapping. The original idea had been for it to convey no information whatsoever, but EMI prevailed and the album came emblazoned with a sticker depicting robot hands locked in a hand shake from which all humanity is absent. The black outer wrapping was then peeled away to reveal images of absence and loss. A wind blown piece of fabric is devoid of purpose, and the iconic image of the business deal gone wrong with one man already burning away. Inside the album was a postcard depicting the legs of a diver in mid dive projecting from a shallow pool. Closer inspection reveals that the splash is absent from the image.

The other striking image was the faceless record salesman devoid of any sense of identity or morals. It seems slightly hypocritical that Hipgnosis should harness such images critical of the commercial nature of the record industry in order to er... sell records.

John Rowntree, reviewing the album in *Records and Recording* published in November 1975, was typical of the many journalists who seemed to genuinely enjoy the album. "Depending on your age and your head, the music of the Pink Floyd will probably be etched deep into your just-post-adolescent consciousness. After *Ummagumma* the band vacillated: *Atom Heart Mother* was too full of gratuitous effects to count for much; *Meddle* seemed full of *Echoes;* and, despite their concerts, the odd soundtrack album seemed to confuse the band's direction. *Dark Side of The Moon* proved the major recovery point – at the risk of pulling their heads far out of conventional rock into classical muzak, the Floyd concentrated on what they could do best – arranging and the technical side of recording. On this album came *Money*, a no-holds-barred, motherfuckers-to-the-wall rocker that turned many a cynical head.

"By extension they came to *Wish You Were Here*, undoubtedly their best album since *Ummagumma*, crammed with beautiful and surprising things. As ever, form easily outstrips content: the kernel of *Shine On You Crazy Diamond* is a neat little exhortation to a lost colleague (Syd Barrett), on most other albums a three-minute filler. Preface with a hugely atmospheric jam, eating up a spectrum anywhere from David Bedford to Savoy Brown, add a scary little laugh after the first line of the lyric and you have a concept that dominates the album – around a quarter of an hour to begin with and another ten minutes at the end. Another such device, on paper painfully obvious, translates Roy Harper's guest vocal on *Have a Cigar* via the effect of tuning across a radio waveband to a sinister acoustic rendition of the title track. The use of extended saxophone solo against a Moog backdrop and much simpler exploitation of the lead electric guitar as pure sound confirm experiments attempted on *Dark Side of The Moon*. *Wish You Were Here* gives no clue as to where rock is going in the future; but then it did take about two hundred years before they ran out of ideas for symphonies."

David Gilmour is on record as stating that *Wish You Were Here* is still his favourite Floyd album and it was no surprise that the title track from the album was chosen for the reformation concert at Live 8. Even on that emotional evening Roger Waters remembered to dedicate the song to Syd. It's now 30 years since the launch of the album and it certainly looks to have stood the test of time. *Wish You Were Here* proved beyond all shadow of a doubt that *Dark Side* was no fluke. Pink Floyd have justifiably gone on to be one of the most successful bands on the planet. Syd lived quietly in Cambridge until his death in 2006....

Chapter 11
ANIMALS

The year 1977 marked the beginning of a difficult era for Pink Floyd. It had begun auspiciously enough with the release in January 1977 of Animals. This particular album however, was never destined to be hailed as the greatest Floyd offering ever. It received a respectful if not overly warm welcome from the fans and critics alike, yet it still proved itself to be both a commercial and an artistic success. True, the album had not scaled the heights of Dark Side of The Moon either financially or creatively; but it was still a huge accomplishment by any standards reaching number 1 all over Europe, number 2 in the UK and number 3 in the States.

Ironically 1977 was also the year in which the band had finally cemented the stellar status which every would-be rock star dreams of attaining. The *In The Flesh* tour had confirmed the stadium filling status of Pink Floyd and crowds of 60-70,000 were commonplace. Although it was never destined to be hailed as one of the truly great moments in Floyd's career, *Animals* had succeeded as a project and for the first six months of 1977 the band toured the stadiums of the world promoting a tour which, given the huge size of the venues, was ironically dubbed *Pink Floyd - In The Flesh*. Tickets for the *In the Flesh* tour sold in huge numbers further reinforcing Pink Floyd's status as one of the biggest acts on the planet.

Animals will forever be associated with images of flying pigs. Under Roger Waters direction Hipgnosis had again managed to infuse an ordinary everyday image with such potency that the band did not even have to put it's name on the cover. In many respects the *Animals* album cover and the promotional activity surrounding it, marks the finest hour for the Hipgnosis/Floyd partnership. *Animals* is remembered as a triumph for Hipgnosis, the unpromising image of a disused power station was sprinkled with some design magic which transformed it from an unremarkable and unloved industrial relic into something iconic.

The album was a distinct evolution in style from Floyd. Waters lyrics were increasingly important and had come to enjoy equal prominence to the music on the album. The lyrics were already full of vitriol and bile which would dominate the next two Floyd albums.

Of the five tracks which make up the album, four are credited solely to Waters with the writing credits shared with David Gilmour only on the epic *Dogs*. *Animals* therefore marks the first Floyd album which was devoid of any compositional input from Rick Wright, a trend which was set to continue on to *The Wall*. The music is definitely poorer for it. *Animals* has never really hit the spot with the Floyd crowd although in the live arena the album was given every chance to make its mark. The album was performed in its entirety for 1977's *In The Flesh* tour and was very well received. With the tour concluded however, Floyd abandoned the material from *Animals* to scarcely a murmur from the massive Floyd fraternity. Not a single scrap of *Animals* was ever again performed live on stage. Only Roger Waters kept the faith with the material he had written performing *Dogs* in its entireity for his solo shows in 2000 which were also entitled, with some lack of imagination, *In the Flesh* , but without the rest of the band the material never sounded the same. *Animals* was the first of three Floyd albums to be, not only master minded by Roger Waters, but also to be built mainly around Waters compositions. Fortunately the album also coincided with Roger beginning the climb towards the very best of his form as a writer. The

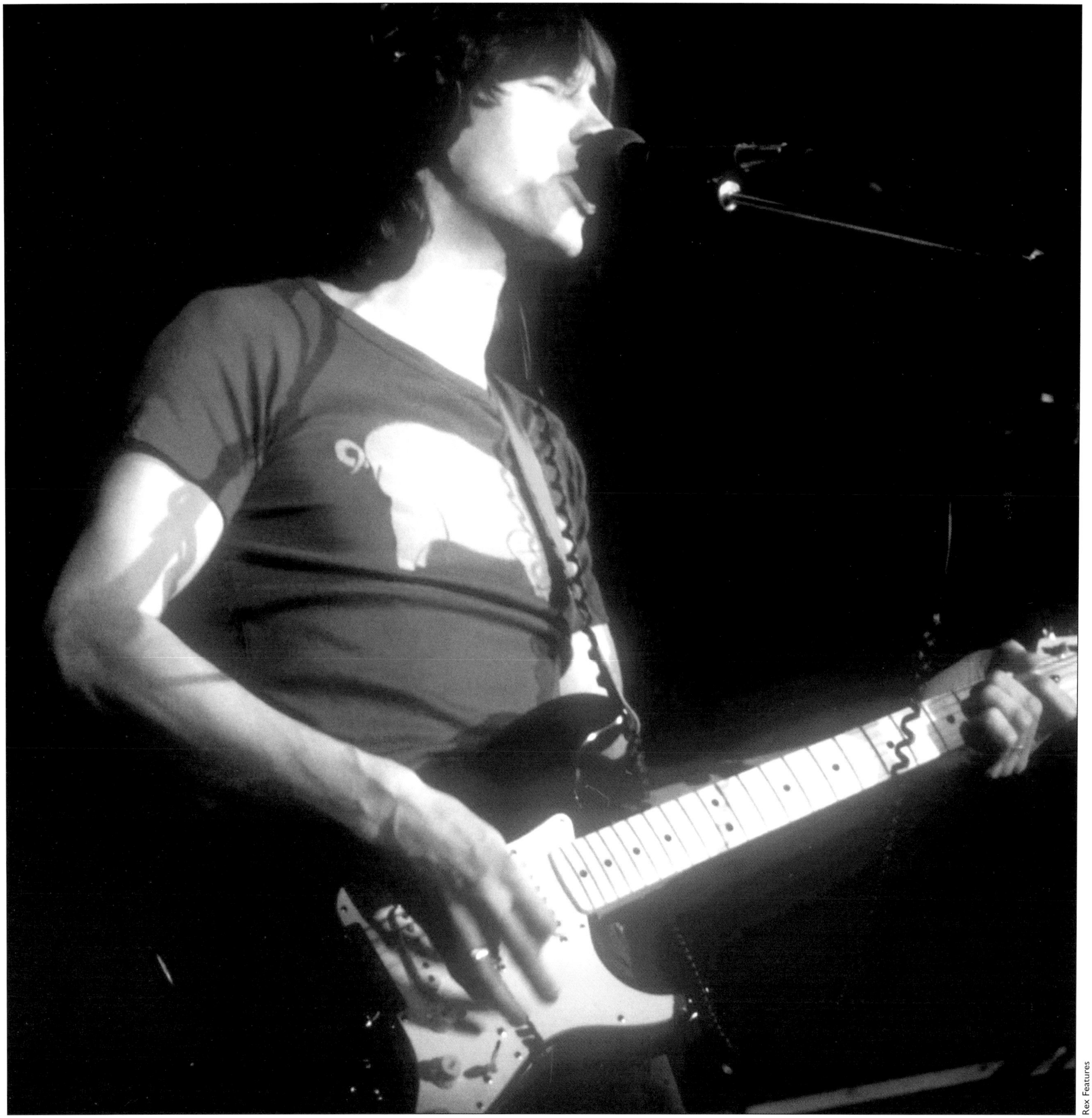

Rex Features

The publicity poster from the ill-fated Olympic Stadium concert at which Roger Waters infamously spat on a member of the audience.

choice of subject matter is typically bleak and joyless but instrumentally the band continued to shine as brightly as ever. Rick Wright did not contribute as a writer but his instrumental performance is among the best of his entire career.

Often overlooked in favour of what came before and after, *Animals* represents another milestone in the run of amazing Floyd albums which stretched unbroken from 1970 to 1981. Nick Mason recalled this as a difficult record to make - "we were getting older, there was much more drama between us."

There was also drama out on the road. In 1979 Roger Waters met with Tommy Vance to tape an extended interview for broadcast on BBC Radio One. Included in this amazingly insightful broadcast is Roger's account of the infamous incident at the end of the *Animals* tour which gave birth to the whole idea of *The Wall*. "The idea for *The Wall* came from ten years of touring with rock shows. I think, particularly the last few years when, in 1975 and 1977, we were playing to very large audiences, some of whom were our old audience who'd come to hear us play, but most of whom were only there for the beer. All this was in big stadiums and, consequently, it became a rather alienating experience doing the shows. I became very conscious of a wall between us and the audience, and so this record stemmed from shows being horrible."
From his elevated position on the stage Roger sensed that, to a good proportion of the audience, what happened on stage was unimportant. They were there to have a good time and were ready to yell, scream and throw firecrackers. In this crazy party atmosphere art came a poor second. Waters began to despise the party animals in the crowd.

Increasingly frustrated by the boisterous party antics of North American stadium crowds Roger had grown progressively more alienated from his audience. He finally snapped at one particular devotee in Montreal who screamed and yelled like a demented banshee throughout a performance which included the sensitive pianissimo passages of *Shine On You Crazy Diamond* alongside the rockier moments from *Dogs*. Regardless of the demands of any given musical moment, Waters' tormentor kept up a stream of noisy shrieks and bellows intermingled with demands for old standards. Eventually the bassist could stand it no longer. This one individual had come to personify the crass, boorish behaviour of stadium rock concert goers who are simply there to 'party on' regardless of the nature of what is being performed. Roger later filled in the exact details of the incident for Tommy Vance. "The basic idea behind it all is this story. Montreal 1977 at the Olympic Stadium in front of 80,000 people, the last gig of our 1977 tour, I personally became so upset during the show that I spat at some guy in the front row who was only doing what he wanted to do, but what he wanted to do was not what I wanted to happen. He was shouting and screaming and having a wonderful time, and pushing into the barrier. What he wanted was a good riot. And what I wanted was to do a rock and roll show. I got so upset that I finally spat on him, which is a very nasty thing to do to anybody. I got him as well, it hit him right in the middle of his face." Ironically it was Waters who had written the line in *Dogs* which describes the conditioned animal as one "Who was trained not to spit in the fan."

Almost twenty-five years later, writing in his book *Inside Out*, Nick Mason recalled the same concert with remarkable clarity and his version of events corroborate with Water's account of that unhappy day. "The moment that sparked *The Wall* happened at a show at Montreal's Olympic Stadium during the Animals tour of 1977. This was a gigantic sports stadium, overlooked by a futuristic tower, that had been constructed for the Olympic Games of the year before. There was a relatively small but over-excited group in the audience close to the stage, who were probably high on chemicals and definitely low on attentiveness. Being right at the front they were audible and defined our sense of the audience's mood. During the break between a couple of numbers, this group were shouting out suggestions for songs. When Roger's eye was caught by one particularly vocal member of the claque yelling, 'Play *Careful With That Axe*, Roger,' he finally lost patience, and spat at the offender. This was more than unusual, it was weird. Roger had always been the spokesman on stage since Syd's departure, and handled the introductions, the gaps in proceedings when the projectors broke down or the hecklers with some aplomb, and often with some droll observations. This incident just indicated that establishing any kind of bond with the audience was becoming increasingly difficult."

David Gilmour too recalled the events surrounding that unhappy affair in Montreal and his version, although told to *Mojo's* Sylvie Simmons twenty-two years later corresponds closely to the recollections of his band mates. "I can remember not enjoying it much as a show. They'd just finished building this big stadium and the crane was still in there, they forgot to dismantle it and couldn't get it out. I was so un-enamoured that I went and sat on the mixing desk for the encore - that might have not contributed to Roger's mood. I think Roger was disgusted with himself really that he had let himself go sufficiently to spit at a fan." Interestingly it was not just Waters who was frustrated by the over animated crowd at this particular show as Nick Mason later recalled in his autobiography. "Roger was not alone in feeling depressed about this show. Over the years we had evolved a definitive final encore, where we played a slow twelve-bar blues while the crew gradually removed all the equipment and instruments, leaving one lone, silent musician to walk off stage. On this occasion, David was so upset by the mood of the concert that he refused even to take part in the encore."

After the gig Roger poured out his sense of frustration and alienation to Canadian producer Bob Ezrin and in his frustration suggested he would like to construct a wall between the band and the audience. Ezrin's reply was direct and to the point, "well why don't you?"

The Music

PIGS ON THE WING (PART ONE) *(Waters)* - The *Animals* album opens with the plaintive strains of Roger Waters' *Pigs On The Wing (Part One)*. This is a very untypical Floyd song, sung by Roger Waters over acoustic guitar accompaniment sounding for all the world like some 1960s singer-songwriter, is a kind of palate-cleanser. He would later reveal it was a love song to his then first wife Carolyne. There is a kind of symmetry at work here. As with *Wish You Were Here,* the album rests on four principal compositions and as with the previous album where *Shine On You Crazy Diamond* acted as the musical book ends opening and closing the album, so too does *Pigs On The Wing* which crops up again at the end of *Animals,* albeit in a single, final verse.

DOGS *(Waters/Gilmour)*- follows and takes up the rest of the space on the vinyl release. This is a joint Gilmour Waters composition of epic proportions and was one of two songs on this album that had already been performed (and bootlegged) live on stage for almost two years under the title *You Gotta Be Crazy*. It had now been formalised under it's new title as a song depicting the barbaric behaviour humans are capable of, it featured the noise of barking treated by a Vocoder effects unit, with eerie results.

PIGS (THREE DIFFERENT ONES) *(Waters)* - is next up, the lyric of the vinyl side two opener rhymes 'house-proud town mouse with 'Whitehouse', the latter a clear reference to moral guardian Mary Whitehouse. This bespectacled old lady was constantly in the media bemoaning the lack of morality on television and radio, and had already attracted the ire of Deep Purple's Ian Gillan whose 'Mary Long' combined her name with that of fellow moral crusader Lord Longford. While Gillan asked when she lost her virginity, Waters bottles out and semi-obscures a 'fuck you'!

SHEEP *(Waters)* —This track had begun life as *Raving And Drooling* and was already familiar to live audiences long before the release of the album. Depicting sheep grazing peacefully before being sent for slaughter, it includes a parody of the 23rd Psalm ('The Lord Is My Shepherd') again delivered through the machine-like Vocoder. By this time, Orwell's *Animal Farm* looked more of a relevant reference point than the Bible. Roger has said it had more to do with *The Wall*, the album that followed it, than to predecessor *Wish You Were Here,* even though two songs had been imported from those sessions. He also said that *Sheep* in which the sheep revolt and kill the dogs, foretold riots in Brixton and Toxteth.

PIGS ON THE WING (PART 2)- closes the album and almost feels like an afterthought which ends the album on a slightly lighter note and even suggests the whole thing might have been a dream - make that nightmare - sequence told by one dog to another. According to *Sounds'* review, it offered the listener 'words of comfort'. The concept of a pig on the wing had, through accident or design, become reality the previous December when an inflatable porker, part of the unique cover photo-shoot, had slipped its moorings and allegedly appeared in Heathrow Airport's flight lane! All good publicity for the forthcoming release…

Although the album is critical of many aspects of the commercial world, journalists hoping to review the album were subject to a regime every bit as bleak and totalitarian as the world inhabited by the *Dogs* of Water's imagination. *Record Mirror* anonymously parodied the high handed behaviour of EMI Records when it came to organising listening sessions. Given the behaviour of those organising the reviews when

Rex Features

juxtaposed against the subject matter of the album the *Record Mirror* review of the album became as much a review of the irony free process of obtaining a review as of the music itself. The piece was entitled *A Short Story by Johnny the Fox - An Animal Yarn*. No doubt the writer was an admirer of Orwell. "They have, we are led to believe, been working on this project for most of the past year. Speculation as to the content and eventual arrival date has been rife since the autumn. Then last week the world's Press and his wife were invited to Battersea Power Station for a preview (Why Battersea? Well, friends, its tall chimneys, plus a large inflatable pig, will feature on the album's cover).

"The playback started and the furtive scribes commenced note-taking. 'We can't have this,' sneered the man from *Harvest*. 'We don't want them to review it on just one listen. Go and tell everyone to desist at once.' The sheepish scribes obeyed the dog's order and the music played on. After a chicken meal, the album was played again. 'No note-taking again if you don't mind, gentlemen,' grinned the big dog, now walking on two feet and sporting a string of medals across his chest. A raucous laugh from the rafters over-awed the music. The sheep looked up and at each other, mouths open; the dogs strutted about and showed their teeth.

"All agreed it had been a pleasurable evening. The grazing had been particularly good and the assembled sheep were now bleating to one another. 'It's a Dave Gilmour album,' mused a woolly wonder from the Moors. 'OK – as the second album in a double set,' assured a bespectacled ram and the adoring ewes shook their fuzzy heads, bleated and went off into the night, telling themselves over and over that what the EXPERTS had said was right. As I was leaving, a leather-clad dog caught me by the scruff of the neck. 'You want another listen? It can be arranged. Come up to HEADQUARTERS tomorrow afternoon.' 'Does this apply to the whole flock?' I retorted curiously. 'No. All sheep are equal, but some are more equal than others. YOU have been chosen.' I left at once for the funny farm and found myself humming the rural licks from *Animals*.

"The following day I went to HEADQUARTERS as instructed. There, there are many sheep who sit obediently at typewriters and a handful of dogs who are allowed to put their feet on the desks and bark orders at the woolly ones. I was handed the ULTIMATE ARTICLE – a white label of *Animals*. I played it over and over all afternoon and well into the evening. I also obtained a copy of the lyrics. *Animals* has four tracks, is an allegorical LP and will inevitably be compared to *Dark Side of The Moon*. The words are strong, bitter and they ask questions. The instrumental interludes are at times powerful; Gilmour's guitar work does predominate. It asks questions, but never really gives the answers.

"The words must come from Roger Waters. I don't know, they wouldn't tell me. In fact, the pigs just didn't seem to want to let us know much at all about the album. In the words of the opening track (vocals over acoustic guitar backing)... 'If you didn't care what happened to me, and I didn't care for you...' Do the pigs care, or did they produce this album to fulfil contractual agreements? I think not. This is a powerful and thought-out album. It will be as big as *Dark Side*. For your information, the tracks are *Pigs on the Wing (part one), Dogs, Sheep* and *Pigs on the Wing (part two)*. Who are the pigs, who the sheep and who the dogs, you must decide for yourself. This album may disturb you. It did me, even though the ideals and thoughts behind the words have been raised before.

"The sheep looked from dog to dog and they all looked the same. It was five-thirty. The ANIMALS left HEADQUARTERS two by two. The little dog laughed to see such fun and life went on just the same, day in, day out. Where were the pigs? Who were they? The questions were soon forgotten and never answered."

If Sartre is to be believed and Hell is indeed "other people", the rowdy rock audiences of the US are the ultimate nightmare for an artist of sensitive disposition. For Roger Waters the task of trying to communicate his art to 80,000 concertgoers, many of whom were intent on getting high by any means necessary, was simply a bridge too far. The band were now the objects of extremely high regard and in distant sections of the crowd the devotees were desperate to demonstrate their excitement and admiration by a barrage of whistling which they kept up even in the gentle moments of the set. Interviewed some 10 years after the last of the stadium shows the audience reaction still played on Roger Waters mind. "It took me until ten years ago to stop being upset that people whistled through the quiet numbers, I used to stop and go, 'Right! Who's whistling? C'mon, be quiet!'"

In December 1999 the British magazine *Mojo* ran a major retrospective feature on Pink Floyd to coincide with the forthcoming release of the live CD version of *The Wall*. Journalist Sylvie Simmons enjoyed the rare privilege of access to all four band members as well as the key members of the production team. David Gilmour described the troubled attitude of his former colleague to Sylvie. "Roger never liked touring anyway very much, he was always rather tense and irritable. He was disgusted with the business in many ways, as we all were. The big change came with the huge success of *Dark Side of The Moon* the audiences liked to 'interact', shout a lot. Previous to then, even though we played large places, 10, 000-seaters, you could hear a pin drop at appropriate moments. So it had been a shock - but four years on I was getting used to the idea that that's the way it had to be."

It was not just on stage where too much stress had crept into Waters' life. Inside the band all was not well either, especially in the hot house climate of the sound studio. Recording *Animals* had proved to be something of a grind. Rick Wright had confessed himself to be devoid of any new material whatsoever and consequently Roger Waters was beginning to exert a greater and greater degree of control over the creative output of the group.

David Gilmour was increasingly frustrated by what he felt was an increasingly autocratic style. There was also a distinct impression that Pink Floyd may well have run its course. Nick Mason writing in his book *Inside Out* summed up the feelings of apathy within the band at the time. "We were certainly given the impression that we could put off the next album forever because of the revenue we were earning. The end of the *Animals* tour marked another low point. David now says that this was one period when he really felt that it might be all up for Pink Floyd. His view is that we had achieved and sustained the success we had originally wanted as a band, and accordingly were finding it difficult to see what more we could do."

For Pink Floyd there would unfortunately be a great deal which they would have to do. Circumstances were about to dictate that Floyd would have to get back into the studio and record the next album sooner rather than later. The studio environment no longer exerted the same pull it once did. As the band had matured, the members found themselves less inclined to compromise. Creative differences of opinion were now less easy to resolve and creative arguments on *Animals* had grown heated as entrenched positions were taken. In 1978 it was obvious to manager Steve O'Rourke that the four members of the group were not too desperate to spend a great deal of time working together in the confines of the studio.

Chapter 12
THE WALL

By all accounts Animals had not been a particularly enjoyable experience. By the time of the recording of The Wall, relationships in the group had deteriorated to the extent of barely concealed animosity especially between Roger Waters and Richard Wright. Waters harboured a deep sense of resentment that Wright was not pulling his weight in the studio and was no longer entitled to his share of the revenue reserved for the producer. This nagging doubt was to surface fully when the sessions for The Wall finally began late in 1978.

To compound the personal wrangles there were other problems facing the band. It was discovered that a series of disastrous financial investments coupled with a remorseless tax regime had brought the group close to bankruptcy. It's almost beyond comprehension for a band which had found the keys to a goldmine in the shape of *Dark Side of The Moon* and the hugely successful *Wish You Were Here*, but in 1978 Pink Floyd already one of the biggest bands on earth were teetering on the edge of bankruptcy. The group had invested the fruits of their labours to date in a series of speculative investments with financial advisors Norton Warburg which had gone bad one by one. Steve O'Rourke's judgements had proved to be extremely sound with regard to the band's musical career and the group had earned considerable sums. However O'Rourke's intuition seemed to desert him completely with regard to exactly how that money should be re-invested. Norton Warburg was a disastrous choice. By late 1978 Pink Floyd were desperately in need of an influx of cash; and they needed it fast.

O'Rourke now had the task of informing the beleaguered musicians that the recording of the next album was no longer a luxury, it was now a pressing necessity. Nick Mason recalled the prevailing air of financial obsession during 1977 and 1978 in his book *Inside Out*. "We returned to the UK to find that the top floor of the Britannia Row building was beginning to silt up with accountants, as business matters became increasingly obtrusive in our lives. Noel Redding, the bass player with

Pink Floyd at All Saints Hall, Notting Hill, London, October 1966. The speed of colour film around that time resulted in about 80% of live shots in artificial light taken at gigs being rejected, but Pink Floyd's use of early strobe effects exacerbated the problem.

THE PIPER AT THE GATES OF DAWN

This album sleeve could only have been produced in 1967. The composition by photographer Vic Singh simply reeks of psychedelia with the image of the band shot through a multiple lens to produce the desired and suitably way out effect. For the non-drug user the result was intended to simulate the distorted visions enjoyed by the legions of listeners who were supposedly out there enjoying a never ending succession of LSD trips. Presumably the tripping fraternity experienced multiples of the multiple image.

Pink Floyd performing at Steve Paul's 'The Scene', New York, 1968. Roger Waters on bass and Nick Mason on drums.

A SAUCERFUL OF SECRETS

A Saucerful of Secrets was the first sleeve to be designed under the auspices of the Hipgnosis partnership. Hipgnosis were formed by Storm Thorgerson and Aubrey "po" Powell. Storm and Roger Waters had also played together in the same school rugby team. The services of the Hipgnosis partnership were not exclusive to Floyd and the design partnership went on to produce some of the most innovative and distinctive record sleeves of the seventies. This early effort produced a more distinctive identity for the Saucerful album than the undistinguished Piper At the Gates of Dawn sleeve but there was still very little to suggest the superb work which was yet to come.

Roger Waters performing at Steve Paul's 'The Scene', New York, 1968.

MORE
The second sleeve from the Hipgnosis stable was for the soundtrack to the film More. This was another unspectacular effort which simply took a still from the film as its subject and sloarised the image to produce this odd cover with a strange orange sky.

UMMAGUMMA
The Hipgnosis partnership really began to find its stride with this brilliant sleeve which was striking, thought provoking and innovative with its clever handling of the theme of infinite regression. In many respects the quality of the sleeve may have been somewhat in advance of the music which lagged behind the creativity of the artwork department. The image on the reverse of the sleeve with all of the bands equipment arranged to suggest the shape of a menacing military craft or possibly the spaceship which was destined to crash into the heart of the sun on the live album, is especially memorable.

David Gilmour was to become a major contributor to the music of Pink Floyd as a producer and a writer.

Pink Floyd on stage in the early seventies. It's hard to credit the fact that a group which had received such colossal sums of money was teetering on the brink of insolvency by 1980.

Attendences at Floyd shows grew rapidly throughout the seventies. By 1975 Floyd had outgrown indoor arenas and had moved on to the vast sports stadiums. It was Waters' unease with these events which would ultimately give birth to The Wall.

ATOM HEART MOTHER
For the sleeve of Atom Heart Mother Hipgnosis took an everyday image and by the excellence of the art direction turned it into something strange and disconcerting. This was the first sleeve which carried neither the name nor any other form of visual reference to the band which served to underline the enigmatic qualities of the sleeve. The sleeve has been described as being "totally cow" and who are we to argue?

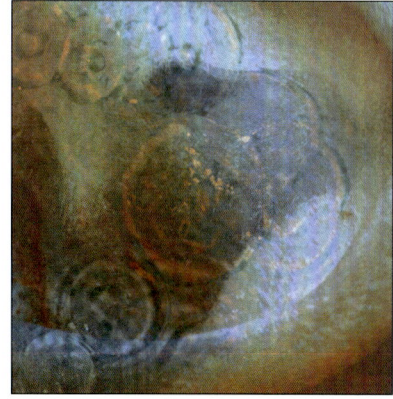

MEDDLE
The second sleeve to feature an image without a reference to the band. This time the image was seemingly abstract but on closer inspection resolved itself to be an ear under water. With Atom Heart Mother already having gone to number one in the UK, EMI were in no position to argue, and the trend was set to continue.

OBSCURED BY CLOUDS
The cover was built around an out of focus still from the film. Obscured by Clouds was not one of Hipgnosis' most inspired offerings

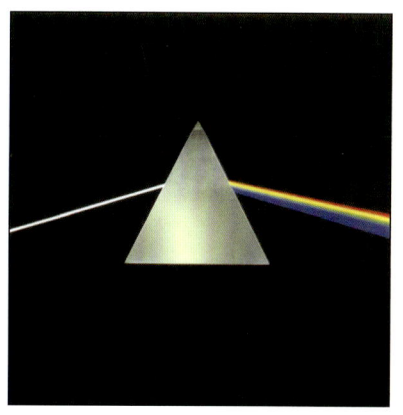

DARK SIDE OF THE MOON
The prism motif was unanimously approved by the band when it was first shown to them by Storm Thorgerson. It has gone on to become an iconic image totally synonymous with Pink Floyd.

WISH YOU WERE HERE
Originally produced in a shiny black plastic wrapper there is some debate over the actual sleeve design of the album and which image actually constitutes the cover. The CD (shown here) reproduced the sticker and the wrapper.

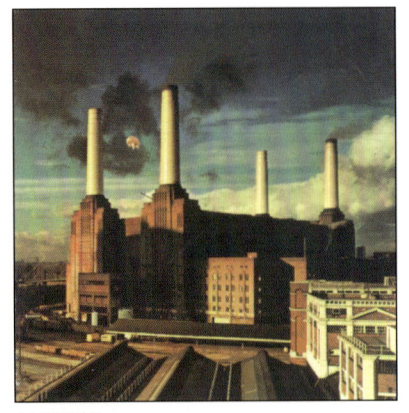

ANIMALS
Considered by many to be the finest moment in the Hipgnosis/Floyd relationship this striking image has become instantly recognisable..

David Gilmour on stage circa 1975. This was the period when the band was still functioning as a cohesive writing and performing unit.

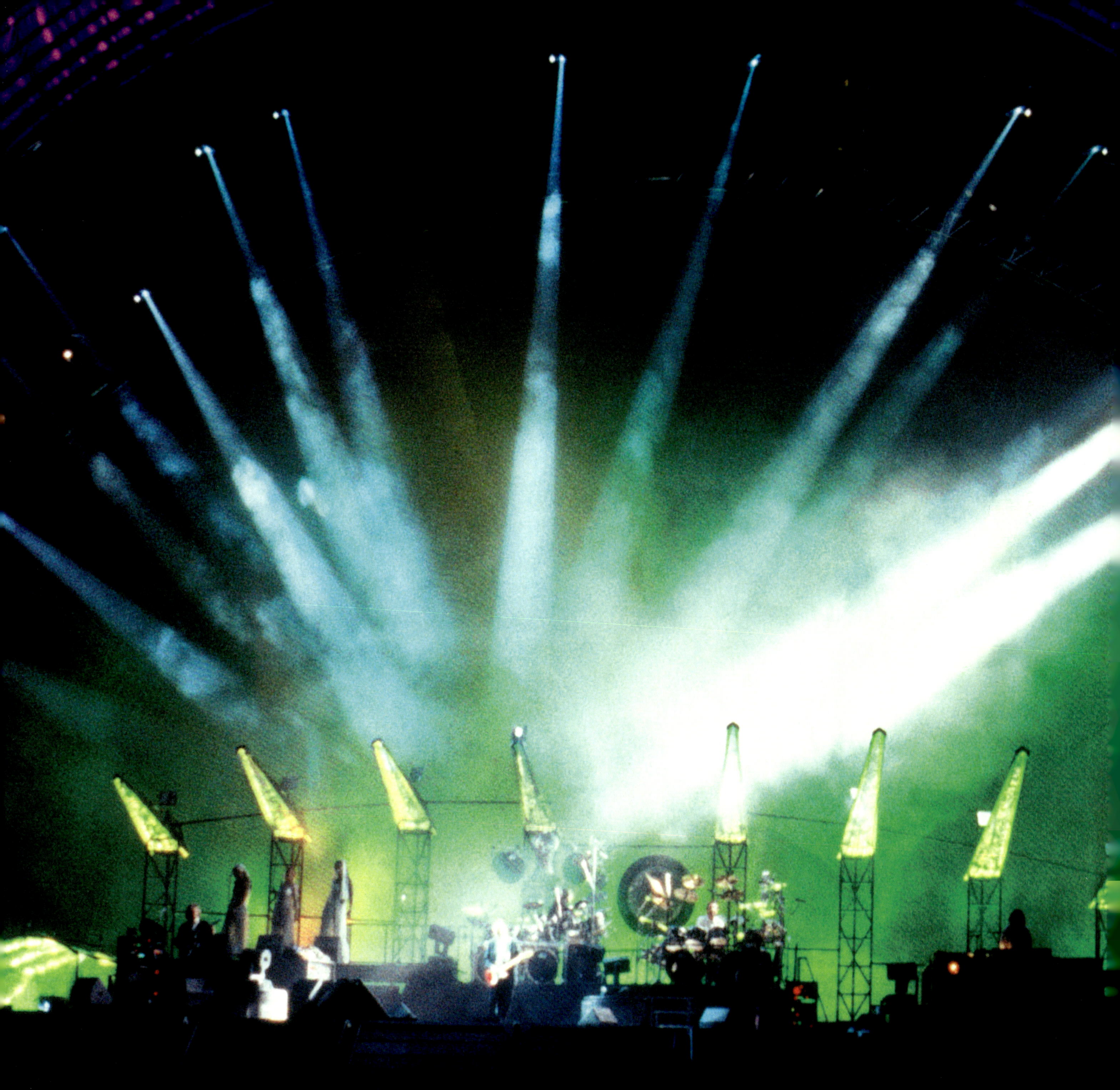

THE WALL
A radical departure for Pink Floyd when for the first time in a decade an album was released without a Hipgnosis sleeve. In the highly capable hands of Gerald Scarfe the cover for the album effortlessly ascended to the same dizzy heights of creativity as previous outings. This is the CD cover; the original vinyl release was devoid of graffiti and utilised a completely plain wall motif.

The live shows concluded with a bizarre country-tinged take on 'Outside The Wall' performed on acoustic instruments, featuring the only known clarinet performance by Roger Waters.

With construction of The Wall well underway the first half of the live show begins to build momentum with the forlorn figure of Pink already outside The Wall.

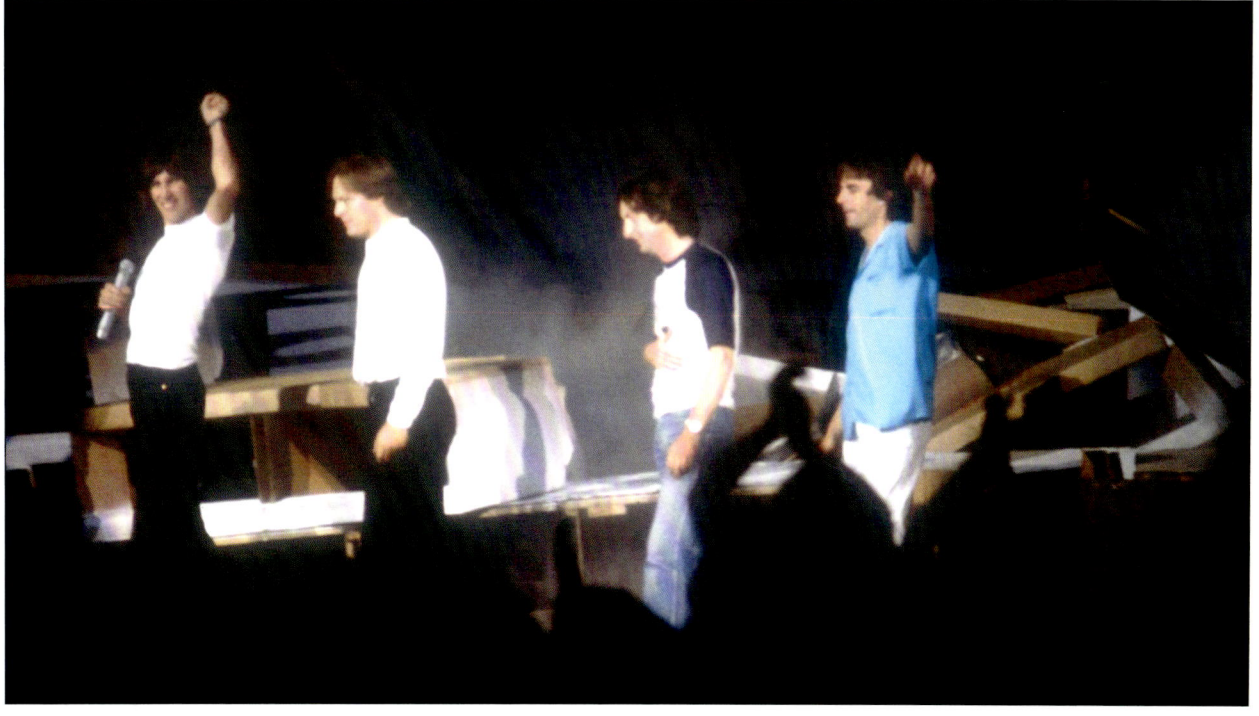

The Wall is now approaching completion. At this point in the live show the dramatic possibilities of back lighting from behind the wall were harnessed to great effect.

In the aftermath of another successful show, the delight on Roger Water's face tells the whole story. The Wall shows were a creative triumph, a dazzling tour de force which has never been equalled.

63

The regrouped Pink Floyd backstage at the Rose Bowl, Los Angeles, basking in the reflected glory of a successful tour and album.

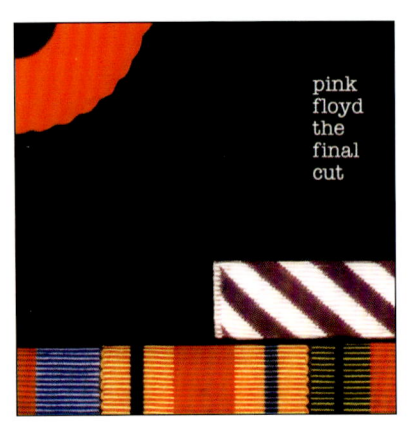

THE FINAL CUT
In addition to creating the music Roger Waters also art directed the sleeve for the album. The design depicted the medal ribbon of a British war veteran and part of a poppy in close up. This was the first Pink Floyd sleeve to feature the band's name since Ummagumma eleven years. The sleeve is as uninspired as the music.

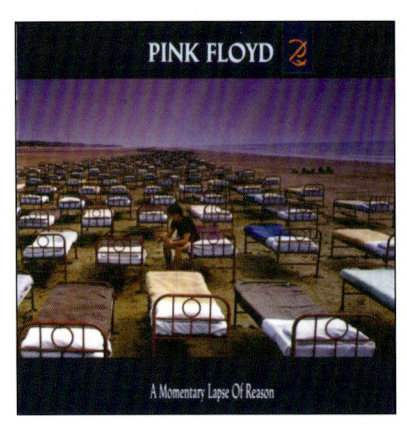

A MOMENTARY LAPSE OF REASON
Hipgnosis was no more, but Gilmour brought Storm Thorgerson back for the cover of A Momentary Lapse Of Reason. It was to prove an inspired decision. The image produced by Thorgerson and his team was breathtaking even if the music couldn't quite match the excellence of the imagery.

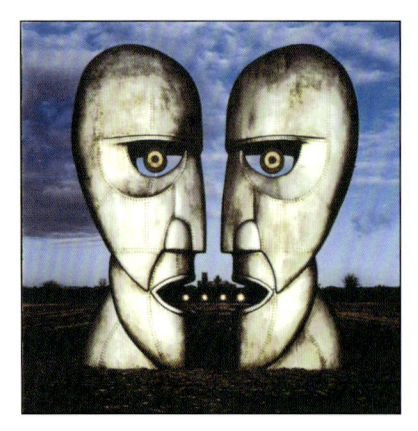

THE DIVISION BELL
There is a strong argument to suggest that Storm Thorgerson saved the best for last. Distinctive, striking, enigmatic and superbly realised, The Division Bell is everything that a Pink Floyd sleeve should be. The perfect visual compliment to a great album.

IS THERE ANYBODY OUT THERE
The front cover from the CD release of 'Is There Anybody Out There - The Wall Live', was arrived at after a great deal of diplomatic wrangling and cannot be said to represent the more striking of Pink Floyd's sleeves.

the Jimi Hendrix Experience, always had a quote handy for anyone wanting to enter the music business: 'Study law. Buy a gun...'" Those same accountants who 'silted' up the Floyd offices were soon telling O'Rourke and the band just how much the group needed the advance for a new album. The only place where they could be guaranteed enough money in the short term was from their record labels. EMI in the UK and CBS in the USA were well aware of the value of Pink Floyd and Steve O'Rourke soon ascertained that the labels were willing to advance the group the then staggering sum of £4.5 million pounds which was more than enough to get the album made and stave off the worst of the financial fall out.

Rick Wright was candid with the financial details when he spoke to Sylvie Simmons for the *Mojo* feature in 1999. "At that time we were, in theory, bankrupt. Our accountants had lost our money, we owed huge amounts of tax, and we were told we must go away for a year, make an album to try to repay the tax we owed, so it was a pretty scary time for us all."

So the band which had all but disbanded in 1977 was forced to come back together again for the worst possible reasons. Even the normally fastidious Roger Waters was to bow to the pressure of time and tax. On this album, for once, even the famous Pink Floyd quality control was sacrificed to the pressure of the immutable financial deadline which resulted in mistakes in the track listing and lyrics printed on early editions of the album's artwork. A clearly embarrassed Roger Waters was forced to explain the reasons to Tommy Vance in a promotional interview circulated to the press. Almost the entire interview was also published in the US magazine *Music Express*. With the benefit of hindsight it's not too difficult for the reader to look between the lines and spot the reason why the album had been promised to 'lots of people' presumably a large number of whom worked for Her Majesty's Inland Revenue. "So that's why those lyrics are printed in the wrong place, because that decision was made afterwards. You will find that, in 'The Show Must Go On,' there are some extra lyrics because we had to edit the side an awful lot. So we just took those lyrics from the album, but left them on the sleeve. For people out there who read the lyrics, I'd tell them not to worry about it. I should explain, at this point, the reason why all these decisions were made too late was because we'd promised lots of people a long time ago that we would finish this record by the beginning of November, and we wanted to keep that promise. In this instance, I am sorry they are out of place."

Artwork mistakes apart, it was Roger Waters who had again come

An original ticket from the Dortmund shows.

to the rescue of the band. His grand design was a sprawling concept which from the outset was envisaged as a daring multi-media extravaganza. In 1999 Roger Waters explained the evolution of the project to Sylvie Simmons of *Mojo*. "Initially I had two images - of building a wall across the stage, and of the sado-masochistic relationship between audience and band, the idea of an audience being bombed and the ones being blown to pieces applauding the loudest because they're the centre of action, even as victims. There is something macabre and a bit worrying about that relationship - that we will provide a PA system so loud that it can damage you and that you will fight to sit right in front of it so you can be damaged as much as possible - which is where the idea of Pink metamorphosed into a Nazi demagogue began to generate from."

The scope and scale of Waters' vision was part of a finely tuned master plan. This was no happy accident in creative terms. The whole concept was carefully planned and fully thought out in a stepped programme of interlinked creations, this was certainly clear to Nick Mason as he later recalled in his autobiography *Inside Out*. "*The Wall* as a piece, represents a large amount of material spread across a range of media: the record, the concerts - enhanced with film, stage effects and props - and a movie. This had been Roger's intention from the outset. He had already shown his fondness for exploring the possibilities of multimedia, but *The Wall* took things considerably further. The whole project also covered a large amount of time, a period of work that actually lasted from mid-1978, when Roger was creating the initial version, until 1982, with the release of the movie."

Various terms have been used to try and define *The Wall* which has been described as a 'rock opera', a 'musical', 'a concept piece' and even an 'oratorio'. None of the terms is wholly appropriate but there are elements of truth in all of them. It's certainly not a 'rock opera' but there are without doubt operatic elements. Gilbert and Sullivan would have had no difficulty in recognising this in *The Trial*. The truth seems to be that *The Wall* takes on a different character at each stage of its development. In the standard lexicon of rock music it begins life as a 'concept album'. On stage *The Wall* was clearly more than a concert, it was a genuine mixed media event, a powerful son et lumiere experience which advanced a strong narrative but which stopped a long way short of being an 'opera'. The film is almost totally devoid of dialogue and could conceivably be described as a musical; but only if one accepts that this is the bleakest, gloomiest most nihilistic 'musical' in the history of cinema.

The subject matter of *The Wall* is remorselessly bleak. In many respects it is autobiographical but those details are intertwined with an equal measure of complete fiction. It is not Roger Water's life story, but parts of it certainly are.

The central protagonist is a rock star called Pink. Each of the individual tribulations suffered by Pink is shown as another brick in *The Wall* of increasing isolation which eventually cuts the star off from the outside world. The process transforms Pink into a confused, insular and drug ravaged individual who, in his own mind cannot distinguish between reality and the illusion which transforms him from a rock star performing to a welcoming audience into a megalomaniacal demagogue leading his doting worshippers into ever greater acts of fanaticism.

Like the real life Waters, the fictional Pink has lost his father in the Second World War. This is just the first of many blows dealt by ordinary life which continue to pile up on Pink. As Shakespeare had noted almost four hundred years earlier when trouble comes it comes in battalions and the emotional blows soon pile up for Pink. They include tyrannical schoolmasters, a suffocating matriarchal relationship, drug dependency, unfaithfulness, matrimonial breakdown and bouts of depression. All of this leads to feelings of paranoia which are only overcome by a massive effort of will and self analysis - an inner trial in which Pink confronts his demons and finally tears down *The Wall*.

It is a message with little hope of redemption. Side one of *The Wall* double album opens with the quiet voice of Roger Waters intoning "...we came in?" It's actually the end of a sentence which is completed by the words "Isn't this where..." which appear at the end of side four. The significance is clear, the process of building and tearing down walls is a cyclical process which we are all doomed to constantly repeat.

In conjunction with the disquieting themes of the album, Roger Waters announced his bold vision for the stage show in which a wall would literally be built brick by brick across the stage eventually obscuring the band from its audience. It was an extraordinarily striking idea which Waters later recapitulated for Nick Sedgwick in an interview conducted for the sleeve notes of the live album release in 2000.

"*The Wall* is part of my narrative, my story, but I think the basic themes resonate in other people. The idea that we, as individuals, generally find it necessary to avoid or deny the painful aspects of our experience, and in fact often use them as bricks in a wall behind which we may sometimes find shelter, but which we may just as easily become emotionally immured, is relatively simply stated and easy to grasp. It's one a lot of people grapple with themselves. They recognise it in their own lives."

Roger's initial idea was to build *The Wall* with the band quietly leaving the stage as the last brick was put into place leaving the audience to seethe in frustration. Eventually, with the input of producer Bob Ezrin the narrative was altered and softened to the point at which there was a resolution of sorts in which *The Wall* came tumbling down; but it was still a powerful, bold, thought provoking and disturbing concept.

With such an enormously successful track record behind him there was little doubt that Waters could be relied on to produce some excellent musical ideas. In order to help him realise the visual aspects of his bold new concept Roger surprisingly turned away from Storm Thorgeson, Floyd's usual designer who had served the band so well, and instead enlisted the help of Gerald Scarfe, a well known political cartoonist. Scarfe's work for *The Wall* was first seen on the minimalist album sleeve which featured the stark image of the outline a bare brick wall. Inside was the familiar lettering style and grotesque cartoons which were Scarfe's hallmark. Scarfe too recalled his initial impressions for Nick Sedgwick for the sleeve notes which accompanied the release of the *Is There Anybody Out There?* CD.

"Roger's ideas appealed to me at once. The story also seemed to make obvious sense. It's about Roger, but that didn't trouble me since one of its virtues is that it is capable of wider interpretation. I took it as a story about every man."

The Gerald Scarfe inspired sleeve (the design of which credited jointly to both him and Roger Waters) was striking and effective, but the real reason for Scarfe's selection lay in Roger's vision for the stage show and the movie which would accompany the album.

Scarfe's idiosyncratic animations were to become a key motif for *The Wall* stage shows. Once the huge wall had been built the audience could not be expected to just sit there, so *The Wall* itself was to be transformed into a giant projection screen for Scarfe's amazing animations. It also served as the base from which giant Scarfe-designed marionettes of the characters would emerge.

We are fortunate that the story of how *The Wall* evolved is so well documented. Like all artists, Roger Waters had misgivings and self doubts about his work. He was concerned over the cohesiveness of the story and how well it all hung together as a concept and frequently felt himself compelled to explain its shortcomings. In late 1979 just as the album was being released, Tommy Vance conducted a lengthy promotional interview in which Roger Waters attempted to explain *The Wall* from the perspective of its chief architect. The interview formed the basis of a lengthy article which first appeared in the US magazine Music Express.

"In a way it's a shame for anybody who might read this, that they hear how I feel about it, because, in a way, it would be nicer if it's just vague. I hope there are lots of other conclusions that can be drawn from it. I'm doing this interview because I think the thing is very complicated and not very well done. But having said that, I don't want people to get stuck with how I feel about it. I'm sure people have their own feelings about it. I hope they will."

The artist's perspective on the crowd is shared by a very small and pretty select bunch of human beings. Few people on earth have experienced the drawing power of the huge bands who can fill football stadiums. It's no surprise that Waters found it difficult to engender universal sympathy for his vision of a rock star as a beleaguered victim. Time and time again he had to go to great lengths to explain the reality of a stadium rock concert as perceived from the lofty point of view of the musician. In 1979 he made yet another attempt to explain the loneliness of the long distance performer, this time in conversation with Tommy Vance. "It's all because the people who you are most aware of at a rock show are the front twenty or thirty rows of bodies. In large situations, where you use what is commonly known as 'festival seating', they tend to be packed together, swaying madly. It's very difficult to perform in a situation where people are whistling and shouting, screaming and throwing things, and hitting each other and crashing about, and letting off fireworks. I mean, they're having a wonderful time, but it's a drag to try and play when all that is going on. But I felt at the same time that it was a situation that we'd created ourselves through our own greed. The only reason for playing very large venues is to make money."

In late 1979 when he gave his interview to Tommy Vance, Waters had not been on stage for a year and a half and had begun to forget the worst stresses of life on the road especially those brought about by over exuberant crowds. At this stage in the cycle Waters was uncharacteristically forgiving of the worst excesses of the lunatic fringe. "I'm actually happy that they do whatever they feel is necessary because they're only expressing their response to what it's like. In a way, I'm saying that they're right, you know, that those shows are bad news. There is an idea, or there has been an idea for many years abroad, that it's a very uplifting and wonderful experience, that there is a great contact between the audience and the performers on the stage. I don't think that is true. I think that, in very many cases, it's actually a rather alienating experience for everybody."

By sharp contrast to his rested and calm pre-tour persona, early in 1980 Janet Huck encountered a very different Roger Waters who was back in full swing with touring. In researching her account of Floyd on tour with *The Wall* she was to discover how almost immediately the old tensions had risen to the surface. Janet's highly readable account of *The Wall* tour *Up Against The Wall* lay unpublished for almost twenty years until it was rescued and printed in Bruno McDonald's well recommended book, *Pink Floyd through the eyes of it's fans friends and foes*. Janet was aware of the strong focus on the importance Waters placed on the interaction between the band and its audience. "Waters expects the same rapt attention from his audience. When asked what was the role of a rock audience, he quickly snapped 'Passive', throwing his head forward as if he were spitting once again on that odious fan. 'Like they're in a theatre. You bloody well sit there. I hate audience participation. I hate it when they want you to sing along: it makes my flesh creep. Yelling and screaming and singing is great in church, but not at our shows, thank you very much.'"

Waters himself keenly felt the need for his audience to be able to listen to the music and fully comprehend his new vision. He clearly saw *The Wall* not just as another rock 'n' roll show but as an important piece of theatre. The darkness of the subject matter only enhanced the need for an environment which allowed the listener to concentrate on the work free from the distractions of the party animals filling the stadiums of the lucrative North American circuit. Filled with murky deeds and distressing observations from the dark corners of our psyche, *The Wall* was not a piece which was likely to bear fruit amidst a screaming stadium crowd as Roger explained to Tommy Vance in 1979.

"Maybe I'm just paranoid or maybe I pick on the darkest side of things to think about or to write about. What I hope is that, when people listen to this thing, there are feelings inside them so that they can understand what I'm talking about and would be able to respond to it and say, 'Yeah, I feel like that sometimes, too.' This show that I've been working on in parallel to working on this album is going to be like that. I think a lot of people in the audience may get very uncomfortable during it because most of them won't be able to see most of the time. It will be just like it normally is for a lot of people who are packed behind PA systems, like when every seat in the house is sold and there are thousands of people at the sides who can't see anything."

What Roger mischievously failed to make clear was that his original uncompromising vision meant that, despite the fact *The Wall* tour would be playing in what were relatively much smaller venues, it wasn't just some people who wouldn't be able to see the band. This time literally all of the crowd were about to find themselves in the restricted view section.

Nick Mason was naturally among the first to be let in on the secret as he later recalled in *Inside Out*. "Although the spitting incident was unnerving at the time, it did serve to set Roger's creative wheels spinning, and he developed the outline for a show based around the concept of an audience both physically and mentally separated from their idols. Whether the confrontation in Montreal had any life-changing impact on the hapless spat-upon fan remains unknown; suffice to say that he has never employed a lawyer, nor claimed any royalties for creative inspiration."

In later years David Gilmour fell out of love with *The Wall* famously describing it on at least one occasion as "whingeing." Much closer in time to the event Gilmour was honest enough to admit his respect for the subject. "I don't think any of us differed all the way through on the subjects Roger approached. We were pretty much of a like mind. On *The Wall* although I didn't agree with that part of the concept - *The Wall* between us and the audience - I still thought it was a good subject to do. My father didn't go off to the war and get killed in it. So that area of it did not apply to me. But I could get into it as fiction."

As a release from the hothouse world of Pink Floyd in late 1977 and early 1978 both David Gilmour and Richard Wright had pursued solo projects. During the extended hiatus after the recording of *Animals*, Richard made his solo album called *Wet Dream* which despite the superstar selling status of its creator's main band, had produced barely a ripple of reaction as a solo project. David Gilmour had also produced the first of his solo albums the eponymously titled *David Gilmour*. It had not been a great success either, and outside of London the audiences for the supporting concerts were frankly embarrassing.

Neither solo project was to meet with any great success either financially or commercially. Roger Waters too harboured solo ambitions and as an artist he was approaching something of a peak of creativity. His song writing muse was in such a creative ferment that in 1988 his unrecorded works could easily have been stretched to fill six sides of vinyl. Meeting with his semi-alienated band mates in July 1978 Roger presented the demos of two alternative concepts which he had spent the previous year writing and recording. The first was a cycle of songs with an American theme called *The Pros And Cons Of Hitch Hiking*. The other was *The Wall*.

In their hour of need, Waters was therefore able to offer the band a choice of two well developed projects. Rick Wright and Nick Mason in particular couldn't get to grips with the *Hitch Hiking* idea and *The Wall* was duly chosen as the next Floyd project.

Subsequent events have coloured the views of all concerned, but in 1978 all four members had enough confidence in the subject matter to get squarely behind the new album. After the merest of hesitation caused by Gilmour's belief that *Hitch Hiking* was the stronger musically, the band came down firmly on the side of *The Wall*. It was to prove an inspired choice. History records that while *The Wall* has gone on to become recognised as Pink Floyd's magnum opus, *The Pros and Cons of Hitch Hiking* was destined to be remembered as a painful flop both on vinyl and in the live arena where not even the presence of Eric Clapton could sell enough tickets for what was widely considered to be a substandard work.

Writing in *Inside Out* Nick Mason later recalled how *The Wall* project was unveiled by its creator. "Roger had learnt from experience that one maxim for work was to know when the time was right to push an idea ahead. At some point during 1978 he clearly felt that it was that time and set to work in his home studio. By the time he played the results to us - I remember going to his house on at least one occasion to listen to them, and he also brought the tapes into Britannia Row - he actually had two records roughed out, one being *The Wall* and the other *The Pros And Cons of Hitch-Hiking*. The level of contributions by other members of the band would become a bone of contention. Perhaps the very completeness of Roger's demo made it difficult for David or Rick to contribute much. But certainly David later felt that his musical contribution, especially to *Run Like Hell* and *Comfortably Numb* was not being fairly recognised. This potential volcano of future discord was, however, still dormant when we started making rough versions of some of the tracks for *The Wall* at Britannia Row during the autumn of 1978." David Gilmour explained his early reaction to Sylvie Simmons of *Mojo* and confirmed that he had initially been enthusiastic over the concept although it was clear that Gilmour's enthusiasm had cooled over the years. "It is true that we had some financial crisis, but I don't think that happened until after we'd started putting together the first bit of *The Wall* at Britannia Row studios between September and Christmas. I thought it was a very good concept at the time - I don't like it quite as much now; with the benefit of hindsight I found it a bit whingeing - and well worth exploring. I was willing - have been before and since - to let Roger have full rein of his vision."

The one major composition which was not present on Roger's demo for *The Wall* was, of course, *Comfortably Numb*. The lacklustre *David Gilmour* album could certainly have been better had Gilmour been able to include a powerful new song conceived just as the production process was coming to a close. The finished result testifies to the fact that this new composition clearly had great potential; but in 1978 the song existed only as an instrumental demo. It was conceived very late in the recording process and with his band now departed for home and no more time available on the recording sessions the guitarist shelved the song for later use. It was to prove a fortunate judgment. Audiences all over the world now know the song by its more familiar title of *Comfortably Numb*, universally recognised as a Pink Floyd masterpiece. Gilmour later acknowledged the birth of the song. "I actually recorded a demo of *Comfortably Numb* at Bear Les Alps studio while I was there doing my first solo album, but it was only a basic little chord pattern which was really not much else." Bootleg copies of David's sketch for *Comfortably Numb* have been widely circulated among the Floyd fraternity for many years and as anyone who has heard it will testify, the demo bears little resemblance to the majestic show-stopper which it would ultimately grow into.

It is of course a moot point, but it is interesting to speculate what might have been had *Pros And Cons* been chosen as the next Pink Floyd project ahead of *The Wall*. It's most unlikely that the album would have been such a failure had it benefited from the full Pink Floyd treatment including the addition of joint compositions like *Run Like Hell* and *Comfortably Numb*. What might have been will always remain unanswered but what we do know is that in 1978, for the time being at least, Gilmour's creative energies had been exhausted by his solo album. As a composer Gilmour was close to running on empty and there was very little left in the tank. As he later told Nick Sedgwick in the autumn of 1988 only his pale blueprint of a possible *Comfortably Numb* and a few ideas for what would later become *Run like Hell* were on offer to the band from David Gilmour. "They are the musical high points of *The Wall*-but then I would think that, wouldn't I?"

In 1999 Rick Wright revisited the moments when he was first introduced to the concept and explained to Sylvie Simmons how the prevailing financial climate had influenced his reaction. "There were things about it where I thought, 'Oh no, here we go again - it's all about the war, about his mother, about his father being lost.' I'd hoped he could get through all this and eventually he could deal with other stuff, but he had a fixation... Every song was written in the same tempo, same key, same everything. Possibly if we were not in this financial situation we might have said, 'We don't like these songs,' and things might have been different. But Roger has this material, Dave and I didn't have any, so we'll do it."

Rick was certainly not understating the case against him. There was no new material at all on offer from either Wright or Mason and very little from Gilmour, so it was no surprise that Roger Waters seized the helm totally. When the desperate need to produce a new album had suddenly descended on the band, only Roger really had enough material available. This left Richard Wright in particular in a very vulnerable position. His personal relationship with the strong willed Waters had been in decline for some time and this new development was certainly unwelcome as Wright confided to Nick Sedgwick in 2000. "It's a matter of historical record that my relationship with Roger collapsed during the time the band was making the album. There had always been a personality clash, but apparently the tensions now became insurmountable. Part of this was down to me. I hadn't contributed any material to *Animals*, nor did I have any to offer for *The Wall*. I simply wasn't very creative throughout that period. I have enormous respect for Roger who works extremely hard on his own, but I find that process difficult."

The importance of the break down in the relationship between Waters and Wright cannot be underestimated when approaching the end result of their last collaboration. Not for the last time, life began to imitate art in the most painful and unhealthy way. Just as they were about to embark on a piece which had at it's heart the subject of isolation and non-communication caused by the cumulative effects of the emotional blows dealt to a fictional rock star, a series of troubles brought about by everyday life had come crowding in on the keyboard player.

Like the fictional Pink, Wright was undergoing a divorce, dabbling with drugs, suffering from loss of confidence and becoming increasingly isolated from his colleagues. Waters response seems to have been less than understanding; he zeroed in on Wright's declining studio contribution and snatched away Wright's producers credit and fees. The explanation he later gave to Sylvie Simmons in 1999 for her *Mojo* piece sounds particularly heartless. "What actually happened was *The Wall* was the first album where we didn't divide the production credit between everybody in the band. At the beginning of the process, when I said I was going to bring Bob Ezrin in and he was going to get paid, I said, 'I'm going to produce the record as well, so is Dave, so we're going to get paid as well, but Nick, you don't actually do any record production, and Rick, neither do you. So you're not going to get paid.' Nick said fair enough, but Rick said, 'No, I produce the records just as much as you do.' So we agreed we would start making the record and we would see. But who would be the arbiter? We all agreed on Ezrin. So Rick sat in the studio - he would arrive exactly on time, which was very unusual, and stay to the bitter end every night. One day Ezrin said to me - he was slightly irked by this brooding presence very occasionally going 'I don't like that - Why's Rick here again?' I said, 'Don't you get it? He's putting in the time to prove he's a record producer. You talk to him about it.' So he did. After that Rick never came to another session, unless he was directly asked to do keyboard tracks. And he became almost incapable of playing any keyboards anyway. It was a nightmare. I think that was the beginning of the end."

In Roger's harsh words we can almost hear a sinister echo of the schoolmaster screaming "If ye don't eat yer meat, how can ye have any pudden?" It seemed as if *The Wall* concept had grown wings of its own and begun to build a wall between two of the men who would give birth to the work.

In the most practical sense the friction in the studio was always going to work against Wright. It seems that Rick Wright's confidence was the first to go, resulting in the total absence of the creative flourishes which had embellished *Dark Side of The Moon*, *Wish You Were Here* and even *Animals*. Despite not writing the material Wright's distinctive playing was still very much in evidence on *Animals* and he had contributed the wonderfully atmospheric jazz tinged intro to *Sheep*. As a result of the absence of Wright as a functioning artist *The Wall* saw Rick's characteristic keyboards take a far less important role than in any other previous Floyd project and the end result is weaker for it.

The breakdown of the relationship between Waters and Wright was also important in the more subtle undercurrents in the studio. It is inconceivable that the effects of a highly strained personal relationship did not manifest themselves in the creation of a concept album which dealt entirely with the wearing effect of combined blows to the psyche of the individual. With his on-going divorce, self confessed dabblings in cocaine, writer's block, creative doubts and increasing isolation from his fellow band members, Richard Wright seems to have far closely matched the blue print for the imaginary Pink than the character's more robust confident and assured creator.

Roger's strangle hold on the supply of new compositions placed Waters firmly in the driving seat as regards the direction and production of the album. Fortunately he was exactly the right man to shoulder the burden at the time and unlike Wright was supremely confident of his own skills as he later told Rolling Stone magazine in 1987. "There wasn't any room for anyone else to be writing. If there were chord sequences there, I would always use them. There was no point in Gilmour, Mason or Wright trying to write lyrics because they'll never be as good as mine. Gilmour's lyrics are very third-rate, they always will be. And in comparison with what I do, I'm sure he'd agree. He's just not as good. I didn't play the guitar solos; he didn't write any lyrics."

As immodest as Roger's self praise may seem, there can be little doubt that Waters is one of the better lyricists at work in rock music. The lyrics of the post-Waters era are certainly unexceptional by comparison to all of the albums from *Meddle* right through to *The Final Cut*. Bob Ezrin had the misfortune to work with a number of artists who were not terribly effective in the lyrical department so discovering the ability of Waters was something of a revelation for him as he recalled for Michael Watts of *Melody Maker* in August 1980. "He's the finest wordsmith in music right now. There's no one to touch him. Absolutely brilliant. You may not like the subject matter that he finally decides to go with, but I've seen other things he's written and he does have a capacity to write anything, right down to simple rock and roll. He has a facility with language like no-one else."

Before he embarked on the task of completing *The Wall*, Roger Waters also made the time to listen to the previous work by Pink Floyd. "I listened to the last three records all the way through because I thought it would be a useful exercise to listen to them before completing *The Wall*. You get so immersed in a thing like a double album or a project like this that, sometimes, it's hard to see it clearly. I didn't listen to anything pre-*Dark Side of The Moon*, though. I know I still like *Echoes*, as a piece, but from *Dark Side of The Moon* till now, I liked it all. I was amazed. I expected to be annoyed or at least embarrassed by it, but I wasn't. I thought it was all pretty good, particularly *Animals*. I was not amazed, but I was surprised that it is as good as it is because when we did it, it was all done very quickly. It's not a masterpiece, but it's a bloody good album, and I think *Wish You Were Here* was too."

Now that the die was cast it was time to get down to the serious business of making it all happen. With the *Animals* experience still scarred into their minds, neither Waters nor Gilmour was too keen to embark on another major product without the presence of an independent producer, though in reality he was to be more of a peace keeper and arbiter. From the outset *The Wall* was very much Roger Water's project, but David Gilmour was not about to relinquish total control of anything which carried the precious Pink Floyd name. As the creative friction escalated it was clear to Steve O'Rourke that a peace keeper had to be sought and as he was the supplier of the lion's share of the material for the project Roger Waters naturally got the casting vote. Roger promptly selected Bob Ezrin, the Canadian producer of such luminaries as Kiss and Alice Cooper and for whom Roger's new wife had once worked as a secretary.

In 1999 when he spoke to Sylvie Simmons, Waters was clearly still upset over the possibility that the over arching nature of his artistic contribution might be undermined and he sought to set the record straight from his point of view with regard to both his own contribution and that of Bob Ezrin. "Rick didn't have any input at all, apart from playing the odd keyboard part, and Nick played the drums, with a little help from his friends. And Dave, yeah, Dave played the guitar and wrote the music for a couple of songs, but he didn't have any input into anything else really. We co-produced it, I think, Ezrin and myself-the collaboration with Ezrin was a very fertile one, his input was big - and Dave got a production credit - I'm sure he had something to do with the record production; he had very different ideas about that sort of thing. But there was really only one chief, and that was me." For the creative artist, recognition for his creative input is something which is of paramount importance. For his part David Gilmour was bitterly opposed to the expression of the idea that he hadn't played a full part in producing the album. He made the alternative position abundantly clear to Sylvie Simmons during his 1999 interview. "Roger was obviously one of the main producers because it was his idea and he was very, very good about many things to do with production, like dynamics. I've always been one of the producers on Pink Floyd records, and while I might not argue with Roger much over lyrics I think I know as much as anyone in or around the band about music and would certainly give my opinions quite forcibly. Bob Ezrin was in there partly as a man in the middle to help smooth the flow between Roger and I, whose arguments were numerous and heated."

On the surface, the connection with Roger's wife might appear as the pat answer for the choice, but Roger's selection of Bob Ezrin had deeper roots. As we have seen, Ezrin had actually been present with Roger at the infamous concert in Montreal on Wednesday 6th July 1977 when in front of 80, 000 Roger had undergone his on stage epiphany which was to have enormous consequences for the group. Over twenty years later Ezrin described his introduction to *The Wall* to Sylvie Simmons for the *Mojo* feature. "Roger invited me down for the weekend - he had a lovely house in the country with an appropriately dark studio area. It was one of those wonderfully moody, grey fall weekends in England. He sat me in a room and proceeded to play me a tape of music all strung together, almost like one song 90 minutes long, called *The Wall*, then some bits and bobs of other ideas that he hoped to incorporate in some way, which never made it to the album but resurfaced later on some of his solo work. The English countryside under the weight of humidity and cloud was the perfect setting for this music and I was transported. It wasn't complete, it wasn't even in anything like the final form of the work, but it captured the atmosphere and I just knew after listening to it that it was going to be an important work - and that it was going to take a lot of work to pull it into something cohesive."

Waters felt that Ezrin was a forceful character who could hold his own in the event of creative disagreements. Roger later explained the reasons for his choice of producer in *Rolling Stone*. "Bob Ezrin would be prepared to argue with me about things. It's no good arguing with me in the studio and saying, 'I don't like that '; you 've got to explain why you don't like it and why we should do it a different way. Bob is articulate and quite able to do that, so we had a good lively relationship making the record. He was a very good musical and intellectual sounding-board for me, 'cos he's very bright and quite tough as well. We could sit and talk about what it was about ad nauseam - which was absolutely invaluable, because I don't think anybody else in the band had any idea of what it was about, and I don't think they were very interested. In fact, I know they weren't interested."

To an extent Roger's view that the band "weren't interested" is echoed by the recollection of David Gilmour who does recall being roused to anger, but only where it concerned his own material. "We argued over *Comfortably Numb* like mad. Really had a big fight; went on for ages... These things that seemed so important at the time, I can hardly remember why we thought they were. Roger and I had a real shouting match at this Italian restaurant in North Hollywood. We 'd gone there with Bob Ezrin to have it out over something - probably *Comfortably Numb*, because the only thing I 'd really argue with Roger over was my own music, otherwise I wouldn't bother."

Roger Waters had by this time clearly emerged as the leader of the band. Janet Huck witnessed this at first hand for herself when she interviewed Roger Waters in February 1980 for her piece entitled *Up*

Against The Wall. "I make the decisions. We pretended it was a democracy for a long time, but this album was the era of the big own-up. It was a mildly painful experience for some of us because we have been pretending we are all jolly good chaps together. It's a load of rubbish. Ten years ago it was true, but not for the last six or seven years."

In David Fricke's *Rolling Stone* article Waters was prepared to expand further on the subject of control within the group. "I suppose it comes down to the fact that we are people in rock 'n' roll bands and people in rock 'n' roll bands are greedy for attention. We never managed to come to a common view of the dynamic that existed within the band, of who did what and whether or not it was right. It was an irritation to start with, and it became an impossible irritation towards the end."

When it came to the creation of *The Wall*, Bob Ezrin was the exception to the "Roger Waters decides" rule as he explained to Sylvie Simmons for her *Mojo* feature. "What I did was write a script for an imaginary *Wall* movie - as distinct from the film; I had nothing to do with that and was actually opposed to the idea of codifying it in any fixed imagery. I just had this sense of a narrative soundscape - saw it, more than heard it - and organised all the pieces of music we had and some we didn't, plus sound effects and cross-fades, into a cohesive tale. I felt who the central character was and I came to the conclusion that we needed to take it out of the literal first-person and put it in the figurative - resurrecting old Pink to whom they had referred in the past. I came in the next day with a script - which, by the way, is in the Rock and Roll Hall of Fame, handed it out to everybody and we did a table-read of *The Wall*. It was a whole other way of doing things when you 're making music, but it really helped to crystallise the work. From that point on we were no longer fishing, we were building to a plan."

Artistic control is only one part of the equation when it comes to the creation of great compositions. Regardless of who controls the mix or chooses the takes, the music has to be spot on, especially if it is to carry the listener through such a bleak concept piece as *The Wall*. Despite the cheerlessness of his subject matter, there was little doubt that Waters was capable of getting the music right but it was not proving a smooth process. Aside from the strained relationship between Waters and Wright, there was the continuing stress of the more fruitful partnership between Roger Waters and David Gilmour which also had it's moments. Both Gilmour and Waters are impeccably polite Englishmen never known as a breed to conduct themselves in a dramatic manner, but beneath the surface lay incredible turmoil as Bob Ezrin later explained in the *Rolling Stone* article by David Fricke. "It was all done under that English smiling, left handed, adversarial stance they take, with smiles on their faces and soft voices. But basically they were saying, 'I hate you, and I'm going to kill you.' The war that existed between those two guys was unbelievable."

It is widely believed in some sections of the music industry that drugs aid the creative process, although remarkably few performers endorse this as a long term view. Tension in the studio holds a similar place in the mythology of music making. Classic albums are often cited as having been enhanced as a result of the creative frictions between the key players. In the absence of a copy of the same album made in the warm fuzzy atmosphere of a friendly studio environment there is no way of knowing what the alternative may have sounded like. The human race is not well conditioned to stress, we don't thrive on it and it seems much more likely that great albums get made despite creative friction rather than as a result of it. *The Wall* may just be the exception which proves the rule. That was certainly the view expounded by Bob Ezrin when he spoke to Sylvie Simmons. "Once we got out of Roger's house and into the studio, it was very much a collaborative effort, everybody had their opinions and contributions. It got very exciting sometimes. Often we'd have these bash-'em-ups where we'd get into furious arguments about an approach to a song that would go on for weeks - as they're English and I'm Canadian we were very gentlemanly about it, but no-one would budge. But the conclusion when there was that kind of conflict - the synthesis of two opposing ideas - was very much stronger than the original idea itself."

Mr Ezrin seems to have overlooked the possibility that opposing ideas can equally be fused together in a friendly manner in an atmosphere of co-operation and mutual respect. Bullying in the workplace is discouraged by any respectable business and every corporation on earth places great store on the positive results from teams working in harmony and goes to great lengths to achieve just that. Obviously many great albums have been produced under convivial working relationships. Arguments, aggression and schisms are over rated commodities when it comes to making great music; after all we 'll never know if the music might have been even better without them.

The stress in the studio however was not just apparent between Gilmour and Waters.

As the weeks passed and grew into months, Bob Ezrin had come to dread the arrival of the moment when he had to step back into the lions den and re-join the seething mass of tension which was *The Wall* recording process.

Roger Waters in the guise of the doctor performs "Comfortably Numb".

Waters and Gilmour together on stage for one of their last performances together as Pink Floyd. It would be twenty-four years before the pair would appear together on the same stage.

He was frank with Sylvie Simmons when he recalled the unhappy days spent recording the album in France. "Roger and I were having a particularly difficult time. During that period I went a little bit mad and really dreaded going in to face the tension, so I would find any excuse to come in late the next morning. I preferred not to be there while Roger was there."

On the recording of *Mother* new cracks began to appear in the veneer of the band in an altogether unexpected direction when it came to the recording of this particular track. The demands of the unusual rhythms meant that there was a measure of strain between Gilmour and Mason. *Mother* is a seemingly innocuous country tinged ballad but the song doesn't quite fit a recognised time signature and in strict musical terms the number of beats in the bar shifts constantly. When the drums enter, the piece represents something of a challenge to set down in standard musical notation. It is probably best expressed as alternating bars of 5/8 and 4/4 time with a sudden switch to 6/8 on the "mother will she break my heart?" line before moving to the familiar 12/8 country blues tempo for "mommas gonna make all your nightmares come true" section. Even then the lyric requires a bar of 9/8 time to hold the phrase "mommas gonna check out all your girl friends for you." before settling back into the 12/8 rhythm for the word "clean". (see figure one) Understandably getting the drums right on this one soon began to eat up a disproportionate amount of time. Gilmour later revealed the resolution to the problem. "Nick played well on the album but *Mother* was one track on the album which he really didn't get ...so I hired Jeff Porcaro to do it."

The real serious stress in the creative team arose in the dwindling embers of the relationship between Rick Wright and Roger Waters. For many years the rumours have circulated that the cause of Wright's departure was a high intake of cocaine. In her interview conducted for *Mojo*, Sylvie Simmons broached the thorny subject with Roger Waters who seemed to be pointing in Rick's direction. "There were people who were doing a lot - some of us had big, big problems. I certainly wasn't doing drugs at that point."

Asked by Simmons for his reaction to Roger's statement, Wright gave a typically frank response. "It would been quite easy to say, 'Oh he left because he had a cocaine problem or a drink problem.' I can honestly say that it really was not a drug problem. It was taken without a doubt by him, me, Dave, Nick, Bob Ezrin, but purely socially, it wasn't lying around in the studio."

Setting the drugs issue to one side, the *Rolling Stone* article by David Fricke published in November 1987 again delved into the causes of the friction between them, but even the respected music journal could shed little clear light and Fricke seems to have been fobbed off with a few platitudes. Wright tactfully attributes the causes of the tension between Waters and himself to 'a heavy personality problem.'

The personality problem it seems was so heavy that Waters finally unsheathed his long threatened sword of Damocles. Despite the fact that the recording process was fully underway, Waters threatened to pull the plug on the whole of *The Wall* album and make it into a solo effort if it was not agreed that Wright had to be dismissed on conclusion of the project. Gilmour and Mason by this stage knew Waters well enough to know that he was capable of acting in just such a manner, and with the threat of bankruptcy once again looming, Wright was officially removed from the group.

Nick Mason gave his own version of the painful circumstances surrounding Rick's departure when he spoke to Sylvie Simmons for *Mojo*. "What I think had been the case is there had always been a sort of philosophical division within the band: Roger effects the show, the technology, the non-music in a way, whereas Dave and Rick took a more musically pure position. That's a very broad generalisation, but since this was conceived from the beginning as a big theatrical production, I think that's where the conflict started - because Rick is absolutely not someone you would have a fight with, he's extremely mild. He was his own worst enemy but I think Roger manoeuvred brilliantly. He made Stalin look like an old muddle-head. We all felt fairly helpless at the time to change it or do anything. Roger made it fairly clear that if Rick stayed, he and the album would not, and I think the threat of what was hanging over us in terms of financial - not just losses but actual bankruptcy - was pretty alarming. We were under a lot of pressure. I felt guilty. Still do really. In retrospect one likes to think that one would have behaved better and done things differently. But probably we would have done completely the same thing."

On early copies of the album neither Wright or Mason even appeared on the credits. This unhappy oversight was quickly rectified but fortunately Richard Wright took a much more thoughtful view of his departure as he told Fricke and *Rolling Stone*. "I wasn't particularly happy with the band anyway the way it was going, the feeling. I'm in no way trying to put this man [Roger Waters] down. I think he has great ideas. But he is an extremely difficult man to work with."

Not surprisingly, there are differing accounts of Wright's exit from the group. Roger Waters was naturally outraged to be painted as the villain of the piece and he told *Rolling Stone* as much. "The story that gets out is that it was a personal whim of mine, which is absolute bollocks."

Figure one
Mother (Waters) - 2nd verse

Figure one: The constantly changing time signatures of 'Mother' were varied to fit Roger Water's lyrics. This seemingly innocuous country tinged number is difficult to pin down to a standard time signature and presents an interesting challenge in standard musical notation. Shown here is the likeliest formal solution.

Wright was clearly underperforming at the time of *The Wall* and had not contributed at all to the composition of Animals as he explained to Sylvie Simmons for *Mojo*. "I think he would tell you that I'd lost interest in the band - there are times around *Animals* where I would sit down with our manager and say, 'I've got to leave this band, I can't stand the way Roger's being,' but I wasn't really serious about leaving, though sometimes I wasn't happy. At the time I was going through a divorce, I wasn't that keen on *The Wall* anyway and I didn't have any material. He might have seen my situation as not having contributed everything, but he wouldn't allow me to contribute anything."

Clearly Wright contributed to the frustration which culminated in his sacking but the evidence certainly seems to mitigate against Roger having totally clean hands with regard to Rick's departure. Bob Ezrin has famously described Rick Wright as - "a victim of Roger's almost Teutonic cruelty." As a first hand observer, Ezrin was in the perfect position to view the inner workings of the band. His words on the subject were reported by David Fricke for *Rolling Stone*. "No matter what Rick did, it didn't seem to be good enough for Roger. It was clear to me that Roger wasn't interested in his succeeding."

There are always two sides to every story and Waters expounded a totally different view when he spoke to Sylvie Simmons for *Mojo*. "Anyway, it was agreed by everybody. In order not to get a long drawn-out thing I made the suggestion that O'Rourke gave to Rick: either you can have a long battle or you can agree to this, and the 'this' was you finish making the album, keep your full share of the album, but at the end of it you leave quietly. Rick agreed. So the idea of the big bad Roger suddenly getting rid of Rick for no reason at all on his own is nonsense."

Not surprisingly David Gilmour had an altogether different view of the event as recalled by his former band mate. This diametrically opposed version is what Gilmour had to say to Simmons on the same subject. "I did not go along with it. I went out to dinner with Rick after Roger had said this to him and said if he wanted to stay in the band I would support him in that. I did point out to Rick that he hadn't contributed anything of any value whatsoever to the album and that I was not over-happy with him myself- he did very very little; an awful lot of the keyboard parts are done by me, Roger, Bob Ezrin, Michael Kamen, Freddie Mandell - but his position in the band to me was sacrosanct. My view, then and now is, if people didn't like the way it was going it was their option to leave. I didn't consider that it was their option to throw people out."

In or out of the band there does seem to have been a tendency to overlook the importance of Wright's contribution to all of the previous Floyd albums to date. Rock groups are accidents of fate which occasionally throw up tremendous results from the chemistry of the interactions of all four musical personalities. Like Led Zeppelin, Floyd were really only a band when those four particular musical personalities were at work. Admittedly, Wright was always a more low key player than rivals like Keith Emerson, Rick Wakeman or Jon Lord but Wright's input to the music was built into the fabric of the Floyd sound. It was in his wonderful jazz sense of timing and his unexpected choice of obscure minor chords which didn't often appear in a rock setting which made his contribution so unique. Like Waters and Gilmour, Wright had a great

Figure two: The notable "Another Brick" theme (in grey on the bass line) is used to underpin the superb guitar solo on "Hey You".

gift for timing. His contribution was often made in what he left out of the Pink Floyd sound, resisting the temptation to fill every space with little flourishes crafting exactly the right phrase to play only when the most propitious moment arrived. The amazing sonic architecture of *Shine On You Crazy Diamond* with each note carefully considered, polished and selected by four consummate craftsmen is the ultimate testimony to the supreme artistry of Pink Floyd as a group.

It is obvious that by accident or design Wright was in any event incapable of playing his part. The other three members simply had to carry on and complete the work. There would be little difficulty in hiring other keyboard players more technically proficient such as Freddie Mandell who was hired for some of the sessions. Waters, Ezrin, Gilmour and Michael Kamen were all capable of adding the required keyboard parts and did so; but as soon as Wright stopped making a contribution something of the essence of Pink Floyd went with him, the band had lost a quarter of its soul.

After *The Wall* Pink Floyd was never to fly so high again. In his own way Wright was to prove irreplaceable and the proof would lie in the next album, the lack lustre assembly which was the *The Final Cut.*

Richard Wright may well have had a point when he observed to Sylvie Simmons that *The Wall* tended to favour the same key and tempo. The most obvious musical trait of the entire album is that it makes no use of the minor keys at any point. Much of the album is indeed in G major, a key which Waters often favours. The chief exception to that rule is *Another Brick (parts 1, 2 & 3)* which are all in F major, although we also hear a neat variation on the *Another Brick* theme, this time in E major when it appears underneath Gilmour's breathtaking solo in *Hey You*. (See figure two)

Like Waters, David Gilmour favours a major key (D major) for his work which brings a measure of variety but doesn't add significantly to the light and shade of an album like *The Wall*. Stage musicals tend to make great use of the minor keys as an obvious device for adding colour and texture and a sense of drama. The old trick of changing key at a particularly dramatic point in a number is as old as the hills, but Waters steadfastly avoids these noticeable devices. His creative vision was for a cohesive piece which flowed almost like a single song and by limiting the number of keys used to essentially G major and F major, the few moments of contrast are all the more effective. The overall mood is intense grey and downbeat which is helped by the relatively unchanging nature of the major keys which pull the work together.

Wright also had a point with regards to the tempo of the album which rarely breaks into a trot. With the notable exception of *Mother* much of the album is presented in a sedate 4/4 time signature. This barely contrasts with an often even slower 12/8 blues which is used as the basis for most of the other tracks.

As an avant garde composer and co-writer of *Atom Heart Mother* Ron Geesin had once famously noted that Waters is a "master" of timing. His genius lies in knowing exactly when the moment has arrived to increase the tempo and the resulting contrast brings its own drama. As we have seen, all three parts of *Another Brick* are in F major but each time the piece is presented it is with a differing rhythm and each makes a fascinating use of the rhythmic possibilities inherent in the composition and brings it's own sense of contrast even when the drums are silent as with *Another Brick (part 1),* with a disco beat as in *Another Brick (part 2)* or in a straight ahead rock tempo as we hear in *Another Brick (part 3)*. *Run Like Hell* and the violent 4/4 passage which erupts during *One Of My Turns* are the two obvious moments when the tempo quickens bringing a complete change of atmosphere exactly when the music and the narrative demand that it should happen.

The Music

IN THE FLESH? *(Waters)* - The album version of *The Wall* opens with the posturing of *In The Flesh?* The presence of a question mark immediately establishes a mood of uncertainty. Lyrically the theme soon unfolds with it's desolate motifs of alienation and ambiguity which right from the outset is highlighted by the appearance of a surrogate Pink Floyd. "Tell me is something eluding you sunshine? Is this not what you expected to see?" The bombastic G major guitar chords and Hammond organ flourishes and plodding slow blues 12/8 tempo which heralds the song itself, quickly builds the impression of a brooding overture and serves as a powerful introduction to the piece as a whole. The opening vocal section modulates into A major as Roger Waters voice enters for the first time sounding like a menacing circus ringmaster about to lead us into the most desolate hour of entertainment we have ever experienced, which looks forward to a similarly theatrical performance on *The Trial*.

In his lengthy promotional interview with Tommy Vance, Roger approached the album on a track by track basis and explained the background to the story. "*In the Flesh?* is a reference back to our 1977 tour, which was called *Pink Floyd In The Flesh*. That was the logo we used for the tour. That is supposed to set the whole thing up. On the album, I can't imagine anyone would actually get that because when we do the show, at this point we should be recognisable but disguised."

THE THIN ICE *(Waters)* -The second track on the album stays with the 12/8 blues rhythm established by *In The Flesh?* We are now in C major with the result that the recapitulation of the *In The Flesh* theme which we briefly hear following the words "claw thin ice" sounds slightly less dramatic. *The Thin Ice* represents the very beginning of Pink's life as Roger Waters explained to Tommy Vance. "In fact, at the end of *In The Flesh,* you hear somebody shouting 'roll the sound effects,' and you hear the sound of bombers. And so it gives you some indication of what's happening. So it's a flashback and we start telling the story about it, which in terms of this, it's about my generation; war babies. But it can be about anybody who gets left by anybody. My father was killed in the war and although it works on certain levels, it doesn't have to be about the war, I think it should work for any generation, really. The father is also... I'm the father as well. People who leave their families to go and work, not that I leave my family to go and work, but a lot of people do and have done, particularly in rock and roll. It happens in all kinds of businesses, really. So it's not meant to be just a simple story about somebody getting killed in the war, and growing up and going to school, but about being left, more generally."

ANOTHER BRICK IN THE WALL (PART 1) *(Waters)* - is the first appearance on the album of a straight 4/4 time signature which is given an extra crispness by the driving rhythm of the understated guitar. The feeling of freshness is by the choice of the F major key which is also introduced for the first time on the album. The main *Brick In The Wall* theme is also introduced here but in a wonderfully understated manner helped by the absence of drums which forces the guitar to develop the rhythmic qualities of the song.

THE HAPPIEST DAYS OF OUR LIVES *(Waters)* - The album moves on to tackle the issue of the misuse of power in the educational system with the ironically titled *The Happiest Days Of Our Lives* in 4/4. Set in the key of F major this powerful track utilised the sound of a roaring helicopter motor as an aural metaphor to introduce a sense of overbearing supervision; we are under no illusion we now know we are being watched at all times and from every angle. This is Water's first tilt at the educational system and obviously "happy" was not a phrase which Waters would ever associate with his own schooldays as he later told Tommy Vance. "*The Happiest Days of Our Lives* condemns school life, my school life was very much like that. It was awful. It was really terrible. When I hear people whining on now about bringing back grammar schools, it really makes me quite ill to listen. I went to a boys grammar school. I want to make it plain that some of the men who taught there were very nice guys. It's not meant to be a hard condemnation of all teachers everywhere, because I admire a great many teachers. But the bad ones can really do people in for a long time, and there were some at my school who were just incredibly bad and treated the children so badly. They wanted to systemise them and crush them into the right shape so that they can go to university and do well. I'm sure that still happens and there is a resurgence of it right now in England. You know, terrible panic, because the little dears can't read and write, and the resurgence of 'right, we've got to regiment them,' and this nonsense about interesting them in things and treating them as individuals. There is a resurgence of the idea that that's all rubbish, and that all you 've got to do is sit them down and keep them quiet and teach them things, which is what I object to. I'm in the privileged position of being able to pick and choose how my kids are educated. But most people aren't. Most people are stuck with a system of state education. But my feeling is that our system of state education is improving. There are a lot of paradoxes in all of this. But, you know, maybe we shouldn't be really talking about my political beliefs. Maybe we should. I don't mind. I've nothing to hide. It's not just political. It is also sociological. But for me they are the same thing, really."

ANOTHER BRICK IN THE WALL (PART 2) *(Waters)* - further expands the theme of systematic failures in education. The 4/4 time signature and F major key is again presented, this time with drums and school choir, an innovation added by Bob Ezrin. *Another Brick (part 2)* was to provide an unexpected foray back into the world of the commercial pop single and in fact gave the band their first UK hit since 1968. Nick Mason recalled the unlooked for event in *Inside Out*. "*Another Brick* appeared as a single partly due to the influence of Bob Ezrin, who curiously had always wanted to produce a disco single. We, on the other hand, had abandoned the idea of releasing singles in a fit of pique in 1968 when *Point Me At The Sky* failed to dent the charts. Bob maintains that such was the lack of enthusiasm to make a single that it was only at the last minute that the piece was tailored to the requisite length. The tempo was set at a metronomic 100 beats per minute, which was considered the ideal disco beat, and so the concept of a hit disco single was forced through rather to our bemusement, a bemusement made even stronger when we ended up as the UK Christmas Number One for 1979."

MOTHER *(Waters)* - changes the mood and the up tempo disco tinged flavour of *Another Brick In The Wall (Part 2)* recedes into the soft embrace of *Mother*, the closing track on side one, which reinforces the sense that all is not well with a razor sharp portrait of an over protective parent. Here we are back in the embrace of the G major key which opened the album. Musically the piece may have presented the band with some real challenges in the studio especially in regard to the constantly shifting time signatures, but in his extended interview with Tommy Vance, Roger Waters revealed he had a very clear idea of the lyrical direction and meaning of the song. "She's over-protective, basically. That's what she is. All enveloping and over-protective, which most mothers are. If you can level one accusation at mothers, it is that they tend to protect their children too much, in my opinion, and for too much and for too long. That's all. A woman that I know phoned me up the other day saying that, on hearing the album and the track *Mother*, she liked it and that it made her feel very guilty. Now, she's got three kids. I was interested and glad that it had got through to her. If it

The 'real' Pink Floyd, complete with a jack-booted Roger Waters, and the 'surrogate' band together on stage perform 'In The Flesh' and 'Waiting For The Worms' in the second half of the show. The possibilities offered by The Wall as a screen for projections are clearly seen here.

The progenitor of The Wall puts his full heart and soul into one of the performances of his masterpiece. The overwhelming logistics and the expense of playing relatively small venues limited the number of shows to a modest total of just twenty-nine performances.

means that much to people, then it's good. It makes it difficult, and more difficult for you as you grow up and in your later life, to respond to people as an individual in your own right, rather than being an extension of your mother. In the same way that over-bearing school teachers will crush you down. Mind you, that's completely different because I feel very antagonistic towards the teachers at my school who tried to put me down when I was a kid. I never felt like that towards my mother, although I recognise certain things that she did may have made it harder for me to be myself as I grew up."

GOODBYE BLUE SKY *(Waters)* - Side two of the album opens with *Goodbye Blue Sky* and we find ourselves back in World War Two territory. The gentle sound of the nylon strung acoustic guitar introduces the D major key although the time signature is now a more uniform 4/4. In his interview with Tommy Vance even Roger Waters himself was rather vague on the reason for the inclusion of this song. "Since we compiled the album, I haven't clearly tried to think my way through it, but I know this is very confusing. I think the best way to describe this is as a recap, if you like, of side one. It's like setting off from childhood at this stage."

EMPTY SPACES *(Waters)* - We rejoin with the now familiar G major key and 4/4 time signature. This is where the confusion begins. The running time of four sides of vinyl proved insufficient to house the full piece. The album therefore retained Empty Spaces in favour of the originally proposed track *What Shall We Do Now* which was included in both the stage shows and the film. Despite the fact that the track had been deleted the lyrics still appeared on early versions of the artwork. Roger Waters attempted to clear up the confusion in his interview with Tommy Vance. "That is the track that is not on the album. It was quite nice and, although it is not on the album, we do it in the show. It's quite long, and this side was too long. It's basically the same tune as *Empty Spaces*. And although *Empty Spaces* is quite nice to listen to within its context, it isn't particularly strong. We've put *Empty Spaces* where *What Shall We Do Now?* is listed. The lyrics to that one are, sort of, very crude. *Empty Spaces* works better there, instead of that track. What is really different between those two tracks is that list where it says, 'shall we buy a new guitar, drive a more powerful car,' etc. That is about the ways one protects oneself from one's isolation by becoming obsessed with other people's ideas. The idea is whether it is good to have a powerful car, or whether you are obsessed with the idea of being a vegetarian, or going to be analysed. Whatever it might be, you are adopting somebody else's criteria for yourself without considering them."

YOUNG LUST *(Waters/Gilmour)* - heralds a complete change of mood. The tempo of the album lifts again with the arrival of the first Waters/Gilmour composition *Young Lust*. Again we are in 4/4 and the favoured G major key for a swaggering rocker of the type which the imaginary Pink would use to win over his fans. On the album the song is sung by David Gilmour. In the movie Parker handled the underlying atmosphere of lust, passion and desire with great skill and created one of the strongest sequences in the film. Building on Water's strong lyrical base *Young Lust* is a pastiche of young British life in the sixties. "It reminds me very much of a song we recorded years and years ago called *The Nile Song*. Dave sings it in a very similar way and I think Dave's singing on *Young Lust* is terrific. I love the vocals, but it's meant to be a pastiche of just any rock 'n' roll band out on the road. When I wrote this song, it was actually quite different lyric-wise. Originally, it was about leaving school and wandering around town and hanging around outside porno movies and dirty bookshops and things like that, and being very interested in sex but never being actually able to get involved because of being too frightened. That song exists somewhere on a demo, but now it's completely different on the album. That was a function of us all working together on the record, particularly with Dave Gilmour and Bob Ezrin, who co-produced the album with me. Dave didn't like the chord structure of the song that I had originally written, so we changed it and then it never seemed it could quite fit in anywhere."

ONE OF MY TURNS *(Waters)* - visits altogether different territory musically. The geriatrically slow C major intro in a 3/4 waltz time signature conjures up the atmosphere of a particularly decrepit tea dance. Water's reference to love turning grey "like the skin of a dying man," only adds to the sense of moribund decay. The turgid opening is in stark contrast to the sudden burst of energy as the band kicks in and we modulate into B flat major and switch to 4/4 time for the menacing orgy of destruction which begins on the phrase "Run to the bedroom..." Unable to make the connection to his wife, *One of My Turns* sees Pink grow tired of the attentions of yet another groupie and turn his frustrations on the objects in the room. "*One of My Turns* sounds like a viscous acid song, it actually happened to me years ago, may be six or seven years ago. That was a bit like me but I would have never said it, to actually come out with anything like that, because I was much too frightened of everything, really. I think a lot of people in rock and roll are, sort of, very frightened of most things. But it's one of the very safest places in the world, standing on the stage with a few thousand watts of amplification behind you. It's like driving a very powerful car. Anything with a lot of power makes you feel safer, temporarily. I referred to all that in *Young Lust*. On *One of My Turns* it's all terribly confusing." On the album, the track closes with an inspired piece of drama in which Pink repeatedly tries to call his unfaithful wife. The concerned voice of a real AT&T telephone operator dialled from the studio is heard as she continues doing her job blissfully unaware of the real purpose of the call as Waters revealed to Tommy Vance. "At the end of *Young Lust,* there is that telephone call. There is an enormous leap, conceptually, from *Young Lust* to somebody calling home from an American tour. And although nothing is said, it implies a sort of 'Dear John' phone call. I have experienced that sort of thing, not that particular phone call, because that is just a theatrical device. I love that operator. I think she's wonderful. She didn't know what was happening at all. I mean, it's been edited a bit, but the way she picks up all that stuff about 'Is there supposed to be anybody else there besides your wife?' I think she's amazing. She really clocked into it straight away. The idea is that we've leapt, somehow, into the rock and roll show. It's a lot of years from *Goodbye Blue Sky*. So we've leapt to somewhere on into our hero's career.

"*One of My Turns* is supposed to be his response to a lot of aggravation in his life and not really having got anything together with a woman, although he's been married. He's just splitting up with his wife and, in response he takes another girl back into his hotel room. He's had it now. And on this song, he can't relate to this girl either. That's why he just turns on the TV and sits there and won't talk to her. He realises the state he is in. This is an extremely cynical song. I don't feel like that about marriage now."

DON'T LEAVE ME NOW (Waters). In the wake of this orgy of destruction Pink is left to wail "Don't Leave Me Now" in a drawn out howl of self pity and pain. The key is C major set against a very slow 12/8 blues tempo which contributes to the numbing atmosphere. Waters continued his exposition on the themes of the album for Tommy Vance with a discussion of the role of marriage in building *The Wall*. "A lot of men and women do get involved with each other for lots of wrong reasons, and they do get very aggressive towards each other and do each other a lot of damage. If you skip back from there, my theory is that they do that because they've never really been able to become themselves and there is a lot of pressure on people to get married, at least when they're in their late twenties, not earlier. I think that a lot of people shouldn't really get married until they are strong enough in themselves to be themselves. It's very easy to attempt to be things that you are not. I, of course, as far as I can remember, have never struck a woman, and I hope I never do. But a lot of people have. A lot of women have struck men as well, and there is a lot of violence in relationships that very often aren't working."

ANOTHER BRICK IN THE WALL (PART 3) (Waters) We see the return to the G major key and the familiar 4/4 time signature this time in a rock tempo. Lyrically, *Another Brick (part 3)* continues the theme of building the defences against a cruel world. Pink seems to get his confidence back as the line 'I don't need no arms around me' refers to the realisation that he has to fend for himself as no one else will.

GOODBYE CRUEL WORLD (Waters) The 4/4 time signature remains but the pace slows to a crawl and the D major key which looks forward to *Comfortably Numb* is introduced. Lyrically, as Roger Waters explained to Tommy Vance, the story now moves back to focus on Pink in the present day. "What is happening is this. From the beginning of *One of My Turns*, from where the door opens through to the end of side three, the scenario is an American hotel room. So when the groupie leaves at the end of *One of My Turns*, he sings to anybody. It's directed at women, in a way. It's a kind of guilty song as well. At the end of that, he is there in his room with his TV, and there is that kind of symbolic TV smashing, and then he resurges a bit out of that kind of violence, and says, 'Fuck it. I don't need any of you.' And he sings, 'All in all, you are just bricks in *The Wall*.' So he convinces himself that his isolation is a desirable thing. *Goodbye Cruel World* closes side two of the album and leaves Pink in a dazed state of trance. When he sings, *Goodbye Cruel World* I've seen that happen to people, and *Goodbye Cruel World* is that sort of feeling. He is catatonic, if you like. That's the final thing and he's going back and he's not going to move. That's it. He's had enough. That's the end. So at the end of side two, he's finished. *The Wall* is finished. It's complete now. It's been built, in my case, since the Second World War, but in anybody else's case whenever they care to think of it. If they feel isolated or alienated from other people at all, then it's from whenever you want."

HEY YOU (Waters) - Side three of the album opens with *Hey You* which first introduces the E major key and features yet another variation of the *Another Brick* theme under the guitar solo. The metaphor of worms is used to represent all of the hundreds of uncertainties gnawing away at Pink's brain. The gentle arpeggios of the acoustic guitar gain a menacing edge when mixed with the noise of a million insects buzzing in Pink's brain. The fact that side three of the original album began with a different song from the one listed on the first pressings of the original record jacket naturally caused a great deal of confusion at the time. Back in 1979 Roger Waters did his best to explain the anomaly to Tommy Vance, "I wasn't there when side three was finally put together,

The sense of menace inherent in Waiting For The Worms is enhanced by the looming presence of The Wall constructed during the first half of the show.

but Bob Ezrin called me up and said, 'I've just listened to side three and it doesn't work,' and when I asked him what was wrong with it he said there were too many sound effects. I think I had been uncomfortable about it anyway. I thought about it for a bit and I thought that the thing that was wrong with it was that there was a long scene with somebody in a hotel room with a broken window and a TV, and he sings his thoughts and feelings while he is sitting there on his own. What we are talking about now is nothing, really, conceptually to do with the album. It had just to do with how the side of the album balanced and how to program the thing. I thought about it, and a couple of minutes later I realised that *Hey You* conceptually, could go anywhere, and that it would make a much better side if *Hey You* is at the front of the side, and sandwiched the little theatrical scene of the hotel room between an attempt to re-establish contact with the outside world, which is what *Hey You* is, and not at the end of side three, which we will come to later on. Pink is now behind *The Wall*. He is behind *The Wall* symbolically, and he is locked in a hotel room with a broken window that looks out onto the freeway. Within his mind, *Hey You* is a cry of help to the rest of the world. Dave sings the first two verses of *Hey You*. Then there is a fantasy piece which I sing, which is a narration of *The Wall* which was too high, as you can see. No matter how he tried, he could not break free. 'And the worms ate into his brain. That is the first reference to worms. The worms have a lot less to do with the piece than they did a year ago. A year ago they were very much a part of it. They were my symbolic representation of decay. So that is why there is this reference to worms there. And then I sing the last verse of the song. So, if you like, it's like going back to *Goodbye Cruel World*. At the end of *Hey You,* he makes this cry for help, but it's too late. Anyway he is only singing it to himself. It's no good crying for help if you are sitting in the room all on your own, and saying it to yourself. The theme of isolation and non-communication is rammed home by the next two tracks.

IS THERE ANYBODY OUT THERE? *(Waters)* - After the heady drama of *Hey You, Is There Anybody Out There?*, acts as an eerie mood piece which briefly quotes from *Echoes* from *Meddle* and reprises the insect noise from *Hey You*. Pink is now beginning to emerge from the depths of his catatonic state, he surfaces only briefly to pose the solitary question *Is There Anybody Out There?*

NOBODY HOME *(Waters)* - The homely sounding brass and warm unchallenging C major key set up the feeling of a comfortable armchair and welcoming hearth, unfortunately for Pink we learn that despite the cosiness of the music there is to be no warm welcome for him. We are about to be crushed again by the news that there is indeed "Nobody home". Roger Waters explained the significance to Tommy Vance in these terms. "All of us, I'm sure, from time to time, have formed sentences in our minds that we would like to say to somebody else, but we don't say it. Well, that's no use. That doesn't help anybody. That's just a game you play with yourself. It's useful to me, personally, because that's what writing is. He realises he needs help but doesn't know how to get it." Waters said, "Well, he doesn't really want it. Part of him does, but part of him that makes his lips move doesn't. In the song, *Nobody Home*, he is getting ready to re-establish his contact from where he's started, and to start making some sense of what it was all about. He is getting ready here to start getting back to side one. He does this on the next song, *Vera*. On the surface of this, *Nobody Home* is like having had the song about the non-telephone conversation. This is a re-expression of that. He is not just watching television. Sometimes he is trying to get up and trying to call her. So this is about his wife going off with somebody else. And then this is supposed to be brought on by the fact that a war movie comes on the TV, which you can actually hear. That snaps him back to then. We leave Pink in his hotel suite to revisit the tortured landscape of World War Two with *Vera*."

VERA *(Waters)*- Once again we are back to the comfortable embrace of the G major key favoured by Waters for the creation of his masterpiece. "The stuff about Vera Lynn is a stream of unconsciousness, and it precedes what, for me, is the most important track on the album, *Bring the Boys Back Home*."

BRING THE BOYS BACK HOME *(Waters)* - We stay with the now familiar G major key, but switch time signature to the slow 12/8 blues tempo. In musical terms the piece does not particularly stand apart from the rest of the album but to Roger Waters it was a vital part of the lyrical development of the piece as a whole and he went to some lengths to stress this to Tommy Vance. "The central song on the whole album is, *Bring the Boys Back Home* because it has the most to do with me, because it's partly about not letting people go off and be killed in wars. But it is also partly about not allowing rock and roll, or making cars, or selling soap, or anything become such an important and jolly boy's game that it becomes more important than friends, wives, children, and other people. That's a very, very little vague song, and that's why I like it." After *Nobody Home*, there is a short piece where there are tape loops used.

In the year 2000 David Gilmour was interviewed by Nick Sedgewick for the sleeve notes released with *Is There Anybody Out There?*, the live CD version of *The Wall*. Gilmour gave a typically frank interview which praised the project as a whole. However even in 2000 Gilmour still had his reservations about this section of the material as he told Sedgewick. "There are some weaker sections - all that *Vera Lynn, Bring The Boys Back Home* stuff, for example."

COMFORTABLY NUMB *(Gilmour/Waters)* - Any debate over the preceding two songs is soon forgotten with the arrival of the majestic *Comfortably Numb*, a stunning piece with music by Gilmour and words by Waters. Written in Gilmour's favoured D major key this is his second musical contribution to the album and one which may well contain his finest ever guitar playing. The writing was now on *The Wall* for the Gilmour/Waters partnership but this was certainly the way to finish on a high. Waters again takes up the narrative from his interview with Tommy Vance. "The teacher's voice is heard again, and you can hear the groupie saying things, and the operator again. But there is a new voice introduced at that point. There is somebody knocking at the door, saying, 'Come on; it's time to go.' So the idea, which obviously isn't expressed clearly enough, is that they are coming to take him to the show, because he has got to go and perform. And when they come to the room, they realise that something is wrong, and so they actually, physically, bring the doctor in, and *Comfortably Numb* is about his confrontation with the doctor. The doctor puts him in a condition that allows him to perform. He gives him an injection so as to cool him out, and he can actually function, because they are not interested in any of his problems. All they are interested in is the fact that there are thousands of people, and tickets have all been sold, and the show must go on at any cost to anybody. I mean, I personally have done gigs when I've been very depressed, and I've also done gigs when I've been extremely ill, where you wouldn't do any ordinary kind of work. Even if you were ill, you still did those stadium shows because you were committed. It's nothing to do with being personally committed to do it. It's to do with how much money is at stake because the money is there in the briefcase. That's all it's about. Generally speaking, people in rock and roll don't really cancel concerts at such short notice because it costs a lot of money. To cancel a show at such short notice is very expensive. Some of the lines on *Comfortably Numb* and *Nobody Home* hark back to the halcyon days of Syd Barrett but it's partly about all kinds of people that I've met. All this is about all sorts of people that I've met. But Syd was the only person I ever knew who used elastic bands to keep his boots together, which is where that line 'I got elastic bands keeping my shoes on' comes from. In fact, obviously the 'obligatory Hendrix perm' you have to go back ten years to understand what all that was about. I never had a Hendrix perm, thank God, but they were obligatory for a while. It was unbelievable. Everybody from Eric Clapton to I don't know who, had one."

THE SHOW MUST GO ON *(Waters)*- Side four opens as Pink, pumped full of stimulants by the unscrupulous doctor makes it on to the stage. Again this was at least in part based on a true experience of Roger's who had once played a concert under the influence of medication prescribed by a doctor hired by the band's management in order to prevent a gig being cancelled. The song continues the theme of avarice on the part of unscrupulous promoters and managers.

IN THE FLESH *(Waters)* - A reprise of the main themes of *In the Flesh?* advances the narrative still further. Pink is now so delusional under the medication the gig itself takes on the trappings of a monstrous political rally. The original question mark in the songs title has now been dropped. Pink is certain of his powers but the delusions are about to be uncovered as events begin to drift out of control and descend into violence real or imagined. Pink is now on stage and is very vicious. "Anyway, the idea is that these fascist feelings develop from isolation. So the symbols of decay develop from isolation. So what happens to you is that, if people who are older and wiser than you don't set you straight in the world, it's very easy to become isolated. And if you become isolated, you decay. The end result of that kind of decay is any kind of fascism that you care to think of, and any kind of totalitarianism or violence this is really him having a go at the audience or the minorities of the audience. I've picked on queers and Jews and blacks simply because they're the most easily identifiable minorities

A feature of the live shows were the marionettes designed by Gerald Scarfe which loomed up from behind the wall, dwarfing the performers and creating a powerful visual statement which spoke volumes on the overbearing nature of the educational system.

85

The calm after the storm. Waters certainly kept his word with regard to not performing a encore from any of the Pink Floyd works. The Wall concerts featured exclusively material from that album.

where I come from, which is England. In fact, they are the most easily identifiable minorities in America, as well. Outside the English-speaking world, I don't know, because language has a great deal to do with what you understand and what you don't understand, and I wouldn't care to comment about France or Germany."

RUN LIKE HELL *(Gilmour /Waters)* - *Run Like Hell* lifts the pace on side four of the album. This is the final Waters/Gilmour joint composition, not just on the album, but also as a writing partnership. After *The Wall* the two would never write together again. As with *Comfortably Numb*, the piece begins in D major, but modulates into C major with the entry of the first vocal line and as with *Comfortably Numb* this track was based on another outtake from David Gilmour's solo album which clearly had possessed the potential to produce something truly extraordinary! Roger Waters explained the naggingly familiar qualities of the rhythm to Tommy Vance. "This is meant to be... I don't know whether you have noticed, but this is disco. So it says something about disco, and says something about 'there is a great deal of rock and roll that is kind of unthinkingly paranoid and unthinkingly warning people about all this isolation,' and that's what *Run Like Hell* is. Originally, when we started making the album, I wanted there to be announcements and all kinds of stuff to make this sound live, but when you try to put it on record, you realise that it would be alright if you'd listen to it once only. For instance, when *In the Flesh* finishes, if you put in an announcement like 'Thank you very much,' and then you say 'Here is a tune for all the paranoids in the audience,' it will only last for one or two listenings because a joke wears out quickly. So it's best just to leave them out. *Run Like Hell* is meant to be him just doing another tune in a show. So that is just part of the performance, but still in his drug-crazed state. "In between some of the songs, you can hear things going on, such as before and after *Run Like Hell*. Waters said, "If I don't explain this, nobody will understand it. After *In the Flesh*, you can hear an audience shouting 'Pink Floyd.' After *Run Like Hell* you can hear an audience shouting 'Pink Floyd' on the left-hand side of your stereo, and on the right-hand side or in the middle you can hear voices going 'Hammer, hammer, hammer.' This is the Pink Floyd audience turning into a rally, a kind of fascist rally."

WAITING FOR THE WORMS (*Waters*) - The excitement of Run Like Hell subsides as the next track *Waiting For The Worms* begins to set the stage for the final act. The familiar G major key re-appears and the excitement builds but just as the crescendo is reached the song stops abruptly and breaks into "Stop: a plaintive plea for mercy which heralds *The Trial*. *Waiting For The Worms* is about decay, in theatrical terms, it's an expression of what happens in the show when the drugs start wearing off and his real feelings of what he's got left start taking over again. Because he's been dragged out of the hotel room and put in that position, he is forced by the situation he finds himself in to confront his real feelings. That's the idea. In the show, we've used the hammer as a symbol of the forces of oppression, and the worms are the thinking part of the forces of oppression. "It is interesting to point out that, in *Waiting For The Worms,* you can hear a voice being spoken through a loud hailer. That wasn't done with a loud hailer. I did it with my hands over my nose. None of that stuff was written and I did it all in one take, all through the song. It starts off with 'We will convene at one o 'clock outside Brixton Town Hall.' It is actually describing the route of the march from Brixton Town Hall down Southwark Lane and then Lambeth Road and over Vauxhall Bridge. It's meant to be describing a route to Hyde Park Corner to have a rally by the National Front. I did that because I feel that there are enough people in the world who are isolated and alienated that they find it necessary to join those kinds of organisations, and to attempt to damage other people as much as they really would like to if they were ever to come to power. I thought twice about whether to write all that stuff down on the inner bags of the album and, in the end, I decided not to. But since then, I've realised that people who listen to it can't hear any of it, which, in a way, is a shame. But, hopefully, anybody who listens to it and wonders what it is, this interview will be able to tell them what it's all about. That is a description of a National Front march from Brixton to Hyde Park. And then, at the end of it, there is somebody who is raving and raving about what should be done." The person raving is a fanatic. Waters said, "Yeah, a right-wing fanatic. Although this isn't really meant to be a very political album, I suppose it is a political album in a way, and it does seem to me that right-wing politics always seem to lean more towards alienation between different groups of people, which is what, it seems to me, fucks people up. If you like, on the broadest level, side four is particularly a left-wing statement. Not in any economic terms, but in terms of ideology."

STOP (*Waters*) - Again we remain in the G major key and stay with the 4/4 time signature but slow the tempo to a crawl for this short contrasting interlude which heralds the trial.

"The idea is that the drugs wear off, and in *Waiting For The Worms* there are bits which Dave sings, 'sitting in the bunker, here behind my wall, waiting for the worms to come.' He keeps flipping backwards and forwards from his original persona, which is a reasonable kind of humane person into this 'waiting for the worms' kind of persona, and he is ready to crush anybody or anything that gets in the way, which is a response to having been badly treated, and feeling very isolated. But at the end of *Waiting For The Worms,* it gets too much for him, and he says, 'Stop, I wanna go home.' So he takes off his uniform and leaves the show. But he says, 'I'm waiting in this prison cell because I have to know if I've been guilty all the time, and then he tries himself, if you like.

THE TRIAL (*Waters/Ezrin*) - *The Trial* is the most unexpected twist of style in Pink Floyd's career. It takes the style of a mini Gilbert and Sullivan operetta with Waters dancing brilliantly through the characters of prosecuting counsel, judge, witnesses and defendant. We are now firmly locked into the G major key and the 4/4 time signature, but that is not to suggest for a moment that this breathtaking piece is in any shape or form predictable. It is in fact one of the most uncharacteristic pieces in the entire Pink Floyd canon. "He puts himself on trial, The judge is part of him, just as much as all the other characters and things that he remembers. they're all memories in his mind." None of his memories have any sympathy for him, well the Mother does a bit. She wants to protect him, that's all. She is only being over-protective. She's not attacking him in the way that the teacher and his wife do. There is also the prosecuting counsel. He, in fact, is meant to be the person who is on the record label on side four. He is that rather pompous lawyer figure. The idea is that he is somebody who always follows all the rules and that he ended up in the legal profession because he likes laws and that it has nothing to do with real feelings. It's always amazed me, the idea of barristers who can look at both sides of the case and be able to present either side. There is never anything impartial about it. If you 're a good barrister, you 've got to be able to present both sides partially. That I find very strange. I think that's probably why the trial crept into this piece. Anyway, so there is this trial going on in his head, and it's really just his imagination. He's creating a courtroom for himself. At the end of it all, when he judges himself, he feels extremely guilty and bad about everything that he's been and done. And in the end, the judgement on himself is to de-isolate himself, which, in fact, is a very good thing. *The Wall* is then torn down."

In April 1980 Bob Ezrin was interviewed by Circus magazine and recalled the sense of excitement and satisfaction in the wake of recording *The Trial*. "One thing we went for with the Pink Floyd vocals was an acting quality. For example, Gilmour who's very sober by nature, sang screaming on *Young Lust* in a way he hadn't sung in years and all the characters and accents in *The Trial* are Roger. When we're through, I said to him, 'we've really got to do Broadway.' On the album the track was without doubt a fitting climax to a real tour de force, but it was in the cinema that the piece really came into it's own thanks to the truly remarkable animation by Gerald Scarfe.

OUTSIDE THE WALL (Waters) - A gentle lullaby in a 6/8 time with an angelic children's choir contrasted by Water's almost spoken lyric and very faint beginning of the sentence "isn't this where..." which is concluded on side one with "...we came in?" and so the cycle begins again.

The release of the album in late November 1979 came as a huge relief to Pink Floyd. With their money worries receding into the past, Waters was again able to look forward into the future and the realisation of his dream. The hugely elaborate stage shows were already in preparation, but Floyd had always had great ambitions on the road and had carried off the grandest of visions with aplomb. What Roger was now firmly focused on was the movie and it was here that the greatest trials and tribulations would arise. Before then there was the small matter of the gentlemen of the press…

The music world had changed since the release of *Animals*. The arrival of punk and new wave had supposedly altered the musical landscape forever and the likes of Floyd were now dismissed as "dinosaurs" doomed to extinction. Johnny Rotten defined the mood of the day wearing a t-shirt which loudly proclaimed "I hate Pink Floyd". The mantra among the hip and trendy was that Floyd were now history. Unfortunately no one had seen fit to inform the record buying public and *The Wall* was soon ensconced in the Number 1 album slot in the USA and just about every other market on the planet. Amazingly even the UK hotbed of the short lived punk movement still had an appetite for Floyd. The album peaked at Number 2 but the tickets for the forthcoming Floyd shows were like gold dust. Janet Huck was one of those who in 1980 rejoiced to see the Floyd banner flying higher than ever. "Last year, when rude young punks came of age and respectability, the veteran rock group released their seemingly out-of-date concept album, *The Wall*. Some hip, post-punk observers expected their sales to tumble faster than their own prop, but the old-wave group - which has remained together for twelve years - refused to surrender to the new wave. When the expensive two-album set was released in the last week in November, the flash marker was the biggest-selling, most-played album in the country. Now, after ten weeks in the charts, it is sitting securely in the number one slot, having bumped the Eagles 'Long Run' weeks ago. The soon-to-be-double-platinum album has sold almost two million copies, and it may have a longer run yet. Their most successful album, *Dark Side of The Moon*, which was released in 1973 and made the underground cult stars into over-the-hill superstars, has stayed on Billboard's charts for a total of two hundred and ninety-eight weeks, popping up at a respectable number 45 this week." By this stage in their career Pink Floyd were a big enough noise to attract the interest of mainstream magazines like the hugely influential *Time* magazine. Jay Cocks was assigned the task of reviewing the album and the subsequent live shows for *Time* magazine. Jay's review is interesting as it gives an idea of how the project was viewed by those outside the world of specialist music press. It's worth re-printing at length here as the piece as a whole demonstrates just how far the band had come to be able to command this amount of column inches in a sophisticated news magazine with a worldwide circulation. One gets a distinct impression that the illustrious *Time* Magazine had a rather superior view of itself, not least because of Mr Cocks' insistence on referring to the band as 'The Pinkies'.

"This late burst of activity is directly traceable to the surprise success of the new Pink Floyd album, *The Wall* which has become the country's No. 1 album and which shows few signs of giving way to the competition. This is all the more remarkable because the two Floyd albums between *The Moon* and *The Wall* achieved only modest success. There was every reason to believe that the Floyd had gone under, sunk beneath the collective weight of their cosmic speculations and primal ruminations. The resurgence represented by *The Wall* and by the Pinkies' current tour, which is touching down only in New York City and Los Angeles, is a reminder that the only commercial constant in pop

A seqence of stills from 'The Trial'. Without doubt this is one of the most successful elements of the movie which was perfectly suited to Scarfe's background as a political satirist.

music is unpredictability. Bass player Roger Waters, who writes most of the band's music, has tempered his lyric tantrums somewhat for the new album and has worked up some melodies that are rather more lulling and insinuating than anything Floyd freaks are used to. Spacey and seductive and full of high-tech sound stunts, *The Wall* has a kind of smothering sonic energy that can be traced to *Dark Side of The Moon* and even past that, to the band's early days on the psychedelic front lines. To fans, this continuity must be just as reassuring as the trendiness Waters has grafted onto his lyrics, which are a kind of libretto for Me-decade narcissism. Says Tom Morrera, disk jockey at New York City's pace-setting WNEW-FM: 'The Floyd are not as spacey as they used to be. They're doing art for art's sake, and you don't have to be high to get it. They 'll take you on a trip anyway.' Travellers who may not want to sign on for this particular voyage may find themselves more in agreement with a vice-president at a rival record label who speculated, not without wistfulness, that the Pinkies 'make perfect music for the age of the computer game.'

"*The Wall* is a lavish, four-sided dredge on the angst of the successful rocker, his flirtations with suicide and losing bouts with self-pity, his assorted betrayals by parents, teachers and wives and his uneasy relationship with his audience, which is alternately exhorted, cajoled and mocked. None of the dynamic exaltation of The Who and their fans for the Pinkies. To Waters, the audience is just another barrier, another obstacle to his exquisitely indelicate communion with his inner being. 'So ya / Thought ya / Might like to go to the show,' he sneers at some hapless fan.

Is something eluding you sunshine?
If you 'd like to find out what's behind these cold eyes
You'll just have to claw your way through this disguise.

"Sunshine might just as well try tunnelling out of Sing Sing with a soup spoon. Every avenue of Water's psyche ends up against a wall, a towering edifice whose bricks have been mixed from the clay of emotional trauma, vocational frustration and, apparently, brain damage. Absent fathers, smothering mothers, sadistic schoolmasters, insistent fans and faithless spouses: 'All in all you were all just bricks in The Wall.' Urging caution on 'The Thin Ice Of Modern Life', Waters' lyrical ankles do a lot of wobbling before he is indicted, some seventy-five minutes into the record, on charges of fecklessness, savagery and numbness. The presiding magistrate, a worm, sentences the singer to 'be exposed before your peers / Tear down The Wall'. Lysergic Sturm und Drang like this has a kind of kindergarten appeal, especially if it is orchestrated like a cross between a Broadway overture and a band concert on the starship Enterprise. It is likely, indeed, that *The Wall* is succeeding more for the sonic sauna of its melodies than the depth of its lyrics. It is a record being attended to rather than absorbed, listened to rather than heard."

On the other side of the Atlantic the new wave bug had bitten much deeper than in North America and there was a certain amount of resistance to the very idea of a Pink Floyd record. Magazines like *NME*, *Melody Maker* and *Sounds* which had long been champions of the band had long since moved lock stock and barrel into the new wave camp. Ian Penman reviewed the album for *NME* in an article titles "Pink Floyd: A

The large budget allocated to a full-scale movie verion of The Wall enabled Alan Parker to utilise full-blown set designs such as the human mincer incorporated into 'Another Brick in the Wall (Part 2)'.

band with Walls!" in which he dismissed the entire project as "a seemingly fatalistic piece of work which is a monument of self centered pessimism and hopelessly clichéd."

Over at *Sounds*, things were little better as Dave McCullough sharpened his axe in readiness for a total hatchet job. "This is Pink Floyd's worst album ever. It is full of tired music, features feelings of lethargy and datedness, the solos sound senile and antiquated and the themes are tedious. Gordon Lightfoot meets Pete Townshend on a very bad trip."

Of the three important music magazines only *Melody Maker* held out any hope for the album but even then Chris Brazier confessed himself too confused to pronounce judgement in his article entitled "Floyd: The New Realism". He wrote: "It is an extraordinary record but I'm not sure whether it's brilliant or terrible, but I find it utterly compelling."

Back in the US the band was already gearing up for the first of the live shows scheduled for the LA sports arena in February 1980 but Martha Hume writing in *News* magazine was certainly not doing her best to help ticket sales. "*The Wall* is an album for chumps offering little more than the tired lament 'I am a famous rock star with lots of money so why am I not happy?'. The members of the band are exceptionally talented musicians, but with pedestrian imaginations."

As he revealed to Janet Hucks in 1980, Roger Waters had always been clear in his vision. "*The Wall* album is phase one, the concerts are phase two, and a film will be phase three." Phase two was always likely to be the most successful and relatively easy to deliver. The album had been a huge success and the band were now big enough to sell as many tickets as were put on sale for virtually any venue on earth and the band were hugely experienced at mounting lavish productions. It seemed that nothing could phase the Floyd team and it was probably just as well. The vision for the stage show required a huge leap forward from *In The Flesh*. In keeping with Water's desire to avoid stadiums, the venues were smaller at around 15,000 capacity but the show was exponentially more complex.

Only 29 Wall shows were ever performed. They took place over the course of 1980 and 1981 in just four cities, Los Angeles, New York, London and Dortmund. Technically Richard Wright had been fired at the end of the recording process and was no longer a member of the band so his inclusion on *The Wall* tour was something of a swan song as he later recounted to Nick Sedgwick for the *Is There Anybody Out There* sleeve notes.

"It was a very difficult and sad time for me. Naturally, I didn't want to leave the band, but once I was thrown out I managed to persuade myself that it was bound to happen and that Roger and I couldn't work together anyway. Still, I wanted to finish the recordings-most of my parts had already been taped. I also wanted to do the shows as a kind of final goodbye. That was hard and I'm not sure how I did it. I must have completely blanked out my anger and hurt. It was an awkward situation for all of us to be in, but in the English stiff upper lip manner we just got on with the job."

Rick Wright expanded on this unhappy phase of his career when he was interviewed by Sylvie Simmons for *Mojo*. "Why did I agree to play? Maybe I couldn't actually handle the idea of just standing up in the room and saying, 'Right, that's it, bye-bye.' I thought, if I'm going to leave at least I know I've got another month or so to carry on working - even possibly with the hope in the back of my mind that things might change. On the live performances Roger was being reasonably friendly. It was difficult but I tried to forget all my grudges, and I enjoyed playing *The Wall*. I put everything I could into the performances, and I think Roger approved of that. We would talk civilly to each other. It wasn't too bad at all."

The image of an emotionally crushed Wright as Pink seems to shine through more than ever on this second interview. The on-going stress of his relationship with Waters obviously occupied a large slice of Rick's mental landscape during the concerts and can be seen in his vain hopes of winning back Water's "approval". It was almost as if Rick could see the looming presence of Waters transformed into a giant Gerald Scarfe marionette overshadowing the key-board player's own personal wall. Never had the album's central theme seemed more appropriate. This was life again imitating art with painful prescience.

Before the first of *The Wall* shows had even taken place, Roger Waters sketched out his vision for Tommy Vance, so it is interesting to be able to compare the hopes with the reality. "The live performance of *The Wall* is an enormous project in itself. It's a very enormous thing, and not easy to move from country to country. So it's rather a slow project in many ways, and can't be done very frequently because it's very complex and difficult to do. The sound will be very good, mind you, at these shows, but the impediment to seeing and hearing what is going on will be symbolic rather than real, except for *The Wall*, which will stop people from seeing what's going on. Until it comes crashing down and that final song is saying, 'Right, well, that was it. You've seen it now. That's the best we can do.' That was us performing a piece of theatre about alienation. This is us making a little bit of human contact at the end of the show: 'We do like you really.'"

Waters also explained to Vance that there were no plans for an encore of more familiar material, "I've always been very against it, but everybody else says that we should. It's the writer in me that says, 'That last line is so nice that you should just leave it at that.' We definitely don't want to play any old material as an encore, first of all because it wouldn't fit in with *The Wall* concept, and secondly because we've played that old material so often in the past. We never, over the last few years, have done old material as encores. I mean, the 1977 tour consisted of *Wish You Were Here* and *Animals,* and then I think we played one track of *Dark Side of The Moon* as an encore."

For the shows themselves Waters stuck to his guns. The finale of the shows was a curious adaptation of *Outside The Wall* led by Waters on clarinet and rendered in a country and western style. Definitely not your average Floyd sound but again it worked.

The Wall was destined to be performed at only 12 shows in the US. Seven were in Los Angeles and a mere five in New York. This represented some 150, 000 tickets for a country which could easily have bought millions had one of Waters hated stadium tours been permitted. The shows were so elaborate and labour intensive that they were guaranteed to loose money in those size of venues. The live shows were therefore seen as an expensive publicity event which would underpin sales of the album. As predicted demand for the limited tickets was fierce and Janet Hucks witnessed the phenomenal demand as it hit the box office computer system.

"When their limited tour - one week in Los Angeles and five days in New York - was announced, the computers were pushed to warp drive to handle the demand. In New York, more than thirty-three thousand tickets were sold in a record-breaking five hours. In Los Angeles, more than seventy-seven thousand seats were sold. A few Massachusetts fans, who couldn't get tickets in New York, bought LA seats and came three thousand miles to see their heroes."

The show that the lucky ticket holders were about to witness has gone down in history as one of the boldest and innovative rock shows ever staged. Bob Kirk was present at the London shows. "The London shows were certainly special. Interestingly before the concert even began *The Wall* was already partially constructed at either side of the stage suggesting that, like builders everywhere, the lads had gone off somewhere for a quick tea break. It still looked like a huge task to fill the enormous span especially if, as we were led to believe, *The Wall* would be constructed brick by brick during the show. It seemed an unfeasibly large space to fill in such a short time and the uncertainty added to the tension of the evening."

Perched behind the as yet un-constructed wall was the circular screen which has since become synonymous with Floyd shows. During the first half of the show as the labourers strove to achieve their task the screen showed dazzling Scarfe animations and played host to some of the most amazing lighting effects ever witnessed on a rock stage.

The "surrogate" Pink Floyd rudely interrupted the fake announcer and almost before the audience had time to settle down a World War Two aircraft came screaming down over their heads and crashed into the stage in reference to the death of Pink's father. As the wall grew in size, strobe lighting and equally strong blasts of powerful back light were utilised to project fiercely through specially chosen gaps in which various performers would appear. The grittiness of the lyrics allied to the flawlessness of a live Floyd performance mixed with the stunning visual display to create an all round attack on the senses which left the audience dizzy with sensory overload. As the narrative unfolded gradually the wall took shape until finally the last brick was dropped into place just as Waters sang the last line of *Goodbye Cruel World*; the cue for an unwelcome and overlong intermission.

The second half of the show now utilised the completed wall as a cinema screen and child's peek-a-boo game from out of which slid a mid air platform on which was mocked up a complete hotel room replete with Roger Waters watching endless repeats on a flickering black and white TV. There was also the pure theatre of Gilmour's wall-top solo on *Comfortably Numb* and the gothic melodrama of *The Trial* before the whole thing came crashing down to earth for the band to emerge for a final farewell over a country tinged version of *Outside The Wall*.

Over in North America Steve Pond reviewed the shows for *Rolling Stone* magazine and gave a very positive verdict on the wall itself as "probably the most spectacular prop ever used by a rock band." Steve described the show itself as "startling, overpowering and numbing." As a writer, Janet Huck was lucky enough to be there to witness *The Wall* performed live in North America and her description of the gigs on the other side of the Atlantic matched the London template exactly. "Pink Floyd's concerts are legendary for making the most flamboyant gestures in the biggest stadiums - but this time they've transcended themselves. During the first half of their Los Angeles show, celebrating their new album *The Wall*, a massive, half-finished wall - stretching across the eleven thousand seat Sports Arena - was completed. Slowly, brick by brick, the black-clothed crew walled off the musicians, separating them totally from their audience. The wall stands insurmountable throughout most of the second half. But, at the end, a chant from the Floyd rose up louder and louder: 'Tear down the wall, tear down the wall.' A few people in the audience picked up their call for freedom as a series of Nazi images flashed, faster and faster, on the wall. With a murky low rumbling, the top bricks started to teeter, tumbling backwards in a unit. Then, with a hypnotizing roar, the rest of the carefully built wall crumbled, tossing the large white cardboard bricks dangerously close to the feet of the audience. Through the ominous, warlike devastation and billowing green smoke wove the newly cleansed musicians, dressed in street clothes, walking slowly in single file like medieval minstrels and playing on simple acoustic instruments, no longer 'banging against some mad bugger's wall'."

Obviously Floyd were never going to win over all of the critics. There were a fair number who just couldn't come to terms with the sheer bleakness of the message. Dave Dimartino writing for Creem magazine in the US was one such critic. Earlier in his article Dave had described the convivial atmosphere, the anticipation and the good natured warmth surrounding his first trip to see Floyd since 1973, but as the show progressed Dimartino describes the sense of unease over the subject matter which gradually asserted a grip over him. It was a feeling which was common even among the natural supporters of the band.

"And then comes the wall, of course, now making much more sense in this context. Huge marionettes in the shape of the Oppressors: the School Teacher, the Mother, the Whorish Female, the Judge and Tribunal. And the films, projected on the continually-growing wall, sophisticated animation depicting the same thing. *The Wall* Illustrated, With Quadraphonic Sound, soon to be a major motion picture, all here now for you at the Nassau Coliseum. Five continuous showings.

"And the thing of it is - it's all impressive as hell, it really is. The schoolchildren sing 'We don't need no education,' from speaker to speaker to speaker, behind us, at our right, our left. An airplane flies from the back of the Coliseum, over the audience, crashing over the wall. It is ROCK AS SPECTACLE and, as such, deserves to be appreciated as spectacle. Certainly it's the antithesis of everything immediate about rock 'n' roll - poor Roger Waters even wears headphones through the entire performance because he has to. Tapes are rolling, sound effects must be synchronized with the music the eight musicians on stage are playing. The tapes don't accompany Pink Floyd; Pink Floyd accompany the tapes. But then, there were never any claims put forth that immediacy mattered much here, that Roger Waters was aiming for anything but tightly-controlled, spectacular theatre. And on that level, *The Wall* in concert is a success, an extraordinary one.

"But there is something wrong here, something about this show in Nassau Coliseum that doesn't mesh. Images, emotional undercurrents that seem vaguely unhealthy, not quite right. *The Wall* and what Roger Waters meant by it isn't the same Wall the audience has come to see, hear, and take drugs while watching. 'We don't need no education,' bursts alternately from the quadrophonic speakers and the crowd cheers on, obviously in agreement. 'Mother do you think they 'll try to break my balls?' Same cheers. 'I have become comfortably numb.' BIG cheers. 'I've got a silver spoon on a chain,' and 'There's one smoking a joint' bring the biggest cheers of all, and Roger Waters' message, as the crowd at the Nassau Coliseum interprets it, is TAKE LOTS OF DRUGS, KIDS, BECAUSE EVERYTHING SUCKS OUT THERE ANYWAY.

"And there's more. The overprotective mother of *The Wall*'s first few minutes, the bubble-headed ("oooh - do you wanna take a bath?!?' she coos) groupie, the almost repulsive imagery of Gerald Scarfe's

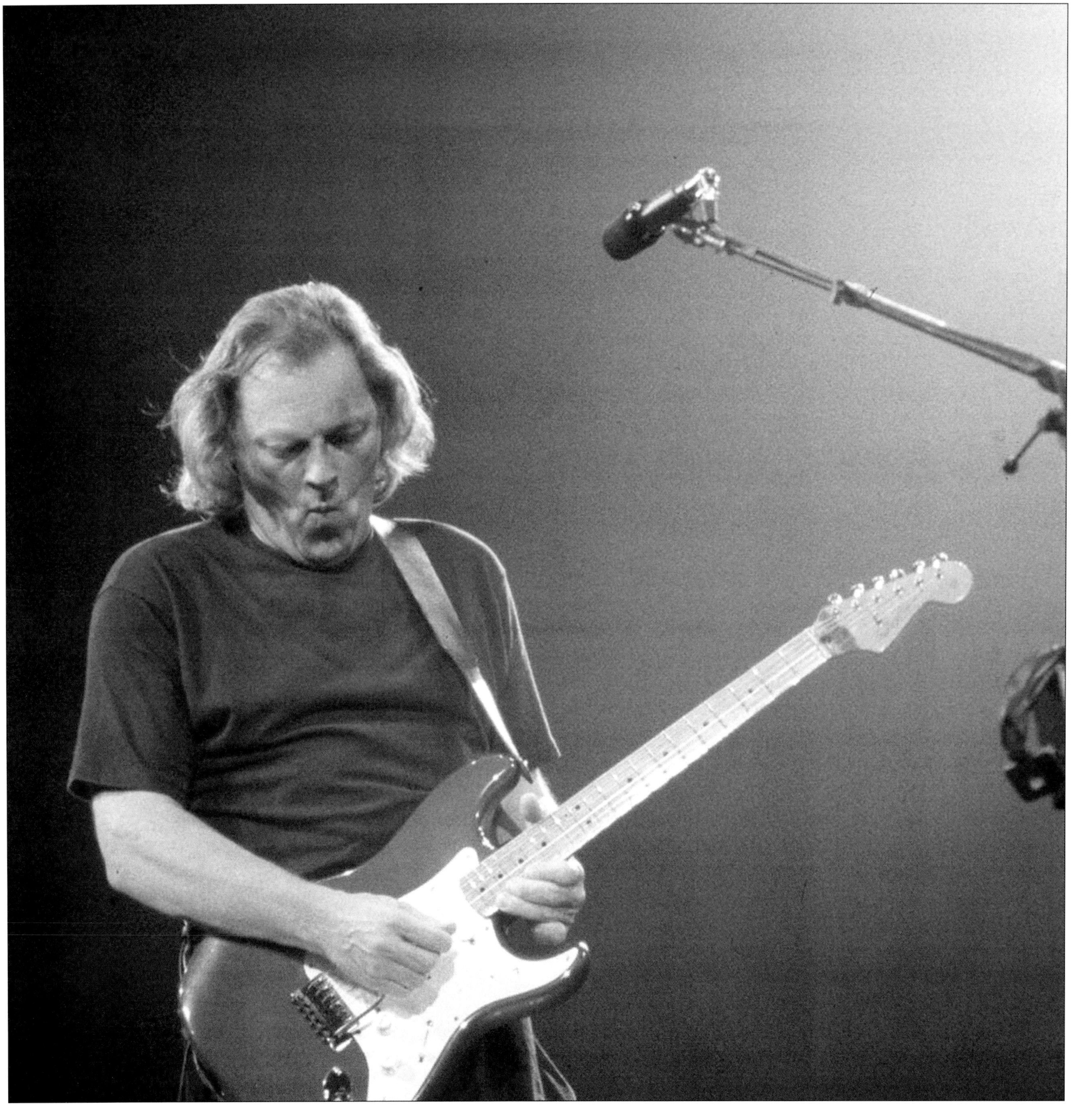
Rex Features

animation - they all share such blatantly misogynist overtones it's frightening. Castration anxiety, oozing vaginas that lure and snip - is this Roger Waters' message? And if it is, why is this message one that elicits the strongest audience reaction? Roger Waters' second message, as the crowd at the Nassau Coliseum interprets it: WOMEN ARE EITHER STUPID OR OUT FOR YOUR BALLS, GUYS.

"That the latter portion of the performance has Waters in almost Hitlerian dress is heavily ironic, as, of course, is most of *The Wall*. Waters was never one for life-affirming messages - *Dark Side*'s lobotomy climax proved that years ago - but there's an element of dark sarcasm running through *The Wall* that at least partially alleviates its overbearing negativity. Unfortunately, few have picked up on it, preferring instead to think that hey, life really does suck, and isn't ol' Roger tellin 'it the way it is?' And if I were Waters, it would disturb me greatly knowing that I was at all responsible for imposing - or at least confirming - such negativity on a young and old impressionable audience. To sing 'I have become comfortably numb' and be cheered for those exact words would make me wince.

"But if you want to talk about walls, talk about this: Roger Waters is a multi-millionaire who never has to see anybody he doesn't want to; his net worth has quadrupled since *The Wall* has been lodging *Comfortably Numb* at the top of the charts; between shows at Long Island he flew by helicopter to Connecticut to 'get away from it all'; he totally ignored the press this time around due to *The Wall*'s success and can go right back home and fly kites for the rest of his life without ever having to work another day. Roger Waters and Syd Barrett both seem to have learned the same lesson, and I wonder who's happier. I already know who's richer.

"At the show's end, the huge white wall is demolished, falling into bits and chunks that cover the stage floor. Waters and the rest of the band move in procession, one by one, across the stage. Waters, the *Piper At The Gates of Dawn*, leads with his clarinet; others follow. The band files offstage, the Colliseum lights turn on, and people leave, buying beautiful $5 programs here and there to prove later to their friends that see, I was there, I even have the program. And envious friends will glance through the elegant four-color program while someone else suggests playing *The Wall* one more time."

Over in the UK the music press reaction was as hostile as ever. *Record Mirror* dismissed the whole show as "a triumph of spectacle over substance," concluding that "the concept is as hollow as the bricks used in its construction." On August 16 *NME* published a particularly damaging review in which Nick Kent felt that *The Wall* had been a dismal failure as both a record and now as a stage show and that among a list of other demands, "Waters should deflate the farce, debunk all the myths, strip the Floyd of their pathetic theatrical devices, inform the audience that the game is over, and offer them refunds..." *NME* could not resist coming back for another kick at the prone carcass when *The Wall* or the "cosmic farce" as Chris Bohn now termed it, returned for its second London run in 1981. "Although it is difficult not to be impressed by the spectacle (and Mr Bohn was certainly trying his best) it leaves a bitter aftertaste. The music is portentous and pedestrian ...Scarfe's puppets are as contemptuously vile as Water's characterizations."

"Play *Comfortably Numb,* they'll say. "I like that best."

Janet Hucks was privileged enough to be able to get behind the scenes and gain a sense of the enormous complexities involved in setting up *The Wall* shows. She was also given an in-depth explanation by special effects assistant Graham Fleming. "A massive white wall which stretches two hundred and ten feet across the Sports Arena floor and rises thirty-five feet off the ground. Waters' symbol of psychological isolation is made up of approximately four hundred and fifty individual fire-proof cardboard bricks that measure five feet by two and a half feet and weigh a hefty nineteen pounds. A crew of six - called The Brit Row Brick Company - lay down three hundred and forty of the foldable bricks every night in about forty-five minutes.

"There were plenty of problems... design a self-supporting wall which wouldn't accidentally crush the musicians on stage, yet would come down on cue when *The Wall* has to crumble. For safety, the top rows are knocked back on the stage, on to giant metal cages protecting the equipment and musicians. The other basic problem is how to lay all the bricks in time to the music. To make sure they could get *The Wall* up and down in time, the Brit Row Brick Company started rehearsal two months ago. In case there are any time problems with *The Wall*, the band have written some expandable riffs to cover the delayed brick-laying; amidst all the gee-whiz effects, Pink Floyd don't act like normal egotistical rock stars on stage. They don't jump around or use flamboyant, Jaggeresque gestures - they tune up carefully and start playing almost exactly on time. At times they act as if it's just another job that has to be done; consequently, some of the audience think they are cold and impersonal. In fact, they pace the show without reckoning on any participation from the audience. The performance is speeded up or slowed down according to problems with the special effects and, like an opera, one song is rolled into the next without any time or space for applause. And Waters almost never addresses the audience - once he yelled 'Is there anybody out there?' but those lines are actually part of the script. Of course, The Wall robbed the audience of any intimacy; towards the end of the first half, you could only see the band through five-foot cutouts, almost as if you were watching them on a television set. During the second half, the audience got only occasional glimpses of the band: Gilmour gave a searing solo on top of The Wall and Waters sang one song in a motel room mock-up that folded out from The Wall. But at other times he just sang with his back to the audience."

David Gilmour did not have the same huge problems with audiences which Waters experienced and his spectacular view of the audience provided Gilmour with one of the highlights of his career as he later explained to Nick Sedgwick for the sleeve notes of Is There Anybody Out There? "For me the best bit of The Wall was standing on top of it. We were a few songs into the second half of the show. The band had been bricked in, the audience left to confront a vast, blank barrier. Then a trick of light, there I was 30 ft up, with the heat of four enormous spotlights at my back, throwing my shadow as far as I could see over the audience while I belted out the solo to one of the best pieces of music I'd ever written: Comfortably Numb. The sensation was certainly incredible, almost out of body. I could simply do the part of my job I enjoy most: playing the guitar, trying to make it a little better every night."

Making it better was not the only thing on Gilmour's mind. The huge array of technical requirements made enormous demands on his concentration and left no room for spontaneity or improvisation. Gilmour explained the reasons for this when he spoke to Sylvie Simmons in 1999. "I was in charge of all the mechanics of making it work. I had a six-foot-long cue-sheet draped over my amplifier for the first few shows which I had memorised after that, so I'd know exactly where a cue would come from, because it could come out of a floor monitor or from film, and I had one control unit to adjust the digital delay lines on my equipment and Roger's, Rick's and Snowy's [White], so I didn't really notice what was going on around me terribly much."

Nick Mason also recalled for Simmons the unusual on stage set up although Nick seems to have had a great time regardless of the odd performing environment. "The drums were in an armoured cage, so when The Wall collapsed it wouldn't destroy them. It was a curious, rather nice environment - almost like being in a studio, except you're interacting, and odd, because it's half live. Not much spontaneity, but we're not well-known for our duck-walking and general gyrating about on-stage."

The lack of interaction and the elimination of the possibilities for improvisation led to a fair degree of grumbling in the press, but by it's very nature The Wall was more akin to a piece of carefully scripted theatre and it was never presented as being a rock 'n' roll show in any event. In fact it was almost the antithesis of the standard rock show. The fans knew what to expect, they knew that Floyd no longer thrived on avant garde improvisation. Here was the intersection between circus, opera, rock and dramatic event. It was the exact opposite of the days when A Saucerful Of Secrets might rumble away up any given musical path which suited the whim of its creators.

In addition to reviewing the album Jay Cocks also ran his slightly jaundiced eye over the live show for Time Magazine. Clearly Mr Cocks was no great lover of the band or their aloof attitude but even he could not but fail to find the proceedings at least interesting.

"The Pinkies' new stage show is an extravagantly literal representation of the album, including a smoking bomber with an eighteen-foot wingspan that buzzes the audience on a guy wire and huge floats representing the songs' major characters, among them a thirty-foot mom who inflates to apparently daunting proportions with the throw of a toggle switch. There is also, of course, a wall, soaring thirty feet above the stage, spanning two hundred and ten feet at the top. At the start of the show, roadies - rechristened 'wallies' for the occasion - start stacking three hundred and forty cardboard bricks until, at intermission, The Wall stands completed. During the second half, a few strategic ruptures appear, through which Waters and his fellow Pinkies - keyboard player Rick Wright, drummer Nick Mason and guitarist Dave Gilmour - can be glimpsed doing their stuff.

"The inevitable apocalypse occurs on cue. The Wall crumbles, bending on its collapsible support columns and bringing a storm of harmless rubble down around the Floyd. Outside the wall, Waters sings, 'the bleeding hearts and the artists make their stand.' The Pinkies would presumably find such company untidy, in the first case, or unflattering, in the

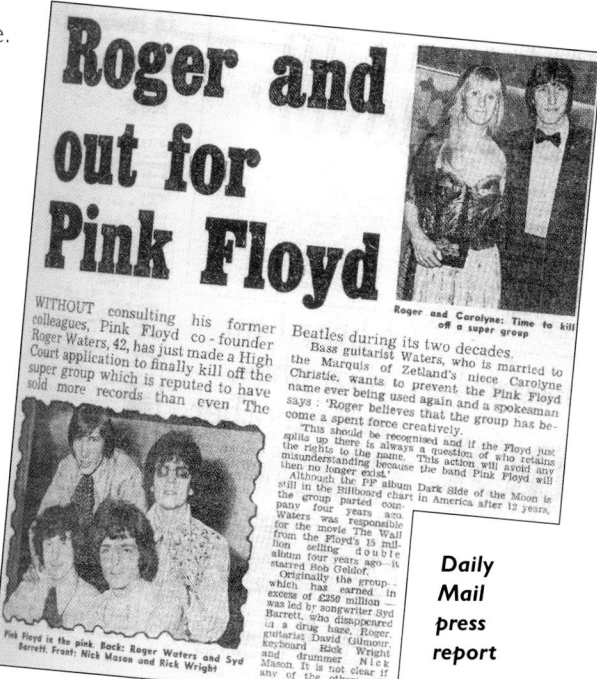

Daily Mail press report

second. As Waters' pipes band and back-up musicians off stage with his clarinet, one recalls with renewed interest the fate of The Godfather's Luca Brasi, who was sent to sleep with the fishes."

Even Roger Waters would surely not have expected to find The Wall compared to the Godfather as he explained to Tommy Vance his own view was that a large number of people would simply be baffled. "I'm sure there were a hell of a lot of people who came to the show and went away thinking, what the fuck was that all about? And they probably aren't interested anyway. There's no reason why everybody should be interested in the same things I am, after all."

The stage shows represented the culmination of what had at times been a very difficult project for Bob Ezrin who was not able to become involved again in the world of Pink Floyd for the live shows. He was nonetheless determined to catch at least one of the shows as he explained to Sylvie Simmons. "I was asked to be involved with the show and I couldn't - I was going through a divorce and fighting for custody of my children. That and another incident, where in my naivety I took a phone call from a friend who happened to be a journalist and broke my non-disclosure with the band when he teased information out of me, so upset Roger, who was already feeling very nervous and was dealing with the Rick situation. That was it. I was banned from backstage. I went anyway, New York was sort of my territory, all the security at the venue knew me from Kiss and Alice Cooper. When the Pink Floyd security said, "He can't come in," they said, "Like hell he can't!" I had to buy my ticket, but I saw the show. It was flawless and utterly overwhelming. In Comfortably Numb, when Dave played his solo from the top of The Wall, I broke into tears. It was the embodiment of the entire experience. In the final analysis it produced what is arguably the best work of that decade, maybe one of the most important rock albums ever."

Despite the huge artistic success of The Wall there was little sign of celebration inside the Floyd camp. Relationships were fast approaching the nadir which would see Waters leave Pink Floyd. In his autobiography, Nick Mason recalled the mood of decline which surrounded those last shows. It should have been an occasion, a wild party in commemoration of a stunning theatrical achievement, instead it seems to have been more like a wake. "By the four nights at Earls Court in June 1981 the show was well honed. However, they also turned out to be the last time Roger, David, Rick and I would play together. As far as group relationships were concerned things had deteriorated even further than during recording. The clearest indication of this could be seen in the backstage area of Earls Court, where each band member had an individual Portakabin. Roger's and Rick's both faced away from the enclosure… I think that we also had individual after-show parties, carefully avoiding inviting each other."

Chapter 13
THE WALL - THE MOVIE

When he spoke to Tommy Vance in 1979 about the album and the live shows, Roger Waters was already looking forward to the movie which would be produced to complete The Wall production trilogy, "I'd like to do it in the open air because I have some ideas for the film that would only really work in the open air. The place certainly needs to be somewhere with a kind of teutonic architecture. Any big stadium would do, really, but it would be nice if it had that kind of German/Roman feel to it because of the culture that we've grown up in. Those will become symbolic of the kind of totalitarianism that part of the record is about."

It was interesting to observe Waters early vision for the movie which he intended to feature the band in performance as well as extensive footage of the audience. Tommy Vance recorded his thoughts. "When Pink Floyd make a film about The Wall, Waters is going to use the audience a great deal probably, the controlled audience will be instructed to turn into a crazed mob, led on by the fascist surrogate band.

Vance touched on the crazy economics of the rock world when he spelled out the topsy turvy finances which meant that even a conspicuous success like The Wall could not hope to recover its costs.

"They have to make a movie about the project in order to recoup the money they are losing on the two-city tour. Every night they put the elaborate show on, each member of the band loses $15,000 apiece; over the twelve nights, the show cost the band $800,000. Waters calculated that they would have to charge $30 a ticket instead of $12 and $15 to break even. 'The audience is really getting more than they paid for,' he remarked, but added: 'The album is selling like hot cakes, so the enormous gamble is paying off.'

Things happen quite differently in the movie from the album. After a brief flash forward sequence in the soulless interior of an American hotel, the film proper begins in the beaches of Anzio with *When The Tigers Broke Free*, a new track composed for *The Wall* movie. This uninspiring piece was later forced onto the EMI Pink Floyd compilation, against the wishes of the other three members, as a result of the horse trading that went on to produce an acceptable track listing. Bizarrely, it was released as part of a Video EP and also as a vinyl single to promote *The Final Cut* even though the track did not actually appear on the album.

This was not the only departure from the blue print which had proved so successful and not all of them would be welcomed by Roger Waters.

Once director Alan Parker had been enlisted for the project creative control began to slip away from Waters. Parker had no intention of making a film for Floyd fans. He was out to create a mainstream cinema film and he brought a very clear creative vision which differed from Waters and set the two men on a collision course. In the film world the director enjoys god like status. His decision is final and as such is usually enshrined in his contract. This situation was accepted on every film set world wide; but Roger Waters seemed to think differently.

For *Inside Out* Nick Mason recalled how he had witnessed the problems unfold at first hand. "Filming of the movie started with Gerald Scarfe and Michael Seresin as co-directors, and Alan Parker as overall producer, but after a week it was clear this system was not going to work. Alan was elevated to director, Michael departed, Gerry was reassigned to other duties, and we started again. Changing the command structure so early on was something of an omen. The stories are legion of the disagreements that occurred on the film. Alan Parker had a strong vision, but so too did Gerry and Roger. Gerry certainly felt quite isolated, as Alan Parker and the new producer Alan Marshall represented one self-supporting faction, and Roger and Steve O'Rourke another. Despite this recipe for disaster, I think the results were a victory for ability over organisation. Gerry's animation managed to make the transition from stage show to big screen, as did Bob Geldof, in the lead role of Pink."

Roger had originally conceived a film for Pink Floyd fans which incorporated live performance footage of Pink Floyd on stage from *The Wall* stage shows combined with live action and Scarfe's amazing animations. In Waters' original vision the dramatic aspects would have enjoyed equal importance to the other elements of the film. This was soon abandoned for an attempt at a main stream film in which live action would take pole position.

Roger had sung all of the parts on the album quite brilliantly and naturally he saw himself in the role of Pink, but here too he was in for an unpleasant surprise. Alan Parker brusquely informed Roger that he couldn't act, but his judgement was to be thrown into question by his choice for the lead role. There was wide consternation among the Pink Floyd fraternity when it was announced that the role of Pink was to be played by a little known new wave singer called Bob Geldof, whose pop career was already on the wane and who was consequently an aspiring actor.

Fortunately the role of Pink required almost no dialogue. Understandably Roger Waters had demanded that Parker use Waters' own voice for the music soundtrack with Geldof miming along, Parker again won the argument although it is highly debatable whether he should have done.

Geldof's feeble rendition of *In the Flesh* must surely rank as a low point in the entire project. His pop career had demonstrated Geldof's singing talent was mediocre at very best and outside of the dumb show silent movie performance of *The Wall*, his acting ability proved to be non-existent. Geldof was famously quoted as stating his opinion that Pink Floyd were "crap" and his appearance in a movie based around their music inevitably reeks of cynical opportunism.

On the film set, relationships between Waters and Parker had become a train wreck. Waters found his vision altered beyond endurance while Parker found the singer to be intransigent and over bearing. The results of this constant creative friction could not be expected to have a positive effect on the film which had now totally abandoned the 35mm performance footage of Floyd's Wall shows specially shot for inclusion in the movie.

There may have been a great deal of debate over the choice of Geldof but Gerald Scarfe's breathtaking animations seemed far better suited to the subject matter. His satisfaction with the end product was apparent in the interview he later gave to Sylvie Simmons of *Mojo*. "*Goodbye Blue Skies* is one of my favourite pieces of animation. For me that was very much a hymn to the Second World War and the sadness of it all. I was a small child during the war so I understood the feeling of bombers and gasmasks - they used to make them for children in the shape of Mickey Mouse because they were frightening, claustrophobic things to wear. I designed some creatures called the Frightened Ones who had heads like gasmasks and were running into air-raid shelters. Animation doesn't have to be little Disney bunnies running around, it's unlimited, surreal. I tried very hard with the open brief that all the guys in Pink Floyd gave me - yes, I dealt mainly with Roger, but all the guys were completely on my side - to give them my very best. Directing animation is a very time-consuming thing, so it took over a year."

The longer running time of the movie also provided the opportunity to reinstate *What Shall We Do Now* a song which had originally been planned for side two but which had been dropped from the album due to running time constraints. Lyrically the song explored the same ideas as *Empty Spaces* but also benefited hugely from the animation of Gerald Scarfe, who produced a powerful and disturbing sequence. His real tour de force of course has to be *The Trial*. A sensational and iconic piece of animation. Although it is Pink who puts himself on trial, mercifully we were spared another vocal interpretation by Bob Geldof. With the ignominy of Geldof's *In The Flesh* so close behind them audiences can only have winced at the prospect of the horror which might have been. As things stand, *The Trial* sequence represents a major artistic triumph.

For Roger Waters, the film had turned into a nightmare. He felt that his cherished vision had been stolen and debased. Despite winning a BAFTA award for best soundtrack Roger always viewed the film as a lost opportunity. Never one to let a grudge slip easily he was to represent his feelings of impotent outrage on the cover for the next Floyd album; *The Final Cut*. As art director, only Roger will ever be able to satisfactorily explain why the military figure depicted on the album cover is holding cans of film, or why he has been plainly knifed in the back...

Once the turmoil of its creation had subsided, it was time to allow cinema audiences to decide for themselves. Brian Mulligan encapsulated much of the highs and lows of the film when he reviewed the movie for the magazine *Record Business*, on 19 July 1982. It slowly becomes apparent in this thoughtful review that what first appears as a hatchet job actually turns out to be a thought provoking, perceptive and ultimately positive view of the film as a piece of art. Mulligan was able to get underneath the skin of the project in a way that few reviewers could, but his words were entirely typical of the many reviewers who appreciated the film but who could not reconcile themselves to the remorseless bleakness of the subject matter. "*The Wall* is a truly nasty film, relentless in its pursuit of depicting the worst excesses of human behaviour, a study of madness and the corrupting effects of violence and alienation. Roger Waters' view of mankind is totally and morbidly hopeless. He offers no solutions, no hope for the future. Love, even that of a mother for her fatherless son, is depicted as being unhealthy. The bleakness of Waters' vision is dramatically underlined at the end of the film when *The Wall* is symbolically blown apart to reveal a scene on the other side no less desolate, with a young boy casually using a Molotov cocktail as a plaything.

"Confusing, overlong, always disturbing and frequently frightening in the way the camera explicitly dwells on blood, rape, war and rotting humanity, *The Wall* is obviously painfully autobiographical. Waters' message seems to be that violence may be the only antidote to the claustrophobic way in which people's lifestyles are determined.

"It catches up with Pink, a burned-out rock star, in his hotel room in Los Angeles, living in his own private hell, a hair's breadth away from madness and suicide. Lacking dialogue in the conventional sense, it leaps from present to past, to nightmarish visions of the future, sequences regularly enhanced by Gerald Scarfe's monstrous animation. Bob Geldof, who plays Pink, is uninhibited and hugely impressive. His destruction of the hotel room and subsequent self-mutilation are two of the film's more chilling moments.

"Such is the awful fascination of what's happening on the screen that it is not always easy to give proper concentration to Pink Floyd's music, but there are certainly occasions when the juxtaposition of visual and sound images, both equally violent, make a stunning impact on the senses. Brilliant though director Alan Parker's film is, it was good afterwards to get back into the street and find that there were still ordinary human beings walking around. Hopefully its message will not be taken to heart by impressionable youth."

As usual the British music press were generally unimpressed by any offering which had the Pink Floyd name attached to it, but even so, Richard Cook writing in *NME* was not entirely dismissive although his views were not exactly favourable with regard to the film overall. "As a rock movie *The Wall* stands high, but as a real movie it is grainy and stolid. Images are cross referenced exhaustively. Technically it's impeccable, and Gerald Scarfe's animations have demonic energy, but the movie tells us nothing new of 1970's excesses."

Needless to say, things were more positive in the more neutral atmosphere of North America. Bruce Kirkland of *The Toronto Sun* gave the film the thumbs up from the country where it had all begun. "The

Rex Features

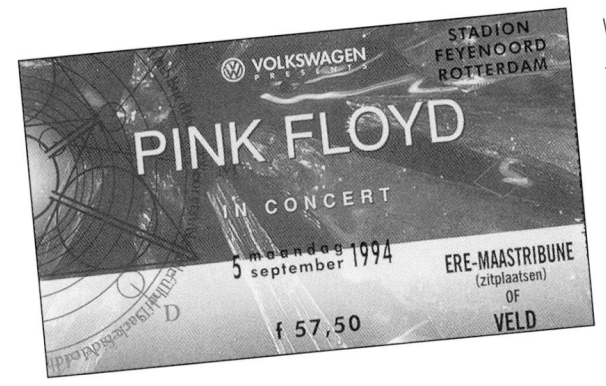

Wall is a beautiful, brilliant film. It overloads your capacity for negative images and feelings but it is one of the few must-see movies of the year." The US trade paper *Music Week (U. S.)* was even more positive stating that "*The Wall* has set the standard by which all future music-inspired films will be judged."

Even the consumer press was positive in the States. Archer Winstein of the *New York Post* was typical of the average critical reaction. "As a one shot entertainment it is overwhelming. The film is an emotional explosion that happens in another place, a different time."

Nick Mason summed up his own feelings on the aftermath of *The Wall* in his autobiography. "After all the work on *The Wall* was complete, my overriding feeling - and by now a pattern may be emerging - was less of elation than exhaustion. Given that we had only performed the show thirty-odd times in two years, it was difficult to blame this on physical exertion. It was more a feeling that the whole project appeared to have been going on for an eternity. However, perhaps another reason for my lethargy and lack of enthusiasm was caused by the thought of confronting each other once again."

For her *Mojo* article Sylvie Simmons explored the last embers of the Wright versus Waters struggle with both Roger Waters and Rick Wright. She talked to Waters first. "It was fait accompli, Rick was being paid a wage, he seemed happy with that, we were happy with that, and that was the end of it - or maybe he wasn't happy with it but it's not something we discussed. Backstage it was all pretty separatist - separate trailers, none facing each other - ha-ha - with all our little camps. The atmosphere was awful, but the job, the show, was so important that certainly on-stage I don't think that affected me at all. Here was the ultimate case of life imitating art. The four men who between them had created, built and performed an iconic piece about non-communication were now it seemed incapable of communicating even at the most basic levels. Wright too summed up the prevailing mood of the day for Simmons, interestingly he does not appear to feel that the off-stage relationships affected the performances in any way. The pre-programmed nature of the show saw to that. " It just seemed to me another example of why I'm not sad to leave, because the band had lost any feeling of communication and camaraderie by this time. But bands can go on-stage and perform music even if they hate each other. It was a band that I felt was falling to pieces - which of course it did."

After *The Wall* the acting world was to be blessed with only one more film before Bob Geldof began to pursue other outlets for which he actually proved to have some ability.

The thousands who have genuinely benefited from Geldof's great work against starvation were of course the real beneficiaries, but in leaving the world of motion pictures behind Geldof also gave future cinema audiences a wonderful gift in the form of his absence from the silver screen. For Pink Floyd fans of course Saint Bob was destined to provide the biggest gift of all when his influence finally succeeded in re-uniting all four original members for the Live 8 charity concert in 2005.

The Wall had claimed five years of Roger Water's life but he was to loose control of his legacy in 1985 when he quit Pink Floyd in a dispute over the management of the band.

The reformed Floyd made full use of the highlights from *The Wall* with *Another Brick in The Wall*, *Comfortably Numb* and *Run Like Hell* enjoying pride of place as exciting elements in the stunning live shows which brought the Floyd name back to life in the eighties.

It was not until July 1990 that Waters would again perform the whole of his most famous work. In a colossal undertaking to benefit the Memorial Fund For Disaster Relief, *The Wall* was performed live from the site of the Berlin Wall before an audience of 300,000 and a live televison audience calculated to be in excesss of 100 million. With hindsight, the cast probably didn't live up to the event and there were embarrassing technical gremlins which no live television director can ever adequately deal with, but in the end the immense scale of the concert worked its magic and above all the work itself shone through. The 1990 performance of *The Wall* is likely to be the last of the massive performances of his magnum opus so it is fitting that Roger Waters should enjoy the limelight of the final performance. Phil Sutcliffe reviewed the performance for *Q* magazine. "Ultimately as a piece of music *The Wall* stood up well, built on the old Pink Floyd instinct for stately weight, offset by everyday sound effects (a phone ringing) and the one great, hypnotic pop song. But nothing became *The Wall* quite so much as its collapse. With a quarter of a million Berliners chanting 'Tear down *The Wall*!' at the top of their lungs, if finally complied in a prodigious avalanche of polystyrene, executed by a dazzling piece of production sleight of hand and the same number of roadies it took to build the pyramids. As pyrotechnicians fired clouds of twinkling tinsel across Potsdamer Platz, the crowd roared long and massively. Americans turned to one another and agreed it was 'Ossome', while a lone, typically English voice said, 'Of course, it was all in the worst possible taste.' If this concert is to celebrate anything, it's that the Berlin Wall coming down can be seen as a liberating of the human spirit,"Waters tells *Q* during rehearsals. So it's not in any sense a 'Top that!' addressed to Dave Gilmour and Nick Mason, now legally established owners of his old band's name and, hence, proprietors of a fabulously successful Pink Floyd comeback in the late '80s? "No it's not 'Top that!' But it certainly will be most gratifying that a few more people in the world will understand that *The Wall* is my work and always has been... Still most of the audience for this show will probably think it's Pink Floyd anyway. The attachment to the brand name is limpet-like. It's just something I live with."

Since that heady evening on Pottsdamer Platz *The Wall* has entered the pantheon of popular music and 25 years on from it's release, the music of *The Wall* has been adapted, arranged and performed by a dizzying array of artists. In 2005 you can find the music of *The Wall* arranged to meet the musical demands of strands as diverse as Blue grass, reggae, disco, classical, dub and even country. It's a trend which looks sets to continue.

As Sylvie Simmons reported, there was even a post script to the Waters/Wright scenario with a resolution of sorts after a Roger Waters show in 1999. Rick Wright finally did what every therapist advises: confronted his Nemesis. "'I think I'm the only one who's actually seen Roger in the last 18 years. John Caron, who was playing with Roger and was on the last two tours I 'd done, said. 'Please come along.' I still had a lot of anger - I haven't spoken to him since *The Wall* - but I thought, Oh shit, why not? I don't have to see him. I was sitting in the audience signing autographs while he performed on-stage. When he did Pink Floyd music it felt very odd - that I wasn't up there, or Dave and Nick." When the show was over Rick Wright decided to go backstage. "It was a difficult one - for both of us. There are a lot of issues that maybe one day we 'll talk about but at the time I didn't want to go into all that. I just said, 'Hello, how are you, you're looking well.'"

For Waters, the ghost of *The Wall* still hung over the proceedings. This was not about reconciliation, it was all about non-communication. From Waters point of view it could almost have been a missing episode from *The Wall*. "He stood in front of me, grinning," says Roger Waters. "I think he 'd had a couple, there was a bit of Dutch courage going on, but he was perfectly gracious. So was I, I think. He introduced me to his wife, I said hello, and that was it. It wasn't uncomfortable. We didn't have much to say to one another."

Chapter 14
THE FINAL CUT

With the departure of Richard Wright, Pink Floyd began the eighties as a three piece but Roger Waters was now the real power in the band. The disproportionate split in control was evident in the next album, The Final Cut, released in March 1983.

The over-riding impression from this ill favoured outing is of a Roger Waters' solo album. *The Final Cut* dwells on the politics and social landscape of Britain in the early 1980s. The focus is incredibly narrow and could almost be lifted from an editorial meeting at *The Guardian*, Roger's newspaper of choice. The listener inevitably gets the distinct impression that we are recycling the same thematic and musical landscape of *The Wall*. In a few cases this was literally true, as Dave Gilmour later confirmed some of the pieces which found their way on to *The Final Cut* had already been rejected for *The Wall*. The album had originally been prepared under the working title *Spare Bricks*. In the accompanying *Final Cut* video EP the late Alex McAvoy was even asked to reprise his role of the School Teacher from *The Wall*. In the Video EP the teacher character is depicted in his unhappy retirement.

Overseas audiences were somewhat mystified by the parochial subject matter of *The Final Cut* especially songs like *Not Now John* which dealt with industrial landscape of Thatcher's Britian. The intensely bitter tone of the lyrics did little to help, but the album has far greater structural faults in musical terms. With David Gilmour relegated to the role of hired hand in a Roger Waters obsessed universe there were none of the flashes of instrumental genius which had made *The Wall* such a complete package. The atmosphere of the album is relentlessly downbeat and with no melodic or instrumental relief the darkness and bitterness are overwhelming.

There is also the constant all pervading feeling that we are revisiting exactly the same thematic and musical landscape as *The Wall*. With its exploration of the damaging effect of the sacrifices made in war we are very much stuck in the same territory as *The Wall*. Even the photograph on the album sleeve with the soldier holding film cans who has been cleanly knifed in the back has been widely interpreted as a reference to Roger's frustrations over the creation of *The Wall* movie. The Hipgnosis partnership had been dissolved but Storm Thorgeson was still very active as a designer and film maker. Roger chose not to employ Storm and instead embarked on a self-designed sleeve.

Not Now John is the only place on the album where the tempo lifts. The song deals with the indifferent attitudes of those who were too oblivious to care about the subjects which troubled Waters so deeply, but it could almost have served as an anthem for all the Floyd fans bored and disillusioned by the relentless diet of earnestness and yearning for an injection of instrumental genius to lighten the mood. The album is a Roger Waters solo album in all but name: "the rest of us just sort of drifted into it," said Nick Mason. The over-riding impression from this ill favoured outing is tension and conflict. Waters had enjoyed the lion's share of the creative input on the previous two albums and carried out those tasks with great aplomb. Sadly, *The Final Cut* fails to live up to its legendary predecessor in any respect.

The album had in fact started out as a band project but Gilmour soon discovered that his input was unwelcome which was the start of a long period of friction which ultimately saw the guitarist relinquish his producer's credit, but not his producer's royalties!

In May 1983, Sounds ran an interview with David Gilmour in which it is not too difficult to read between the lines to see the discontent beneath the surface. "It's very, very much Roger's baby, more than anyone has been before, it's not the way I'd have produced it and we did have an argument about the production on this record, several arguments, and I came off the production credits because my ideas of production weren't the way that Roger saw it being. Obviously the way it is, is the way Roger wanted it to be. It's very, very good, but it's not personally how I would see a Pink Floyd record going. The sound quality is very good, it's very, very well recorded, and the string arrangements and orchestral stuff are very well done. But it's not me. Consequently, I was arguing about how to make the record at the beginning, and it was being counterproductive. We diverge quite a lot. But we do still just about manage to work together. And we still have got things that we can contribute to each other. I think the thing with Rick was that he didn't have anything that any of us felt was contributing to what Pink Floyd do in any way."

The early 80s were also a troubled time for the Hipgnosis partnership which had recently been dissolved in the wake of problems caused by major overspends on a video shoot. Nonetheless Storm Thorgeson was very much active as a designer. His difficulties were not helped by Roger passing over Storm's new design team in order to design the sleeve himself. It has to be said that the results of his efforts are less than striking.

The Music

THE POST WAR DREAM *(Waters)* - The militarily brassy scene-setter name checks the Atlantic Conveyor, a ship sunk by the Argentines in the Falklands War which had just ended, and the fact its replacement will be built in Japan - an enemy, of course, in a previous conflict.

YOUR POSSIBLE PASTS (Waters) - A 'Wall' contender, saved for future re-use, includes chilling sound effects resembling the 'cattle trucks' used to take Nazi concentration-camp victims to their doom.

ONE OF THE FEW (Waters) - Continuing the theme of warfare, 'The Few' of the title refers to the RAF Fighter Command pilots who fought in the Battle of Britain in 1940. The pilots got their name from a famous Winston Churchill wartime speech "never in the field of human conflict has so much been owed by so many to so few."

THE HERO'S RETURN (Waters) - The Hero (or central character) reflects on his war experiences. An extra final verse and chorus for this song turned up on the 12-inch single version of 'Not Now John', identified as 'The Hero's Return Part II'.

THE GUNNERS DREAM (Waters) This was one of 'three good tracks' which Gilmour identified (the others being *The Fletcher Memorial Home* and the title song) from a release which he had publically stated he "didn't think was a good album." Raf 'Baker Street' Ravenscroft is the sax-player.

PARANOID EYES (Waters)- A highly orchestrated number reflecting the Hero's fears ends the first vinyl side of *The Final Cut* on a very downbeat note. The brown and mild of the lyric puzzled overseas listeners who were unaware that this was a reference to a mix of beer which had been a favourite with the war generation.

GET YOUR FILTHY HANDS OFF MY DESERT (Waters) - In echoes of *Money*, a missile moves from speaker to speaker in an impressive sound effect to open side two. This is followed, in complete contrast, by Waters singing over a string section. The lyrics are infinitely better than the music.

THE FLETCHER MEMORIAL HOME (Waters) The title refers to Waters' father, Eric Fletcher Waters, who was killed in action in 1944 and whose demise was re-visited in *The Wall* movie song *When The Tigers Broke Free*. Both these titles were included on *Echoes - The Best Of Pink Floyd* in late 2001 after some poker-style bargaining on the track listing between Gilmour and Waters.

SOUTHAMPTON DOCK (Waters) - Roger Waters pinpointed this song, depicting a war widow (echoes of his own mother?) waving the troopships away to the Falklands, as a personal highlight of the album. Lyrically it's a masterpiece but again let down by the lack of musical light and shade.

FINAL CUT (Waters) - The final repeated line of the chorus, 'Oh Maggie, Maggie - what have we done' refers to Conservative Prime Minister Margaret Thatcher, recently responsible for sending troops to reclaim the Falklands from Argentina. Far too much of it's time for most and too political for many others this track dates the album to the politics of Britian in the early eighties and makes it difficult to appreciate in the 21st Century.

NOT NOW JOHN (Waters) - Released in censored form as a single in May 1983, the line 'Fuck all that' becoming 'Stuff all that', this became an unlikely hit - the Floyd's fifth UK chart single in 16 years. Waters described it as "a very schizophrenic song," saying he identified with the character singing who was "irritated by all the whining and the moaning about how desperate things are." But then a second voice enters…

TWO SUNS IN THE SUNSET (Waters) - The second sun in the title here is clearly the fireball of a nuclear explosion, as Roger Waters contemplates the moment the fabled 'button' is finally pushed. Happily, the 21st century has been lived, so far, out of the shadow of a nuclear superpower stand-off, but in 1983 the real possibility of Mutually Assured Destruction was in the minds of many. A suitably dismal conclusion to a downbeat album which lived down to its title.

Chapter 15
A MOMENTARY LAPSE OF REASON

Despite all of the success which Pink Floyd had enjoyed, in 1986 Roger Waters was far from happy with the state of affairs behind the scenes. In particular he had grown to mistrust Steve O'Rourke's judgement as the manager of the band and now sought to terminate his management agreement with O'Rourke.

Roger had one eye on his projected solo career and he was astute enough to recognise that any future solo work under the Roger Waters banner would always be regarded as a filler marking time before the release of the main event in the form of the next Pink Floyd album. As always, Roger had thrown his heart and soul into the creation and touring of *The Pros And Cons of Hitchhiking* but the public reaction had been confused and overshadowed by requests for information on the

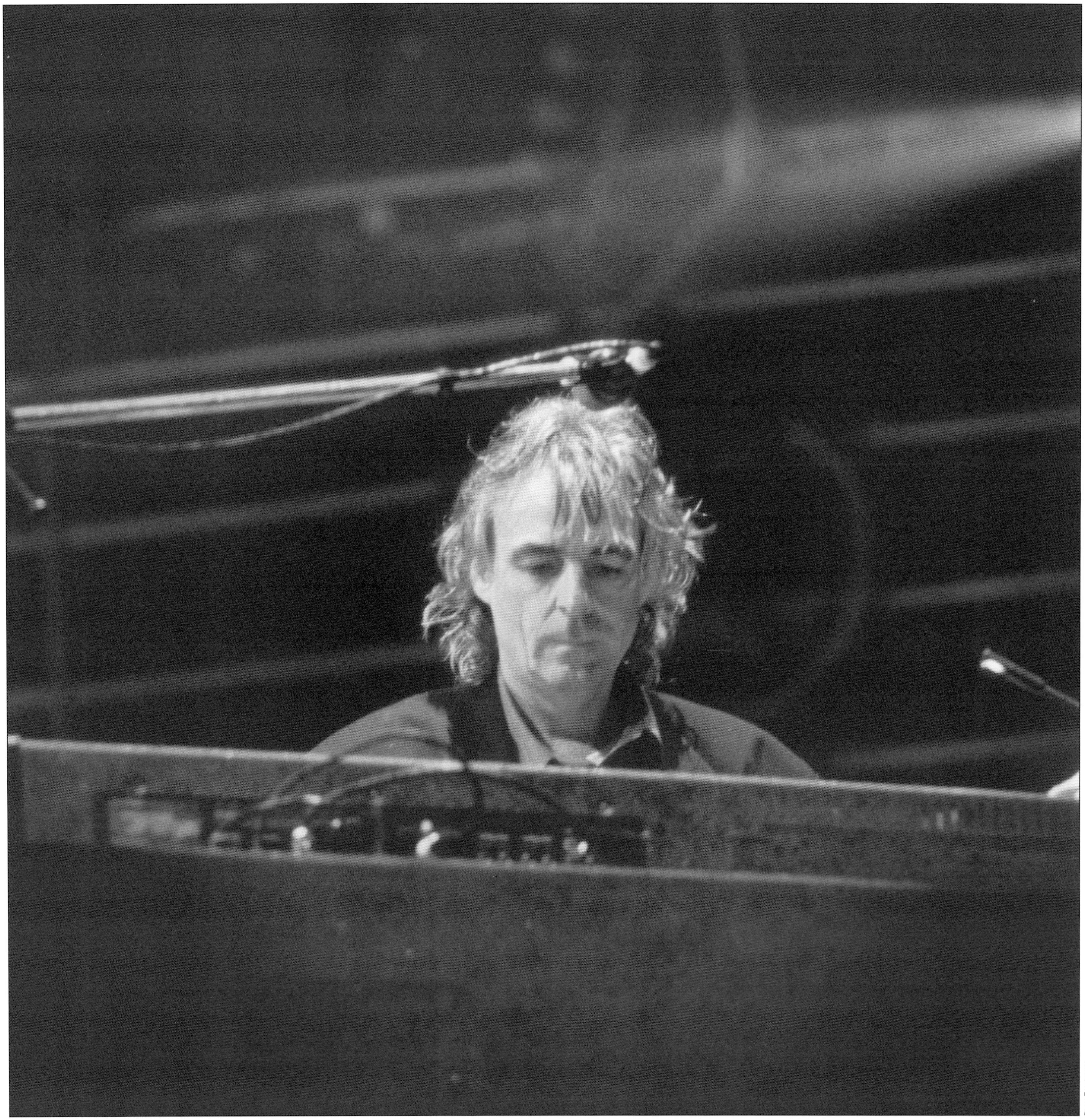

Rex Features

next Floyd project. Roger had clearly taken advice on how to resolve the issue, but he seems to have received some of the worst counsel in history. In order to assist his campaign to terminate his deal with O'Rourke Roger was advised to write to EMI and CBS records stating that he would no longer record with Mason, Gilmour or Pink Floyd.

The implausible logic of the ill conceived scheme seems to have run along the following lines; if Pink Floyd was to be dissolved O'Rourke's managerial function would also be at an end leaving Roger to carry on with his solo career without the spectre of Pink Floyd haunting his every step. The master plan however seems to have made no provison whatsoever for the wishes of the other members. The entire plan seems to have all hinged on Gilmour and Mason simply rolling over and agreeing that Waters was the sole creative force in the band and that without him Pink Floyd was officially and very legally dead. In retrospect it is almost unbelievable that such an unlikely scheme could be considered workable, but somehow Roger's advisors seem to have convinced him that there was a chance that the plan could actually succeed in all its lame brained glory. Consequently in October 1986 Roger's legal team trooped into the High Court and began their attempt to have the Pink Floyd partnership wound up on the dubious grounds that without his input the band was a spent creative force. The great Roger Waters had after all given notice that he would no longer record with Pink Floyd and it was now formally moved that the court should declare that the band should be officially wound up and that furthermore no-one should be allowed to use the name.

Roger's legal team backed up their court assault with a PR campaign which involved setting out their warped reasoning for the benefit of the press. *The Daily Mail* was just one of the many nationals in October 1986 which gave the case extensive coverage, but right from the outset it is clear that the writer was far from convinced. "Without consulting his former colleagues, Pink Floyd co-founder Roger Waters, 42, has just made a High Court application to finally kill off the super group which is reputed to have sold more records than even the Beatles. Bass guitarist Waters wants to prevent the name from being used again and a spokesman says 'Roger believes the group has become a spent force creatively. This should be recognised and if the group splits up there is always the question of who retains the rights to the name. This action will avoid any misunderstandings because the band Pink Floyd will then no longer exist.'"

Tellingly *The Mail* article contained the observation "It is not clear if the others will defend the action." All of this seems to have come as a major surprise to Gilmour and Mason. Their first reaction was to issue a press statement of their own which simply said "Pink Floyd are alive and well and recording in England." The next stage was to mount a proper legal defence. In reality this prevented little real difficulty as it was obvious to all but the most biased observer that the incumbent Floyd's could not be prevented from working and were almost certain to emerge triumphant. Much to Roger's surprise Gilmour and Mason declared that they did indeed intend to soldier on without him. They made it clear they had no intention of retiring and felt they were still entitled to use the all important Pink Floyd brand name. Clearly the remaining Floyds were in the driving seat and it soon became obvious that Roger had a legal mountain to climb. In order to strengthen their claim further, Gilmour and Mason also brought a rehabilitated Rick Wright back into the fold. This had to be done with a great deal of care as it was now apparent that a clause in Wright's leaving agreement prevented him from re-joining the band. There were also tax considerations and the resultant album erred on the side of caution by printing a "band" picture featuring Gilmour and Mason only, with Wright credited as a side man only.

As the legal war dragged on, Gilmour reluctantly moved on to the attack and in conversation with Nicky Horne of London's Capital Radio in October 1987 he spelled out his sense of frustration and the heavy heart with which he was drawn in to all of this nonsense. "I think it's rather unnecessary. There's been many many years together when we have achieved a lot together, and it's a shame when anyone wants to leave of course. But, everyone has to do what they want to do, and of course that's their decision. What is sad and unneccessary about it is trying to prevent anyone else from carrying on with their legitimate artistic and business endeavours."

The outcome was exactly as predicted, no court in the world would have stopped the remaining Floyd members from pursuing their careers and Waters was forced into an embarrassing climb down which allowed him to release the *When The Wind Blows* soundtrack on Virgin Records in return for giving up all claims to the Pink Floyd name.

Roger's advice had been truly disastrous and had resulted in his loosing the very thing he sought to protect, as David Gilmour later explained to Capital Radio's Nicky Horn. "EMI made him sign a piece of paper on the case saying essentially, if you want to put this soundtrack out on another label, not to interfere with Pink Floyd being Pink Floyd, or pursue any activities in the name of Pink Floyd- which Roger agreed to."

It was now that Floyd embarked on one of the most crucial albums in the band's career.

Gilmour and Mason had been sketching out ideas together since October 1986 but there was clearly more than a grain of truth in Roger's claim that the band was a spent force creatively. Without a doubt the Gilmour/Mason axis was struggling to deliver the goods and all the stops had to be pulled out in the form of 18 additional musicians plus co-writers in abundance and of course the return of Bob Ezrin who rubbed salt into Waters wounds by rejecting the proposal that he should work on Radio KAOS in favour of the album which would ultimately emerge as *A Momentary Lapse Of Reason*. There was a huge appetite for Pink Floyd's music and a colossal amount of goodwill. The fans really wanted something which sounded like the Floyd of old and sensing the mood, David Gilmour after an immense effort was able to produce an album which just about passed muster.

Recording was completed in March 1987 after 7 months work, but there was a further 3 months of post production work before the album was finally declared complete. It had certainly been a diifcult birth and the album had gone through numerous incarnations including a tentative stab at a concept album which had been worked up between Gilmour and Eric Stewart of 10 CC fame. Eventually the idea of a concept album was abandoned and for the first time since *Meddle*, Pink Floyd unveiled an album comprising a number of diverse compositions with no overall theme to glue the whole work together.

The estranged Roger Water's notoriously dismissed the album as a "facsimile" of the Floyd sound. The fans reaction may well have been positive over all, but musically the album only just passed the quality threshold, the few stand out tracks were outweighed by the make weights but in quality terms the album was just about good enough.

The music may have been mediocre but the presentation of the album was world class. Storm Thorgeson's Hipgnosis partnership had been dissolved after being dropped for both *The Wall* and *The Final Cut*, but Gilmour was keen to re-establish the link with the designer who was so readily associated with Floyd's greatest work. Storm repaid the compliment by producing some of his best ever work and pulled out all the stops with a breathtaking sleeve and an arresting series of promotional films including an ambitious take on *Learning to Fly* set in the plains of Canada.

Pink Floyd promotional films had come a long way since *Point Me At The Sky* had failed so miserably as a single but it's interesting to note that 20 years on *Learning to Fly* tackled the same subject matter as *Point Me At The Sky* with an equal lack of success in the charts. It seems that the singles buying public just don't warm to songs about the hobbies of rich millionaires. The lesson seems to be that flying is a wonderful and exhilarating experience for those involved, but a somewhat less edifying subject for the average earthbound singles buyer. Despite this minor disappointment, on the whole the reaction of the fans remained positive. With Waters now out of the band Gilmour was determined to carry on. Having overcome the legal obstacles placed in his way the album had to be superb. It wasn't. It was a long way short of being a world beater; but crucially it felt like a Floyd album and in any event it was certainly superior to *The Final Cut*.

Even Gilmour admitted this was not the best Pink Floyd album ever made, but as he truthfully asserted "I gave it the best damn shot I could." It was well received by the Floyd fan base and laid the seeds for the colossal concerts which would see the Floyd juggernaut eclipse Roger Waters solo career. The absent Waters huffily proclaimed that it was little more than an artful facsimile of Pink Floyd. In conversation with David Fricke for *Rolling Stone* in October 1987 Water's expanded further on the new album. "I think it's a very facile, but quite clever forgery. If you don't listen to it too closely it does sound like Pink Floyd. It's got Dave Gilmour playing guitar. And with the considered intention of setting out to make something that sounds like everyone's conception of a Pink Floyd record, it's inevitable that you will achieve that limited goal. I think the songs are poor in general. The lyrics I can't believe."

Fricke himself was far more generous when it came to giving his own views on the album in the same *Rolling Stone* article. "The album is aurally sumptuous and texturally seductive lacking the strident pedagogical edge of *The Wall* or *The Final Cut* which will be reassuring to anyone who was spellbound by the glacial grandeur of *Meddle* or the extended instrumental passages of *Shine On You Crazy Diamond*. With *On The Turning Away* Floyd may also have a hit single of Money proportions. A caressing ballad with a glowing chorus and climactic Gilmour guitar, it is more openly hopeful and loving than anything Waters allowed himself to write for the Floyd."

The Music

SIGNS OF LIFE *(Gilmour/Ezrin)* - With Gilmour's intention "to show the world look, we're still here!" after Waters' departure, one would expect the first track to be a real statement of intent. Perverse to the end, the Floyd went with the sound of a rowing boat and Nick Mason's voice atop guitar and synth backing. The album was nearly called *Signs*

Of Life but changed late on, much to the chagrin of pen-sharpening music writers for whom it would have been a gift from the gods: 'No Signs Of Life from Floyd!

LEARNING TO FLY *(Gilmour/Moore/Ezrin/Carin)* - A fine slice of the new, radio-friendly Pink Floyd, co-written with (among others) Jon Carin, a keyboard player who, says Gilmour, "can do Rick Wright better than Rick can." By the end of the tour supporting this album, Wright had regained the self-confidence Gilmour claimed had been eroded under the previous regime.

THE DOGS OF WAR *(Gilmour/Moore)* Lyricist Anthony Moore borrowed this title from thriller novelist Frederick Forsyth, who himself purloined it from William Shakespeare. The subject-matter is not Julius Caesar, however, but Forsyth's mercenary soldiers. Saxophone is contributed by Scott Page.

ONE SLIP *(Gilmour/Manzanera)* - Long-time friend and former Roxy Music guitarist Phil Manzanera was Gilmour's collaborator here - and unusually Gilmour is the wordsmith of the partnership. Indeed, a phrase from this would name the album which, as previously mentioned, bore the working title of *Signs Of Life*. *One Slip* would also be the third single to be released.

ON THE TURNING AWAY *(Gilmour/Moore)* - The almost folky, unaccompanied introduction to this song soon proves misleading as it opens out into more typical Floyd. Second single from the album, an Atlanta-recorded live version being a CD/12-inch bonus.

YET ANOTHER MOVIE, /ROUND AND AROUND *(Gilmour/Leonard)* - Less a two-part song as one with an instrumental play out, not to mention movie snippets from Messrs Brando (On The Waterfront) and Bogart/Bergman (Casablanca). Co-writer Pat Leonard was an American keyboardist/producer/songwriter hitherto best-known for work with Madonna.

A NEW MACHINE PART 1 *(Gilmour)* - No relation to *Welcome To The Machine*, this shares its non-human like qualities with a disembodied vocal treated with a decoder. This track never really gets going musically, but nevertheless stays in the memory as a kind of primal scream.

TERMINAL FROST *(Gilmour)* - An instrumental apart from the odd wordless vocal that gave Gilmour the time and space to etch his trademark guitar patterns on the windscreen. Sparkling sax and keyboards enliven the middle section but the track begins to overstay it's welcome soon after.

A NEW MACHINE PART 2 *(Gilmour)* - An unremarkable bookend for the unremarkable Terminal Frost instrumental.

SORROW *(Gilmour)* - The album's longest track and one of its more substantial songs. Unusually, Gilmour not only began with a lyric but wrote it himself. The theme of broken promises leads to an automatic connection with Roger Waters (denied, as ever, by Gilmour), but a mighty guitar solo from the maestro closes the album on a satisfying note.

Regardless of the over all quality of the new material the tour proved a huge success and spawned the live album *The Delicate Sound of Thunder* and also the film of the tour which was released on video. The film fails to capture the magnificence of the stage show and compared to the intimate earthy qualities of the Pompeii film the proceedings feel cold and distant. There is a clinical air to the proceedings and despite all of the thought and craft which went into the film there is a distinct impression that the events lack soul. Robert Christgau and Carola Dibbel reviewed the film for the American magazine *Video Review* and neatly encapsulated the problems with this particular film. "We had hopes for Pink Floyd's concert video even though we're not fans of their recent music. This was the model art-school band, and through psychedelic overload, studio obsession, and interpersonal abuse they'd retained their flair for the visual. Their graphic intelligence (especially in the great Hipgnosis covers of the '70s) is unequalled in rock, and they've always had a sense of spectacle - concocting mammoth animations and vast props where workaday rockers posture inanely in the eye of the arena. Perhaps, we thought, they'd defeat the contradictions of the concert-video form as well. But instead they succumb to them. Since the mid-'80s, the rest of the band has been at odds with onetime front man Roger Waters, and the 1987 tour video documentary was designed to show that Floyd didn't need *Another Brick* in *The Wall*. But like the album it promoted, which contributes five consecutive songs to a disastrously dreary opening, all it proved was that guitarist David Gilmour couldn't write Waters' grocery list. Singing has been less of an issue - Floyd's stately, impersonal music doesn't call for much emotion or timbre or melodic acuity. But in concert, it's always lived or died with the visuals, and the enormous, slow-moving effects that complement the songs' ersatz grandeur live are impossible to reproduce on a television screen. Musicians and audience here are better-shot than is customary, and while the filmic distractions provided - South African clips under *Us and Them*, lost-in-an-endless-corridor imagery - are tinged with Floyd's usual pretensions, they certainly look good. It's just that video scale trivializes them - or else makes clear that there wasn't much behind them to begin with. We don't know which, and we don't care. Pink Floyd's audience is now a kind of permanent megacult. *Delicate Sound of Thunder* is for their eyes only."

At the conclusion of the *Delicate Sound Of Thunder* tour the band took a well earned rest. As Gilmour triumphantly declared to *Q* magazine in September 1990, "We wanted to leave no-one in any doubt that we were still in business and meant business-and no one was going to stop us." With the album and tour Pink Floyd had proved they could still make memorable music and they could more than hold their own in the live arena. The task now was to produce an album which was worthy of the legacy.

Chapter 18
THE DIVISION BELL

A Momentary Lapse of Reason had firmly re-established Pink Floyd as a global force, however it clearly did not represent the band's best work. The next album was to address that criticism. After one of the longest gestation periods in the history of rock music, in 1994 after a seven year wait Pink Floyd were at last ready to unveil their new album. There was certainly a great deal at stake. At this rate of output it was clear to many that this could well be the last Floyd album, and the band had yet to produce an album which stood comparison with the best of the Roger Waters era. If the Floyd were indeed to go out on a high the results had to be convincing and to a large extent they were. Gilmour is on record as saying he is unwilling to "lift that weight again," so this looks increasingly likely to be the Floyd swan-song. It is certainly a fitting end to a remarkable career.

The Division Bell was a genuine group effort with all threee musicians gelling brilliantly in the studio where they were again re-united with Bob Ezrin, the architect of their greatest triumphs now guesting as a musician. Released in April 1994 *The Division Bell* was an altogether superior effort. Careful, studied and mannered the album flows together as a suite of songs. There are no dramatic dynamic peaks and troughs or extremes of tempo but the smooth majestic flow of the music worked it's magic on audiences on both sides of the Atlantic, and for the first time in history Pink Floyd had an album which went to number one in both Britain and America.

The theme of this album, the second post-Waters studio venture, was non-communication, "but," insisted Dave Gilmour in a 1995 interview with *Mojo*, "we're not trying to bash anyone over the head with it." Frankly this is not an album which is likely to bash anyone over the head with anything. There is a pleasant ethereal drifting quality to the whole record which seems to echo the gentle currents of the River Thames echoing against the sides of the Astoria, the converted houseboat where the album was conceived.

The recording process began in 1993 aboard the Astoria which was now converted into a studio and moored permanently on the River Thames. Gilmour had recently undergone the trauma of a divorce, and journalist Polly Sampson, his new wife-to-be, contributed a great deal of the lyrics; an input which Gilmour has described as "invaluable" but which was dismissed by a still bitter Roger Waters as, "too Spinal Tap for words."

With a really fine album under their belt it was now time for Floyd to get back out on the road and demonstrate that the group were not only masters of the recording studio they were also masters of the live arena. The stunning impact of *The Delicate Sound Of Thunder* still reverberated around the music world. In the course of over 200 concerts Floyd had played to over 4.25 million fans grossing in the region of £80 million in combined tickets and merchandise sales. Trailing in the wake of Pink Floyd, lesser artists such as U2 had attempted to produce a similar level of spectacle, but they would never be able to aspire to Pink Floyd for musical content. Nonetheless in terms of rock shows, by 1994 the bar had been set very high indeed. Pink Floyd were about to demonstrate once again that they were innovators and visionaries when it came to the live arena. This was the brand which set the bench mark for a whole industry and Gilmour was well aware of the overwhelming responsibility to a powerful legacy which demanded that each Pink Floyd tour was not just better than the last but also better than everyone else in the rock world.

To ensure that the shows were bigger and better than anything which had ever been seen in the rock world Pink Floyd re-enlisted the help of designer Mark Fisher and brought back lighting designer Marc Brickman. In a nod to the roots of the band Floyd had re-introduced *Astronomy Domine* into the set and even called on the services of Peter Wyne-Wilson who had created the liquid ink patterns which had entranced audiences in their UFO days. For this amazing run of shows it was initially agreed that there would be no such thing as a budget. If

Rex Features

the spectacle demanded it then Floyd would provide it. The demands of the show soon grew to encompass a series of new 35mm animated films mixed with live action films especially commissioned from Storm Thorgerson. The list of equipment needed soon grew to epic proportions incorporating a massive steel supporting arch, robotic moving lights, 40 foot projection screen, 400 Vari-Lights, 300 loud speakers, a 70mm Imax Front projector, 35mm rear projector and the latest coloured light laser projectors. All of the gear took three aircraft to transport and these were the largest aircraft in the skies, two 747s and one Russian Antonovv freighter. The show required a staff of 200 to operate the myriad of visual effects which were perfectly synchronised to the music produced by a troupe of 11 musicians. Together all of this combined to deliver the ultimate concert experience to a combined audience of 5.3 million concert goers.

With the enormous scale of the production even the Floyd began to get nervous. As the bills continued to mount, at the urging of Steve O'Rourke, and a tour sponsor was drafted in. Volkswagen, the German car manufacturer, was delighted to be associated with a tour which so closely fitted their target audience. Although the financial input was undoubtedly welcome, Gilmour was unhappy having to bow and scrape to the men in suits. As he told *Mojo* in 1995, "not having thought it through entirely, I didn't want them to be able to say they have a connection with Pink Floyd, that they are part of our successs. We will not do it again."

Despite the reservations Gilmour may have had, Volkswagen undeniably now had more than just a "connection" with Pink Floyd. Nick Mason had a hand in designing the interior for the "Pink Floyd Special Edition VW Golf" which went on sale to coincide with the tour. All 5.3 million tickets also bore the legend "Volkswagen presents Pink Floyd In Concert". But although Gilmour had his concerns, none of this seems to have bothered the fans one bit, they recognised that they were privileged to witness the most imposing rock spectacle ever mounted against the backdrop of the finest rock music ever composed …and all for just twenty five quid!

The show itself included the psychedelic delights of *Astronomy Domine* from *Piper At the Gates of Dawn* and early concerts also included a sublime rendition of *Echoes* (although the band soon tired of the piece and replaced it with the more familiar *Shine On You Crazy Diamond*) besides a generous sprinkling of the new album and a large portion of *Dark Side of The Moon*. As the tour developed and the set list evolved the album began to be played in its entirety.

With its mind boggling scale, technically perfect sound reproduction and dazzling combinations of mesmerising lights, lasers and film projections allied to brilliant music, *The Division Bell* tour could hardly fail to impress; but the written word simply cannot convey the awesome power of actually being present at these stunning concerts.

By turns, majestic, imposing, disturbing and exciting *The Division Bell* tour encompassed all that was great about Pink Floyd. The visual effects complimented and enhanced the music in such a perfect manner that the overall effect of the combination of the two was simply overwhelming. After this there was simply nowhere else to go. Floyd had achieved perfection.

The Music

CLUSTER ONE *(Wright/Gilmour)* - A very rare Wright/Gilmour writing credit kicks off an album which drummer Nick Mason claimed "has more of the feel of *Meddle* than anything else we've done since." This brilliant call and response composition is based on the wonderful interplay behind Certainly. Mason was again playing drums on most tracks although there was still some outside assistance from Gary Wallis. Wright's contributions on the album were pleasingly audible and distinctive. The simple three note theme of *Cluster One* is unusual and carries the Floyd tradition of restraint to new levels by allowing the three notes to be repeated at a time when the listener's brain is screaming to fill in the fourth note to complete the suggested figure.

WHAT DO YOU WANT FROM ME *(Music:Gilmour/Wright- Lyrics:Gilmour/Samson)* - The first Pink Floyd song to feature lyrics from newspaper journalist Polly Samson, now known as Mrs David Gilmour, though both she and Dave are credited; Gilmour and Wright wrote the music. Legend has it the title came from an early marital disagreement!

POLES APART *(Music:Gilmour -Lyrics:Gilmour/ Samson/Laird-Clowes)* - Assistance is rendered here from Nick Laird-Clowes, best known for his tenure as frontman with the Dream Academy. Their *Life In A Northern Town* was homage to the late, great Nick Drake, so can we assume the former colleague who has 'lost the light in your eyes' is Syd Barrett? "Who knows?" says Gilmour. "I like to let the lyrics speak for themselves." And of course he didn't write them! Polly Samson identifies Syd in the first verse, Roger in the second.

MAROONED *(Music: Gilmour/Wright)* - A moody instrumental which confirms co-writer Rick Wright back and functioning as a fully paid-up Floyd member, having recorded *Momentary Lapse* as a session man. A track excerpt deservedly appeared on the *Best Of, Echoes*, while the live version would be played to back projections.

A GREAT DAY FOR FREEDOM *(Music: Gilmour - Lyrics: Gilmour/Samson)* - Placed near the front of the running order for the 1994 tour, this quickly became a big fan favourite. To judge from the newspaper headline visible in the booklet, it was inspired by the felling of the Berlin Wall. In response to relentless and rather crass questioning David Gilmour dismissed any connection with the Roger Waters *Wall* show at that venue which was still fresh in the memory.

WEARING THE INSIDE OUT *(Music: Wright - Lyrics: Moore)* - Rick Wright's first totally self-written Floyd tune (with lyrics from Anthony Moore) also features the familiar saxophone of Dick Parry. Wright, Gilmour and backing singers share vocals on a song that may well be autobiographical but, for whatever reason, would not make it to the live arena possibly because this lightweight piece sounds uncannily like Canterbury rockers Caravan.

TAKE IT BACK *(Music: Gilmour/Ezrin - Lyrics: Gilmour/Samson/Laird-Clowes)* - Producer Bob Ezrin, who first got involved with the Floyd during *The Wall*, crops up in the writing credits of a song that was one of 40 or so routined on Gilmour's houseboat studio on the Thames before coming to full fruition, a track which rapidly became an audience favourite when performed live and was the lead single from the album.

COMING BACK TO LIFE *(Music: Gilmour)* - Unusual in having a lyric composed by Dave Gilmour to match his music, this is a love poem to wife Polly Samson: "The things you say and the things you do surround me." Oh, and the "dangerous but irresistible pastime" referred to "is sex, obviously," he confirms. Maybe we should draw the curtain and leave them to it!

KEEP TALKING *(Music: Gilmour/Wright - Lyrics: Gilmour/Samson)* - The lyrical thread that runs through *The Division Bell* is very much present here. Guest 'vocalist' is Professor Stephen Hawking of *A Brief History Of Time* fame: Dave would use a Peter Frampton-style 'voicebox' to approximate the sound of Hawking on stage.

LOST FOR WORDS *(Music: Gilmour - Lyrics: Gilmour/Samson)* - If *How Do You Sleep* was Lennon's vitriolic note to McCartney, then this is widely interpreted as Gilmour's message to his former partner in song. The lyrics talk of offering to wipe the slate clean, only to be told to "go fuck myself". All such acrimony was finally buried among the friendship of the 2005 Live 8 concert.

HIGH HOPES *(Music: Gilmour - Lyrics: Gilmour/Samson)* Despite the seemingly optimistic title, the bell that tolls at the end of this track is an ominous portent - particularly given the decade of non-recording that has followed. Gilmour describes its creation - in just one studio day - as 'a moment when something happens quickly and wonderfully." Released as a double A-side with *Keep Talking*, but not a major hit.

Floyd fans were delighted with the album, but the same cannot be said for the press. This review by David Bennun published in *Melody Maker* in April 16th sums up the condescending attitude of many of the reviews. "At a secret moonlight ceremony in a small rural churchyard, the reviews editor threw back his cowl and presented to me, on a hempen cushion emblazoned with prisms, the new Pink Floyd album. 'Take this, Brother' he intoned, 'may it serve you well.'

"I raised my right hand and gave him the ritual response.

"'Will Thursday be OK?'

"Onto the coven stereo it went and, bliss of bliss, the rumours were true. A return to the elegant melancholia of *Wish You Were Here*. Hanging in the air like far-off thunderclouds, a track to rank with the most fragrant of modern ambient. A dignified, descending piano phrase curlicued with the distilled anguish of David Gilmour's guitar. *Cluster One*. Magnificent. Unfortunate, then, that the remaining hour should bring all the joy of chewing on a bucket of gravel. This is the frustrating thing. Unlike his contemporaries, most of whom seem to have no clue as to what made their music good in the first place, Gilmour must have a clear idea why people who were but a twinkle in free love's eye when the Floyd were founded cherish those early '70s soundscapes. The delicacy of the instrumental, *Marooned*, which paraphrases *Dark Side of The Moon* to just the right degree, is a dead giveaway. It's as if he's dropping hints, amid the drear and desolate stodge that makes up most of the album, that he can still work magic.

"It's only fair to point out, reading through the lyrics, that *The Division Bell* is a work of genuine gloom. Nobody could accuse Gilmour of being self-satisfied. Bitter, morose and disillusioned, more like it. I say 'reading through the lyrics' because you will quite possibly perish from boredom if you attempt to find this out by listening to the songs themselves. Next to *The Division Bell*, 1987's monumentally turgid Floyd comeback, *A Momentary Lapse of Reason*, sparkles in the memory as a refreshing fountain of light-headed verve. Stupid, I know, to expect any better. And infuriating that the album should bait us with the prospect of it. I can, it teases, but I won't. Sit down and eat your suet.

"No, thanks."

By this stage in their career the odd bad review, even one as negative as that published in *Melody Maker*, could do nothing to affect the Pink Floyd juggernaut. To accompany *The Division Bell* tour there was

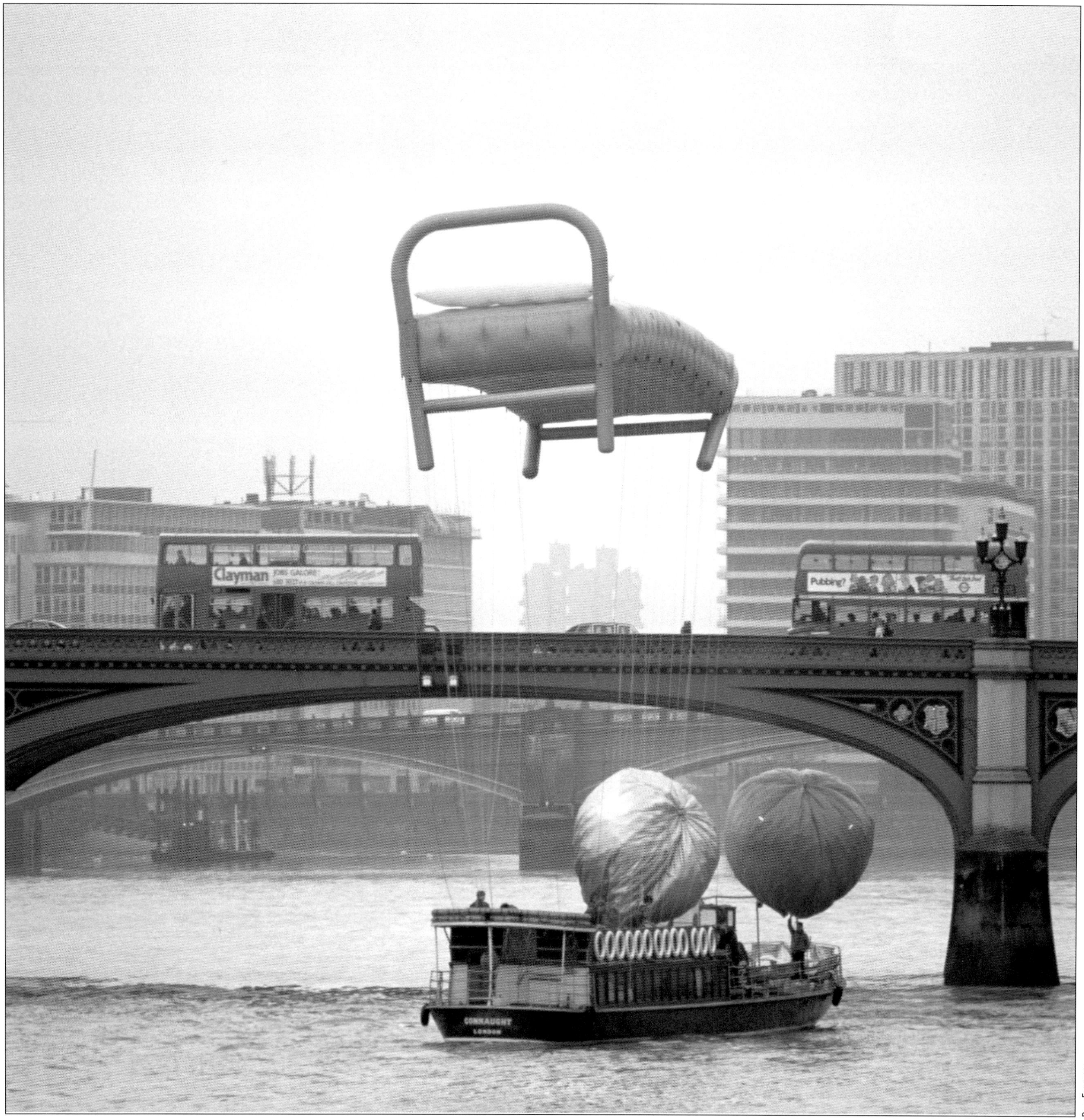

Rex Features

the now inevitable live album and film, this time entitled *Pulse*. *Pulse* was an infinitely superior effort to *Delicate Sound Of Thunder* in every respect. The music is of course flawless and in the film the stage presentation is mind blowing. For once the cameras come close to capturing some of that scale and grandeur of the awesome spectacle which was Floyd in concert. It is interesting to note that in the summer of 2005, *Pulse* was being revved up and fast tracked for a post Live 8 DVD release while *Delicate Sound Of Thunder* continues to lie unmolested in the vaults.

From a fan point of view there was little to set real life pulses racing over the new offering. These were all wonderfully recorded versions of songs which were flawlessly performed by a troupe of remarkably talented artistes, but it was something which had been heard many many times before. There seemed to be very little point in the live album beyond the desire on the part of the fans to be able to buy something with the Floyd name attached and the willingness of the label to sell it to them. Even the packaging in all it's elaborate glory doesn't quite hit the mark. There is a feeling that the whole thing was almost too perfect, too Floydian.

Chapter 19
IS THERE ANYBODY OUT THERE?

From the very outset, Roger Waters had clearly detailed his plans for a Wall album, a Wall stage show and a Wall movie. At no point was there ever a mention of a live album. Then suddenly in the year 2000 without much of the usual fanfare which surrounds these things there appeared a lavishly illustrated double boxed CD entitled Is There Anybody Out There? Why this offspring of a broken marriage should suddenly appear after 20 years in the vaults is an interesting point. The completists of course would obviously jump at the chance to have a proper record of this important era in Floyd history; and it certainly put the brakes on The Wall bootleg industry, even if it was a generation too late. The real answer seems to lie in the straight forward commercial logic of the record companies.

The huge Pink Floyd audience had been starved of new product since the release of Pulse in 1995 and with the band no longer active only live recordings were now available to slake the thirst for all things Floyd, the live tapes of The Wall presented a legitimate "new" release which also provided an interesting historical document. In the process the fans got a genuinely fresh perspective on an album which had now grown so familiar.

Gerald Scarfe's original design for the album sleeve had been bold and iconic, but in the intervening years Storm Thorgeson had been shrewdly drafted back in to the fold to endorse the post-waters Floyd. As *The Wall* in all of its incarnations carried the visual stamp of Gerald Scarfe's design the question of who should design the packaging was to prove a thorny one. With David Gilmour now the de facto leader in the band Thorgerson was brought in to perform his usual Floyd task and produce the packaging. In his book *Mind Over Matter,* Storm recalled his ambivalent feelings on being asked to design the CD release. The mental questions he posed himself were exactly the same as those posed by the fans. "I get to work on *The Wall*…Several questions might spring to mind: like why now? Why this and not a new studio album? Why something from the vaults? Would anybody buy such a thing? Who was behind it? Was Roger top man since it was largely his creation? Or was it David since it was a Pink Floyd project and Roger is no longer officially in the band…If you need a job to pay the rent, like me, then you don't ask too many of these questions out loud..."

For Roger Waters, the creation of his masterpiece had been a painful experience. Revisiting the work was equally painful. As old memories stirred he felt no satisfaction and merely growing unease as he explained to Sylvie Simmons for the *Mojo* feature designed to accompany the album's release. "Since this first upsurge of as-near-as-dammit communal Waters-Gilmour-Mason-Wright activity in the best part of two decades, the web has been buzzing with speculation of a thawing of tensions: a reunion; a millennium show; the Pyramids. 'Ugh!' Roger Waters shudders. 'The idea of having to stay in this big bowl of porridge swimming around - no, I'm going to get out, hose myself down, ah, that's better. Now I can get on with my life. The idea of getting involved with any of them again - and you can imagine, they're constantly trying to get me to leap back into the porridge - even doing this live album, the sleevenotes, it's brought it all back to me how crazy it all is. I don't want anything to do with it or them.' His distaste is palpable."

Roger was not alone in finding the process distasteful. Storm Thorgeson was soon confronted with the suffocating politics which seemed to surround the construction of every element of *The Wall*, even 20 years after it's creation. "What was not so easy to settle, of course, was the politics. Roger was the progenitor, the author, and therefore his opinions were very important. He was not however in charge and could be outvoted if David and Nick decided to do so. David and Nick were respectful of Roger's authorship, but not if it turned to dictatorship. "Roger refused to talk with any of the others, but agreed that the record be released. He reluctantly accepted that I put the whole thing together, but wouldn't talk to me either. The respective managers (Mark Fenwick and Steve O'Rourke) did talk, but usually through expediency. Roger wanted pal Nick Sedgwick to organise the text (this was OK), wanted Gerald Scarfe involved (partially OK) and wanted credit listing like the concert programme (not OK)."

More diplomacy than design perhaps. Things were eventually agreed, but not before the album release was delayed.

Fortunately the four life masks which had been created for the surrogate band were still around and a compromise was finally reached when it was agreed that these relics would form the basis for the new sleeve design. "Finally Roger agreed to the life masks that David and Nick already liked and which were used in the actual show by the surrogate band pretending to be Pink Floyd."

As the old saying goes "a camel is just a horse designed by a committee," and the packaging for *In The Flesh* definitely suffers from the presence of too many contrasting commands and viewpoints. There are elements of Scarfe present in the package transformed into "wall paper" (geddit?) by Thorgeson and the overall effect is of an uneasy mix of the two styles. Since his return to the Floyd fold Thorgeson had been responsible for some amazing work which must rank as some of the best of his career. *A Momentary Lapse Of Reason*, *The Delicate Sound of Thunder*, *The Division Bell*, *Pulse* and *Echoes* all benefited from world class designs. *In the Flesh* unfortunately falls a long way short of the others and the confused chain of command cannot have helped matters.

The recording of the show starts with a fake announcer welcoming the audience to Earl's Court who is rudely interrupted by the surrogate Floyd crashing into *In The Flesh?* The same device in distorted form is reprised for *In The Flesh* on the second disc. The live shows slavishly followed the plan of the studio album with only minor departures. The chief reason for fans buying the album is therefore either as an exercise in nostalgia for those who were there, or for the curiosity of those who weren't to explore the differences between the studio sound and how the music was re-arranged for the stage. In either case *In The Flesh* re-pays the investment handsomely. Without a doubt *The Wall* sounds very different on stage even if it is the same backing tapes as the ones on the album which are re-played in their familiar positions.

Besides the stage announcement, the first of the new additions on disc one is the presence of *What Shall We Do Now*. The track was dropped from the vinyl album due to space constraints and it's fairly easy to see why this song would be chosen. Lyrically it explores much the same territory as *Empty Spaces* and it's another of Roger Waters' list songs. Waters has occasionally demonstrated a tendency to produce lyrics which take the form of a list first demonstrating the technique with *Echoes* and repeating it soon after for *Eclipse* on *Dark Side of The Moon* which begins with-

All that you touch
All that you see
All that you taste
All that you feel

On the *Animals* album *Dogs* had concluded with a verse which begins:
Who was born in a house full of pain.
Who was trained not to spit in the fan.
Who was told what to do by the man.

What Shall We Do Now lists the ever more bizarre alternatives under an increasingly hysterical vocal from Waters.

Shall we buy a new guitar?
Shall we drive a more powerful car?
Shall we work straight through the night?

As the list grows the pitch keeps rising, the questions go on coming at us until we reach the point of "keep people as pets?" by this stage the voice has begun to grate and actually becomes almost painful to listen to as the pitch ascends. The increasing mood of hysteria was of course the outcome planned by Waters. Thanks to the presence of Scarfe's wonderful animation the piece succeeds brilliantly in the film, it works far less well on record.

The live shows made room on *Young Lust* from the soon to be departed Richard Wright which ably demonstrated how different things might have been had Wright and Waters been able to overcome the personal wall which separated them during the making of the album.

Also on disc one is *The Last Few Bricks* - an extendable piece written for the stage shows which took the main themes and wove them into a new piece which could be easily extended to cover any delays in *The Wall* builders schedule ensuring that the last brick would always be popped into place just as Waters intoned the final word of side one "Goodbye."

There are no new compositions as such on the second CD, but

there are numerous re-arrangements and unexpected twists not least the album's finisher *Outside The Wall,* which has been completely re-arranged to suit the live arena. Waters on creaky clarinet leads the musicians in a peculiar country take on the song. This may well have been the original inspiration for the hilarious country/blue grass interpretation of *The Wall* produced by Luther Wright and The Wrongs and which every true Floyd devotee should have in their collection.

Chapter 20
LIVE 8

In July 2005 the band re-united for the Live 8 performance. On the surface the whole event was purely about publicising the existence of poverty in Africa and lobbying governments for the forgiveness of debt. The motives of all of the parties involved in this huge global jamboree were slightly less clear. Puzzlingly tickets for the huge event were free which gave rise to the obvious questions over who actually paid for the event. The initial answer supplied by the press was that the money came from the sale of broadcast rights. The BBC were indeed championing the whole event and had given a huge chunk of their television and radio schedule over to Live 8. Only later did it emerge that the event was in part subsidised by the presale of the DVD rights to EMI. It was this link which made the whole event possible and at a stroke removed any potential contractual obstacle to a Pink Floyd appearance. The BBC were in effect providing a huge free platform for the political message, but they were also providing the biggest free advertising campaign for the DVD which would follow in its wake. Originally scheduled for Christmas release (echoes of the Do They Know It's Christmas message) the release of the DVD was rushed forward to November 2005.

The concert itself provided a fantastic platform for EMI to parade its best selling artists including Paul Mcartney, Robbie Williams, Joss Stone and Cold Play. But none of them could even hope to come close to Pink Floyd. In the wake of Live 8, CD sales of all the artists taking part lept by huge margins. Admittedly much of these sales were helped by the immediate support given to some albums such as the Joss Stone TV advertising campaign which followed in the immediate wake of Live 8 in conjunction with retailers such as Tesco. Even without the benefit of TV advertising, sales of Pink Floyd albums soared by an incredible 1300%. Much to the delight of the moguls at EMI *Echoes, Dark Side of The Moon* and *Wish You Were Here* all crashed back into the charts. An even bigger hidden Live 8 windfall awaited the men in suits at EMI's various publishing interests. Publishing is the huge hidden iceberg of the music business. This is where the real money is made by Publishers who represent the writers of a song and charge TV companies, film producers, advertisers and record labels to use the compositions owned by it's artists. As publishers of much of the material performed at Live 8 the good men and ladies who handled EMI's publishing interests were entitled to fees from Television and Radio stations all over the world. They were also entitled to their share of of the dealer price for every single DVD, or CD sold which featured their repertoire. Pink Floyd Music Publishers Ltd as publishers of the Floyd repertoire could look forward to a similar windfall.

Conscious of the obvious charge of profiteering from a noble cause which was fast becoming perceived as little more than a cynical exercise in commercial exploitation, David Gilmour moved quickly to head off the cynics. The guitarist publicly proclaimed that he would be donating the results of this amazing windfall to charity and urged his fellow multi-millionaires on the Live 8 bill to do the same. Whether all the other artistes and corporate warriors will choose to do the same is still awaiting clarification.

Although there was nothing at stake, Pink Floyd were able to produce a thrilling performance taking in two tracks from *Dark Side,* an exhilarating *Comfortably Numb* and a superb rendition of *Wish You Were Here,* a song from the album written in honour of the man who had started it all - Syd Barrett.

There was a wonderful sense of symmetry about closing the band's performing career with a faultless performance of a truly emotional masterpiece dedicated to the man who had started it all. By the end of this performance the entire world had been given notice of the greatness of Pink Floyd. The band won every single public poll to judge the best of Live8. But with material like this to draw on is it any wonder? ...Well, now you can judge for yourself.

Pink Floyd performing at Live8